CUSTOME

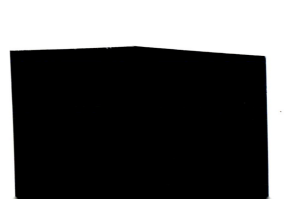

Dynamics *of* Skill Acquisition

A CONSTRAINTS-LED APPROACH

Keith Davids, PhD

QUEENSLAND UNIVERSITY OF TECHNOLOGY, AUSTRALIA

Chris Button, PhD

UNIVERSITY OF OTAGO, NEW ZEALAND

Simon Bennett, PhD

LIVERPOOL JOHN MOORES UNIVERSITY, UNITED KINGDOM

Human Kinetics

Library of Congress Cataloging-in-Publication Data

Davids, K. (Keith), 1953-
    Dynamics of skill acquisition : a constraints-led approach / Keith Davids, Chris Button, Simon Bennett.
        p. cm.
    Includes bibliographical references and index.
    ISBN-13: 978-0-7360-3686-3 (hard cover)
    ISBN-10: 0-7360-3686-5 (hard cover)
    1. Physical education and training. 2. Physical education and training--Psychological aspects. 3. Movement, Psychology of. 4. Human mechanics. 5. Physical fitness. I. Button, Chris, 1973- II. Bennett, Simon, 1970- III. Title.
    GV342.D28 2008
    372.86--dc22   2007020516

ISBN-10: 0-7360-3686-5
ISBN-13: 978-0-7360-3686-3

Acquisitions Editor: Judy Patterson Wright, PhD; **Developmental Editors:** Rebecca Johnson and Kathleen Bernard; **Assistant Editor:** Jillian Evans; **Copyeditor:** Alisha Jeddeloh; **Proofreader:** Pam Johnson; **Indexer:** Betty Frizzéll; **Permission Manager:** Dalene Reeder; **Graphic Designer:** Robert Reuther; **Graphic Artist:** Yvonne Griffith; **Cover Designer:** Keith Blomberg; **Photographer (cover):** © Human Kinetics; **Photographer (interior):** © Human Kinetics, unless otherwise noted; **Photo Asset Manager:** Laura Fitch; **Photo Office Assistant:** Jason Allen; **Art Manager:** Kelly Hendren; **Associate Art Manager:** Alan L. Wilborn; **Illustrator:** Keri Evans; **Printer:** Edwards Brothers

Printed in the United States of America   10 9 8 7 6 5 4

The paper in this book is certified under a sustainable forestry program.

Human Kinetics
Website: www.HumanKinetics.com

United States: Human Kinetics
P.O. Box 5076
Champaign, IL 61825-5076
800-747-4457
e-mail: humank@hkusa.com

Canada: Human Kinetics
475 Devonshire Road, Unit 100
Windsor, ON N8Y 2L5
800-465-7301 (in Canada only)
e-mail: info@hkcanada.com

Europe: Human Kinetics
107 Bradford Road
Stanningley
Leeds LS28 6AT, United Kingdom
+44 (0)113 255 5665
e-mail: hk@hkeurope.com

Australia: Human Kinetics
57A Price Avenue
Lower Mitcham, South Australia 5062
08 8372 0999
e-mail: info@hkaustralia.com

New Zealand: Human Kinetics
P.O. Box 80
Torrens Park, South Australia 5062
0800 222 062
e-mail: info@hknewzealand.com

PART II Applying the Constraints-Led Approach 105

CONTENTS

Preface **vii**

Acknowledgments **xi**

This book is dedicated to the ultimate self-organizing social system, my family: my wife, Anna, and my children, Mike, Jake, Charlie, and India

Keith Davids

For all the researchers past and present whose work has inspired the ideas developed in this book and unknowingly shaped our own academic pursuits

Chris Button

To the many individuals I have had the pleasure and fortune to work with, read of, and listen to, this book is a testament to your efforts and dedication

Simon Bennett

PREFACE

Actions in daily activities such as sport and work differ in the nature of the demands they impose on performers. Some actions, like racket sports or driving on an expressway, are performed at high speeds, and others, like rugby, American football, martial arts, and physical therapy, may involve a significant amount of body contact. Many actions require a high degree of precision and accuracy of movement, such as playing golf or performing surgery, whereas others, like ballet dancing and ice-skating, emphasize the challenge of performing graceful, stylized sequences of aesthetic movement. Many activities pit us against the wild elements of nature when hiking, mountaineering, kayaking, or skiing. Despite the huge variety of constraints imposed by various sports and daily activities, one thing they all share is a requirement for performers to coordinate and control movements effectively.

Movement practitioners in various physical activities understand that skilled learners are able to

- produce functional, efficient, and effective movement patterns that appear smooth and effortless;
- typically demonstrate precise timing between their movements and ongoing environmental events;
- consistently reproduce patterns of coordinated movement, even under severe time constraints or competitive pressures;
- perform movements that are not automated in the sense of being identical from one performance to the next, but are subtly varied and precisely adapted to immediate changes in the environment; and
- integrate different limb movements into an aesthetically pleasing pattern when necessary.

Purpose of the Book

Humans operate in information-rich, dynamic environments and require complex coordination patterns to interact with important surfaces, objects, and events. An important challenge for movement scientists is to understand how coordination patterns are assembled, controlled, and acquired. In recent years there has been an increasing interest in the constraints that shape and influence the acquisition of movement skills. Our purpose in this book is to synthesize and elucidate a constraints-led approach to skill acquisition.

The study of human movement now bridges many related disciplines, including motor development, motor control, psychology, biology, motor impairments, and physical therapy. Although we attempt to apply our discussion of movement as broadly as possible throughout this book, we will often use movement models from sport, exercise, and physical activities as examples to describe key ideas. As sport enthusiasts ourselves, we recognize that movement models from sport can provide particularly rich task constraints in which to study and understand important aspects of movement behavior (Davids, Button, Araújo, Renshaw, & Hristovski, 2006). One of the main objectives of physical educators, sport scientists, movement scientists, psychologists, and physiotherapists is to develop valid conceptual models of human movement behavior that is based on research (Post, Pijpers, Bosch, & Boschker, 1998). The development of a comprehensive model of motor control is necessary before one can consider issues related to learning, but this in itself is not a simple task because "the story of even a simple movement will have intentional, mechanical, informational, neural and muscular chapters" (Michaels, 1998, p. 65). It is becoming clear that a rigorous model of human movement requires a multidisciplinary framework to capture the different interlocking scales of analysis (e.g., neural, behavioral, psychological) and the many different subsystems (e.g., perceptual and movement) involved in producing behavior.

From a practical perspective, understanding how coordination and control is achieved promotes an informed organization of learning and rehabilitation environments and more effective use of practice and therapy time (Davids & Handford, 1994). Studying these processes in human movement systems is vital for considering issues involved in

- ergonomic equipment design;
- organizing and structuring coaching, teaching, and training tasks;
- planning and managing exercise prescription, therapeutic, and rehabilitation programs;
- preventing injury and associated health and safety considerations;
- understanding the nature of individual differences at various levels of performance;
- understanding how to transmit information to learners and patients in rehabilitation;
- getting a feel for children's movement capabilities at various stages of development; and
- interpreting movement disabilities and disorders and their effects on perceptual-motor function.

A conceptual model of coordination and control is not just important for designing learning environments, it is also important for ensuring that learners have positive experiences when acquiring motor skills. Given the alarm expressed at the lack of physical activity and poor movement competency shown in affluent societies (Our Healthy Nation Report, UK Government, 1999; World Health Organization report, 2002; Healthy Eating Healthy Action, New Zealand Ministry of Health Report, 2003), this type of knowledge is vital for the design of physical activity programs to provide the basic skills necessary for subelite sport and exercise participation (see also Clark, 1995). The goal of this book is to outline a reliable and comprehensive model of human movement to provide a valid framework (i.e., concepts, methodological tools, and language) through which students and practitioners can understand and address these issues.

Organization

This book is divided in two parts to facilitate understanding of theoretical and practical concepts. In part I, we describe the theoretical basis of a constraints-led learner model that has emerged within the literature on motor learning. Part II provides several practical implications of the constraints-led approach. We will discuss the relationship between the theoretical concepts introduced in part I and the practical concerns facing the learner and movement practitioner. In part II, we will attempt to bring the constraints-led model to life, especially in chapter 10, where a number of case studies are highlighted.

Audience

This book is written for people with an interest in movement coordination and control and skill acquisition. This includes movement scientists, sport scientists, psychologists, biomechanists, physiologists, coaches, teachers, physical educators, and physical therapists. Advanced undergraduates with a firm grounding in the traditional theories of motor behavior, beginning postgraduates, and academic faculty will all benefit from an understanding of ecological constraints on movement behavior.

The book contains an introduction to many key theoretical ideas that will enhance practical applications. For this purpose, we use examples throughout and case studies in chapter 10 to show how theoretical advances in the natural sciences can help our understanding of the acquisition of movement coordination. Spotlight on Research sidebars and additional readings are presented in each chapter to help readers understand how interacting constraints shape movement behavior. Readers are encouraged to use these features to enhance their learning experience.

ACKNOWLEDGMENTS

The authors would like to acknowledge Maureen Hazelwood for helping us prepare this book. The quality of the book was improved substantially thanks to the insightful comments of William Berg and an anonymous reviewer on early drafts. We would also like to thank the hardworking team at Human Kinetics, and in particular Judy Wright, for their patience and intelligent advice.

Introduction to Skill Acquisition Theory and the Constraints-Led Approach

Part I provides an overview of the key theoretical contributions to the study of skill acquisition and introduces the constraints-led approach.

Chapter 1 reviews the contribution of traditional theories to the study of skill acquisition, including the information-processing approach. In this chapter, we discuss important practical considerations such as practice organization and feedback delivery to provide a basis for comparison in later chapters. In chapters 2 and 3, we explore the relevance to motor performance of some alternative theoretical insights, particularly those offered by Russian physiologist Nikolai Bernstein (1967) and American psychologist James Gibson (1979). By emphasizing the need to adopt a systems perspective on human behavior, their theoretical contributions have had a major impact on our understanding of movement coordination and control. Their insights have encouraged researchers to model the performer as a complex movement system composed of many interacting subsystems. These ideas have focused attention on how coordination emerges between the parts of each person's movement system, as well as the key variables or constraints that the person uses to regulate or guide these coordination patterns.

Clearly, constraints play an important role in shaping the ways in which humans can move to effect change in their environment. In particular, chapter 2 focuses on the physical constraints affecting the performer by discussing key concepts of dynamical systems theory, and chapter 3 describes ecological psychology as a suitable framework for understanding informational constraints on behavior. In chapter 4, we present an overview of the constraints-led approach to skill acquisition, which forms the foundation of part II. Although there are a number of models of constraints, in part I we focus on the implications of Newell's (1986) model as a template for understanding how motor skills are acquired.

CHAPTER 1

Traditional Theories of Skill Acquisition

CHAPTER OUTLINE

Skill Acquisition: Definition and Theories
Association Theories
Neuromaturational Theories
Fitts' Stage Theory of Motor Learning
Information-Processing Theories
Neurocomputational Theories

Common Features of Traditional Theories
Representations of the World and Movements
Learner as Hierarchical Control System
Capacity-Limited Storage
Indirect Perception
Reduction of Error and Noise
Models of Limited Range of Movement

Implications for Movement Practitioners
Amount of Practice
Practice Variability
Practice Organization
Part-Task Practice
Instructions and Feedback
Demonstrations of Technique

Summary

Over the last century, the question of how humans learn to control and coordinate their movements has received much attention, with scientists proposing many different theories. Although there is still considerable debate over which theory is most appropriate (Summers, 2004), the importance of developing a strong theoretical framework for studying skill acquisition and guiding practical activity remains clear. Many practitioners use models of human behavior, either implicitly or explicitly, to plan their decision making for focused, effective practical activity. Theories of skill acquisition can help practitioners develop an appropriate model of the motor learning process that is necessary for understanding how learners acquire motor skills. How do you currently view motor behavior and how does your understanding underpin the way you teach or coach? As part II of this book will show, this knowledge provides a philosophy for structuring practice contexts, providing information to learners, using visual demonstrations, and other important tasks.

This chapter provides a brief historical overview of the traditional theories of movement skill acquisition. This overview will enable us to compile a number of implications for movement practitioners. Summarizing the general features of traditional theories will help us compare them with alternative theories described in subsequent chapters. As you read this chapter, we encourage you to keep an open but critical mind regarding the strengths and weaknesses of the different theories discussed. (For more detailed overviews of these theories, refer to Schmidt and Wrisberg [2004], Magill [2006], and Haywood and Getchell [2005]). Let's start by considering what we mean by the term *skill acquisition.*

Skill Acquisition: Definition and Theories

Motor skill acquisition has traditionally been described as the internal processes that bring about relatively permanent changes in the learner's movement capabilities (Schmidt & Wrisberg, 2004). For example, movement skills such as riding a bicycle, catching a ball, or driving a car require a good deal of practice to allow us to perform them effectively. **Skill acquisition** requires us to interact effectively with our environment, detect important information, and time our responses appropriately. It should result in coordination patterns that are adaptable to a range of varying performance characteristics. Adaptive behavior is important because conditions like the environment, task requirements, and our motivations can change every time we perform a motor skill (Davids, Bennett, & Newell, 2006).

The process of skill acquisition is distinct from execution of the skill (motor control) in that learning is a gradual process that occurs over many performance attempts, resulting in behavior that is less vulnerable to transitory factors such as fatigue, audience effects, and anxiety. One way researchers have tried to understand skill acquisition is by examining performance changes over time. For example, in early research efforts, Bryan and Harter (1897) studied how learners' typing skills developed while practicing to send and translate Morse code. Over a period of 40 weeks, the telegraphers went through distinct phases of improvement and periods where performance levels plateaued. The inference from such performance curves was that learners initially construct simple elements of the skill, interspersed with periods of consolidation (i.e., development of automaticity), before linking individual parts of movements (in this case, individual finger presses) into more integrated patterns of behavior (linked sequences of finger presses typed as words).

Snoddy (1926) proposed that learning can be described in a predictable manner using a mathematical equation ($\log C = \log B + n \log x$, where C is a measure of performance, x is the amount of practice, and B and n are constants). This **power law of practice** predicts a straight-line relationship between the logarithmic functions of practice time and performance (see figure 1.1). The power law of practice simply states that performance improves with practice, although there are eventual physical limits to this relationship.

Practicing a skill such as riding a bicycle leads to performance improvement. Skill acquisition helps us to interact effectively with our environment, detect important information, and time our responses appropriately.

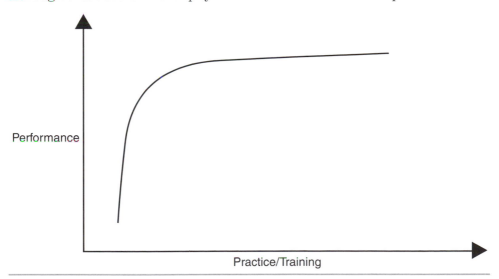

Figure 1.1 The power law of practice predicts a straight-line relationship between the logarithmic functions of practice time and performance.

Despite being researched for some years, the power law of practice has failed to gain universal acceptance because it has become clear that learning is often characterized by sudden jumps, rapid improvements, and even decrements in performance over time. For example, although Crossman's (1959) classic study of cigar makers seemed to support Snoddy's power law, researchers continue to question the generality of this prediction because many types of learning curves have been observed in motor learning experiments as well as practice (see Newell, Liu, & Mayer-Kress, 2001).

Initially, researchers favored a much broader definition of skill acquisition that included movement activities with a heavy emphasis on cognition, such as playing chess or learning new languages (e.g., Bryan & Harter, 1897; Chase & Simon, 1973; Ebbinghaus, 1964). Indeed, research examining such skills has contributed significantly to our understanding of processes such as expertise, attention, and automaticity of movement control. More recently, there has been a tendency to examine the acquisition of movement coordination and control with an equal theoretical emphasis on cognition, perception, and action. Before we discuss this more recent trend in later chapters, we will briefly describe five traditional theoretical approaches to skill acquisition: association theories, neuromaturational theories, Fitts' stage theory of motor learning, information-processing theories, and neurocomputational theories.

Association Theories

Early contributors to the study of skill acquisition were interested in the relationship between movement stimuli (information) and action (e.g., Skinner, 1938; Thorndike, 1927; Woodworth, 1899). In examining this association, researchers employed either relatively simple repetitive movements or reflexes to test their assumptions. For example, to examine the roles of memory and feedback during learning, Woodworth (1899) required blindfolded participants to draw lines of varying lengths. This research demonstrated that repetition of the movement without feedback did not improve accuracy during practice. However, when researchers provided simple right or wrong statements after each trial, participants' accuracy dramatically improved. These findings indicated the important role that feedback plays in reinforcing learning.

Other early researchers on skill acquisition believed that reflexes were the basic building blocks of movement and that people were passive recipients of external sensory inputs that drove their behavior. For example, to study movement in isolation of inputs from higher cortical brain regions, Sherrington (1906) conducted experiments on animals whose spinal cords had been surgically cut in order to study the circuitry of the central nervous system (CNS). Prominent experimental psychologists such as Skinner (1938) and Thorndike (1927) were also influential during this period. However, many researchers criticized these methods for assuming that animal models were relevant for studying motor skill acquisition in humans. Further, the research tended to focus too much on observable performance outcomes rather than understanding of the underlying processes of skill acquisition. In addition, association theories typically lacked explanations to account for the fact that humans can choose when and how to moderate their actions, and they failed to explain that sensory feedback was not always essential for executing some movements, as in the case of rapid reactive actions.

Neuromaturational Theories

During the 1920s through 1940s, research on motor development eclipsed the study of skill acquisition. To some extent, there is no clear distinction between the disciplines of motor development and motor learning because both processes produce durable changes in motor behavior, although along different timescales. In the case of **motor development,** behavioral changes are typically attributed to growth and maturation, whereas in **motor learning,** practice or experience is the determining factor (Haywood & Getchell, 2005). Early research on motor development tended to explain behavioral change from a neuromaturational perspective, focusing particularly on the period from infancy through adolescence (Gesell, 1928; McGraw, 1943). This theory holds that the genetic predispositions that we inherit within our DNA determine the orderly sequence of each person's motor development (ontogeny). Many researchers viewed the stable progression of individuals through key motor milestones as persuasive evidence for the overriding influence of evolution and genetics over environment (see figure 1.2). Theorists suggested that the maturation of the CNS was the catalyst for the development of new movement skills and the gradual disappearance of older, less functional movements

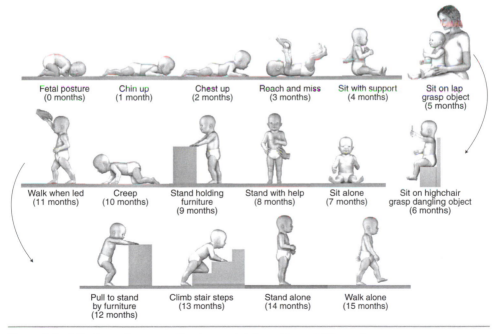

Figure 1.2 Milestones for motor development, infancy through 15 months.

Reprinted from M.M. Shirley, 1963, The motor sequence. In *Readings in child psychology,* 2nd ed., edited by W. Dennis (Englewood Cliffs, NJ: Prentice-Hall, Inc.), 77; adapted, by permission, from M.M. Shirley, 1931, *The first two years: A study of twenty-five babies,* Vol. I., Institute of Child Welfare Monograph No. 7 (Minneapolis, MN: University of Minnesota Press), 100. Copyright © 1931 by the University of Minnesota, renewed 1959.

caused by early reflexes or motor babbling (considered by early researchers as random and incoherent limb movements of young infants).

However, in the absence of any direct measures of such maturation processes in the CNS, research in the field entered a period of descriptive analysis and identification of age-group norms from the mid-1940s to the 1970s. Researchers have subsequently focused more on interesting contradictions to the motor milestones progression (e.g., Thelen, Ridley-Johnson, & Fisher, 1983), which highlight the influence of each person's unique environment during development. Researchers no longer view individual variations in progression rates through motor milestones as potential evidence of pathologies. Instead, they believe that variations reflect the unique interactions between personal characteristics and the specific environmental context in which each person develops (Thelen & Smith, 1994).

Fitts' Stage Theory of Motor Learning

The second World War revived interest in processes of skill acquisition as governments in the United States and United Kingdom asked researchers to study methods for selecting and training military personnel. Due to pragmatic concerns, such as the ergonomic design of equipment and training of military skills, researchers adopted an overriding task-oriented approach that did little to shed light on processes of skill acquisition in humans (Schmidt & Lee, 2005). The emphasis on studying performance and learning in specific tasks resulted in knowledge on practical issues such as the optimal scheduling of practice and feedback delivery to enhance learning (e.g., amount, frequency, duration). Paul Fitts (1964) developed an influential model of skill acquisition that has received a great deal of support in subsequent textbooks and practical literature (e.g., Abernethy, 2001). His three-stage model describes learning as a continuous process with gradual changes in the nature of information processing as learning progresses (see figure 1.3).

During the initial **cognitive stage** of Fitts' model, the learner is exposed to simple rules and verbal instructions to acquire basic understanding of the movement. At this stage, performance is variable and error-ridden as the learner experiments with different movement configurations. When the learner attains the following **associative stage,** movement patterns are refined and more consistent. Depending on the complexity of the task and the learner's abilities, this stage can require varying lengths of practice. Reaching the third **autonomous stage** requires extensive practice. At this stage the learner can perform the skill with minimal mental effort and few errors. As noted in the next chapter, much of the learning process inferred within Fitts' three-stage model has been attributed to the development and acquisition of information-processing abilities (Anderson, 1982) and the construction of relevant motor programs.

Information-Processing Theories

Beginning with the early writings of James (1890), Woodworth (1899), and Lashley (1917), a popular theory postulated that perceptual-motor informa-

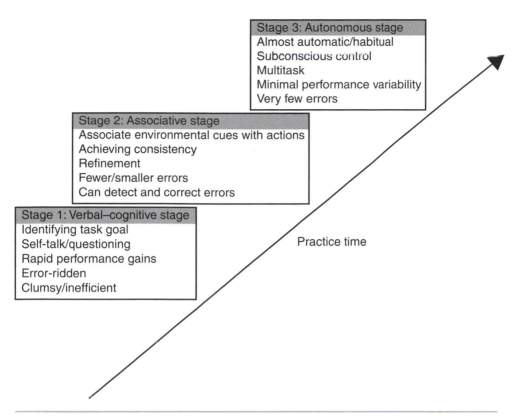

Figure 1.3 Fitts' three-stage model describes learning as a continuous process with gradual changes in the nature of information processing as learning progresses.

tion can be represented within the CNS. Such representations are acquired through learning, which results in the CNS storing a set of motor commands that control movement behavior. Researchers thought that this mode of movement regulation, known as **open-loop control,** was responsible for the control of quick, ballistic movements in which a set of preplanned instructions for action could be executed without feedback modification, for example in the performance of a boxing jab. During the years following World War II, Henry and Rogers (1960) emphasized the importance of centralized instructions for movement with their memory drum theory.

Traditionally, theories emphasizing the role of central structures in movement control have tended to look to electronic and mechanical storage devices to model how information can be stored and represented in the CNS. These devices have served as metaphors for many processes of movement control and demonstrate the influence of physics on psychological theories of movement behavior. For example, memory drums were devices in early computers onto which programs and information could be loaded for storage. Keele (1968) first used the term **motor program,** which he adopted for a popular functional analogy of how the brain produces consistent and reliable movement outputs, again mirroring the technological developments in computer hardware at the

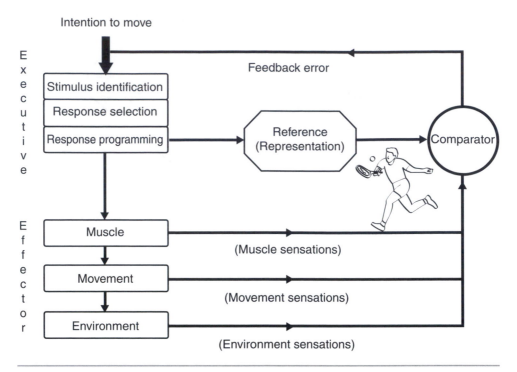

Figure 1.4 Information processing occurs in the CNS through a series of discrete cognitive stages involving perception, decision making, and response execution.

Adapted, by permission, from R.A. Schmidt and C.A. Wrisberg, 2000, *Motor learning and performance*, 2nd ed. (Champaign, IL: Human Kinetics), 95.

time (see the following Key Concept). The basic assumption of the analogy is that the brain functions like a computer to process information and produce outputs in behavior. Information processing in the CNS occurs through a series of discrete cognitive stages involving perception, decision making, and response execution (see figure 1.4). Researchers employed movement reaction time as a key variable to explain the stages of information-processing in tasks that range in complexity (Keele & Posner, 1968; Klapp, 1977).

Key Concept

Motor program describes a set of movement commands that are stored within the CNS. Initially proposed by Keele (1968), the term draws heavily on the analogy of the brain as a sophisticated computer. The generalized motor program was subsequently developed to represent a general category of movements to deal with storage concerns (Schmidt, 1975). Critics of the motor program argue that the concept assumes the existence of a homunculus-type agent (in neurological sciences known as "the little man inside the brain") or executive agent necessary to create and select the programs.

During the 1960s and 1970s, a major paradigm debate raged over the importance of the motor program versus the use of ongoing performance-related feedback to control movement. Adams' (1971) closed-loop theory advocated the role of feedback in both the control and learning of movement. Based on engineering principles in cybernetic science, closed-loop theory implies that normal movement is regulated by a continuous comparison between current sensory information and information generated as a consequence of a successful movement (see figure 1.5). Early learners develop representations (perceptual traces) of the expected movement by using outcome-related feedback (knowledge of results) to gauge their progress. Much published research supported Adams' theory, although it soon became apparent that, in contrast to open-loop theories, mainly slow positioning movements (e.g., steering a car or riding a bicycle) fit closed-loop theory best. In both open- and closed-loop theories, a key assumption is the capacity of the CNS to store a huge number of representations to control the many distinct movements needed in daily life. Just imagine the thousands of distinct movement patterns that humans might be called upon to perform in given circumstances.

Schmidt (1975) attempted to resolve the debate by combining aspects of **open-** and **closed-loop control** in proposing his **schema theory** of discrete motor skill learning (see Spotlight on Research). A **schema** is a set of rules concerning the execution of a movement response linked to feedback received during and after performance. In Schmidt's schema theory, a generalized motor program (GMP) is an abstract representation that contains the general

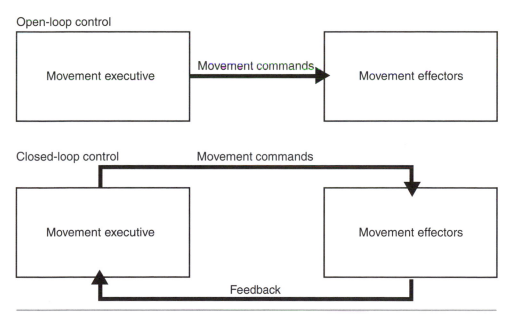

Figure 1.5 In closed-loop theory, early learners develop representations of the expected movement by using outcome-related feedback (knowledge of results) to gauge their progress.

characteristics for a given class of movements such as pointing, balancing, jumping, and locomotion. One implication of schema theory is that variable, rather than specific, practice conditions are necessary for the learner to acquire robust schema that can generate functional movements for a particular class of actions (e.g., driving a car) under a variety of performance conditions. It is believed that driving a car under different environmental conditions will lead to a broader range of experience and allow drivers to cope with novel driving conditions. Schmidt's theory of learning provoked a good deal of laboratory research that tested aspects such as movement parameterization and variability of practice. Once more, however, there was a tendency to employ simple motor tasks involving few motor system components (e.g., limb segments) in restricted learning environments.

 ## Spotlight on Research

SCHEMA THEORY OF DISCRETE MOTOR SKILL LEARNING

In 1975, Richard Schmidt published his original description of schema theory in *Psychological Review*. Schmidt's concerns over the generalization of Adams' (1971) closed-loop theory beyond the learning of slow positioning movements motivated his publication. Subsequent research has cited schema theory frequently, with 782 citations by the end of 2004 (Shea & Wulf, 2005). Further, schema theory has contributed to a large body of empirical research across a broad range of performance domains, testing concepts such as relative timing and variability of practice.

Schmidt proposed the existence of GMPs to counter concerns that every movement would need a separate motor program, leading to storage problems. Instead, a given class of actions (e.g., locomotion, including stepping, walking, running, skipping, and gamboling) could be represented by the same GMP. To produce a response for a given situation, the learner needs to set key specifications or parameters, such as movement speed, duration, and force. Schema theory contends that with practice, learners should rely less on using feedback, instead developing open-loop control via parameter regulation to free this cognitive burden. To explain the gradual shift in control over learning, Schmidt identified two types of schema or abstract rules: recall schema and recognition schema. A schema is constructed from the different information sources that are stored each time a skill is produced, such as the initial conditions, the response specifications, the sensory consequences, and the response outcome. During practice, these information sources can be linked together to construct a recall and a recognition schema that the learner may apply even when performing in novel conditions. The following summarizes the attributes of schema theory:

- Schema theory explains how learners can produce specific movements of a given class that they had never performed previously.
- Variable practice conditions facilitate the creation of a robust, general schema that can lead to enhanced skill transfer.

- Separate memory structures are used for movement production (recall) and evaluation of the accuracy of selected movements (recognition).
- Error-detection capability will improve with practice.

Neurocomputational Theories

The 1990s were designated as the Decade of the Brain by the U.S. Congress, coinciding with the greater integration of neuroscientific evidence of CNS function and psychological modeling of behavior. This concerted integrative modeling effort was reflected in revisions of many motor control theories in the cognitive and behavioral neurosciences (e.g., Kawato, 1999). These internal models address early concerns of how movement representations might interact with rapid environmental changes to provide flexible movement solutions for individual performers. For example, Willingham (1998) proposed a **control-based learning theory (COBALT)** in which the brain creates different types of representations so that important information can be symbolically represented and stored.

According to COBALT, motor learning results in the acquisition of different types of representations in the brain based on features of the world, intentions, or sequential patterns of spatial locations or specific muscle forces (for a more detailed analysis, see Davids, Kingsbury, Bennett, & Handford, 2001). COBALT exemplified a neurocomputational perspective that proposed how representations could allow learners to create mental models of the world and include categories based on environmental features, intentions, and spatial or temporal patterns of muscle activation at different levels of the CNS. For example, a tennis serve is based on a learned egocentric representation (perceptions from the individual's viewpoint) of the "knowledge of a sequence of locations to which one should respond" (Willingham, 1998, p. 574). Arbib, Érdi, and Szentágothai (1998) proposed a similar use of hypothetical structures mediating brain function when they suggested that a schema is a unit of processing that intervenes between the neural structure and movement system dynamics.

In neurocomputational approaches, researchers have been primarily concerned with identifying the regions of the brain that are responsible for controlling action. For example, Muellbacher and colleagues (2002) suggested that the primary motor cortex is the site of consolidation or stabilization of movement representations, particularly in the early stages of learning a new motor skill. Another common approach has been to consider how the brain uses its networked, parallel processing capabilities to cope with multiple information streams (e.g., through neural mechanisms such as cortical cell assemblies and neural net modeling) (Bullock & Grossberg, 1989; Wickens, Hyland, & Anson, 1994).

A major challenge facing computational models concerns the acquisition of coordination during complex multiarticular actions (actions involving many limbs, segments, and joints of the body) in changing environments. Another important question for computational theories concerns the communication among levels of representations, such as spatiotemporal representations of the environment and representations of movement patterns. Where and how does this communication occur in the CNS? More prosaically, how is the neural code transformed from egocentric representations of time and spatial locations into the CNS coding of specific muscle forces used to produce a movement pattern (Flash & Sejnowski, 2001)? In most early computational work, researchers hypothesized that interneurons (perhaps at the level of the spinal cord) acted as code translators for communicating between egocentric representations of the world and the specific muscles used to achieve movement goals.

Recent trends in computational modeling have been driven by attempts to design and engineer biologically inspired robots (i.e., robots that act more like common neurobiological systems, including insects, animals, and humans). This generation of robotic design is tackling the tricky problem of engineering machines that can complete challenging tasks, adapt their behaviors to complex environments and terrains, and even cooperate in teams when engaged in complex tasks like exploration for minerals during mining (e.g., Matarić, 1998). The result is modeling of artificial intelligence that, according to some researchers, provides insights into how the CNS might control movements in humans. Scientific subdisciplines such as robotics and artificial intelligence are now drawing inspiration from research on how neurobiological systems interact with complex environments. Traditional models of robotic design, based on the principles of sense, model, plan, and act, are being complemented by behavior-based control approaches that have the explicit goal of engineering machines to operate in unpredictable and challenging environments, such as during space exploration or RoboCup soccer competitions (Matarić, 1998). Alternative design principles, including situated robotics, draw inspiration from research on how neurobiological systems search for and pick up information to support sophisticated interactions with their environments (e.g., Di Paolo, 2002; Paine & Tani, 2005).

Some behavior-based robotic implementations have been founded on ecological principles in which an agent and its environment are viewed as an inseparable system studied at an ecological scale of analysis. In ecological robotics, adaptive movement behavior is specified by information in the environment that does not need to be represented within the robot in explicit detail (Fajen et al., 2003). There have even been attempts to forgo a central planner for behaviors and to map sensory systems directly to actuators of the robots (Duchon & Warren, 2002).

The influence of neurobiological theories on robotic engineering has not been a one-way street. As a result, these newer models of artificial intelligence

Robots that can complete challenging tasks, adapt their behaviors to complex environments, and cooperate in teams help researchers determine how the CNS might control movements in humans.

have inspired an emphasis on understanding how the coadaptation of the CNS and the body occurs during motor learning (e.g., Davidson & Wolpert, 2003; Wolpert, Ghahramani, & Flanagan, 2001). This advance is significant because it recognizes how cognitive processes can be mediated by the physical constraints of the human body, which changes over the life span as a result of development and over generations as a result of evolutionary pressures.

In this type of computational modeling, anticipating the outcomes of an action forms the basis for planning and organizing goal-directed movement. Communication between sensory representations and motor systems is resolved by requiring two types of representations: forward and inverse models (Kawato, 1999). **Forward modeling** refers to the mapping of motor commands to the related sensory consequences of a movement. Located within the brain, this representation is used to predict the sensory consequences of planned movements. For example, when planning the action of reaching for an object on a high shelf, expected sensory consequences might include information from leaning and overbalancing that would require adaptation of postural muscles and possibly even a stepping adjustment to facilitate the elongated reach to the shelf.

Inverse modeling refers to transforming the anticipated sensory consequences into the motor commands needed to achieve them. From this

Forward models

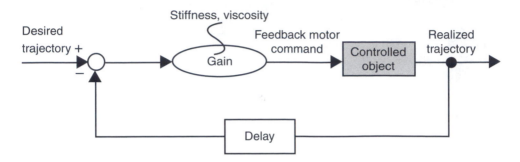

Inverse models

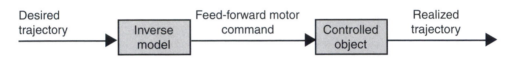

Figure 1.6 With forward models, one learns to use feedback to regulate movements. With task constraints that are too rapid to process information, inverse models provide performers with feed-forward control.

perspective, motor learning involves the acquisition of forward and inverse representations for varying tasks and environments (see figure 1.6). With forward models, one learns to use feedback to regulate movements, whereas under task constraints, which are too rapid to process this information, inverse models provide performers with feed-forward control. The acquisition of forward models enables people to adapt to rapidly changing environments, prevents them from becoming too reliant on immediate sensory information to regulate movements, and possibly forms the basis of using imagery to mentally practice a skill (Wolpert et al., 2001).

As long as environmental perturbations requiring adaptation remain within the performers' experience, feed-forward control allows performers to use "what-if" mental simulations in a kind of preplanned reactive adaptation to a change in the environment. For example, experienced tennis players might predict that an opponent's forehand drive, played with a very low arc at around net height, could just clip the top of the net, changing the flight trajectory of the ball. This possible consequence might lead to feed-forward control of a pickup volley action as one option in those circumstances. Regulated by inverse models, the neural mechanism of feed-forward control recognizes that biological feedback loops act quite slowly and overcomes delays in controlling very rapid or ballistic movements through sensory information. In these neurocomputational models, complexity and storage capacity issues are addressed by the proposal that the CNS actively condenses the detail and complexity of the information it stores by reducing the dimensionality of the forward and inverse representations.

Common Features of Traditional Theories

Traditional theories of motor skill acquisition share several key characteristics. These features are useful to consider when comparing traditional theories with the alternative theories described in subsequent chapters. These commonalities include the role of representations in controlling perception and action, a preference for hierarchical control modeling, information storage within neurobiological systems, indirect perception, noise viewed as system error, and a preference for studying specific types of movements, such as manual aiming, pointing, and reaching and grasping. In this section, we highlight these common features.

Representations of the World and Movements

Traditional theories have been inspired by advances in cognitive science, which tend to compare brain structures to computer architecture and mental processes to computer algorithms. As noted earlier, this theoretical rationale for motor skill acquisition and control uses the base metaphor of an internal representation of the world to describe how perception, cognition, and action can occur. This metaphor demonstrates the influence of physics on psychological science, where the dominant research agenda over the past five decades invoked a view of intentions as representations which function as internal causes of human behavior (van Orden et al., 2003). In psychology, representations have been a popular metaphor for cause-and-effect relations between intentions and movement behavior. This metaphor has not only exerted a strong influence on the design of psychology experiments but also the interpretation and analysis of data and the theoretical explanations preferred by psychologists (van Orden et al., 2003).

Accordingly, these theories infer that learning involves constructing internal models of the world and of movements that facilitate interactions with the environment. Researchers believe that these representations support the internalization of information from the environment that can be used to guide actions. Early representational theories were plagued by problems of specificity, storage capacity, and computational complexity, but recent work has been informed by developments in computational neural network theory, neuroscience, artificial intelligence, and robotics to model how people can acquire adaptive and reliable movements. Developments in this area are taking advantage of increased understanding of the CNS to constrain modeling of representational control of behavior.

Learner as Hierarchical Control System

Traditional theories assume that the coordination and control of movement requires some kind of ordered prescription or representation for action (Anson, Elliott, & Davids, 2005; Newell, 2003). Traditional cognitive approaches deal with this requirement by invoking a central controlling mechanism that resides in the brain. Often known as the **homunculus,** this mechanism is responsible for the creation, selection, and timing of motor programs. Hierarchical control systems operate in a top-down fashion and are analogous to a puppeteer who controls each movement of a puppet by controlling the movement of individual strings attached to the parts of the puppet. Another example of hierarchical control systems exists in the social organization of companies in which all decisions are made by the manager, whose instructions to lower-level supervisors ultimately result in the outputs of workers. In such systems, the emphasis for skill acquisition relies heavily on constructing increasingly elaborate cognitive processes to coordinate increasingly skillful movement patterns. Additionally, hierarchical systems largely ignore a learner's previous experience and the physical makeup of the movement system; feedback processes and the specific properties of each person's body are underplayed (see chapter 2).

Hierarchical control systems regard an executive or external agent as responsible for system organization, as analogized by the puppeteer controlling the moving parts of a puppet.

© John R. Jones; Papilio/Corbis

Capacity-Limited Storage

Borrowing a metaphor from computer science, movements are regulated by symbol-based programs that must be stored within the CNS so that they can be recalled for action when necessary. Despite significant progress in the fields of neurobiology and neuropsychology, how and where motor programs are coded and stored remains uncertain. A further issue arising from cognitive approaches is that, like a computer, the function of the CNS is capacity limited. Researchers have cited this limitation to explain why the allocation of attention is such an important characteristic of skilled behavior (Abernethy, Maxwell, Masters, van der Kamp, & Jackson, 2007).

Indirect Perception

In order to make sense of the world in which we move, traditional theories assume that the performer needs to interpret information internally before responding to it. In other words, meaningless sensory information must be compared with existing representations of the world (memories) that are stored in the brain. For novice learners, such indirect processing would be burdensome as they try to make sense of their environment without previous experience upon which to rely. Conversely, skilled performers have learned to identify key information sources quickly and use their existing knowledge to alleviate the processing burden. For example, experienced mountaineers can look at the face of a rock and detect the most useful hand- and footholds on the surface. Their expertise allows them to perceive subtle information sources concerning size, depth, and width of surface characteristics that less experienced mountaineers do not perceive. Moreover, their speed of perception is enhanced by the strategy of chunking information into larger, more manageable wholes. They do not need to perceive and identify smaller units of information in a time-consuming process.

Reduction of Error and Noise

Traditionally, cognitive science has viewed high levels of movement variability as a problem for humans during task performance (Newell, Deutsch, Sosnoff, & Mayer-Kress, 2006). For example, the information-processing approach views the performer as a sort of human communications channel in which the relationship between input signals and system output is linear and deterministic. In this view, the performer can eliminate or minimize noise through practice and task experience. For this reason, the magnitude of variability in performance has been viewed as an important feature for assessing the quality of system control (Schmidt, 1985). The role of repetitive practice is often conceived of as gradually reducing the amount of movement pattern variability viewed as noise. But is movement variability always bad? As we shall learn later in this chapter, these theoretical approaches have typically neglected the important structural role that variability might play in adapting successful goal-directed movement patterns to changing environments.

Models of Limited Range of Movement

In the field of human movement, a key task is to understand how the movement system achieves coordination among components of the body and among movement patterns and important objects and surfaces in the environment. That is, humans need to acquire skill in coordinating relevant parts of the body into a functional pattern identifiable as a coherent action, such as when performing a triple salko jump in ice-skating, or more mundanely, when stepping onto a surface. However, in both of these examples, even the most coherent movement pattern needs to be coordinated with respect to an environmental surface or obstacle, for example when landing on ice or when placing the foot on a step or curb. Because of the potential for interaction among these subsystems, coordination in the human movement system is characterized by great complexity (Davids, Bennett, & Newell, 2006).

The search for simplistic laws of cause and effect has meant that movement scientists have often struggled to come to terms with the complexity humans must overcome to produce even a simple goal-directed movement. This issue has become known as Bernstein's (1967) degrees of freedom problem. **Degrees of freedom (dfs)** are the independent components of a complex system that can fit together in many different ways. For example, insects in a colony are independent dfs whose actions need to be coordinated to build a nest or feed progeny. In the same way, the large number of available muscles, joints, limb segments, and bones in the body exemplify the dfs of a complex system. This huge number of dfs in the human motor system is a kind of a curse for computational accounts of skill acquisition and performance (Kugler & Turvey, 1987). This is because it seems that a hierarchical control system with an executive agent in charge needs to be aware of so much information on where each individual part is in space, what it is currently doing, and how its position in space might change over time during performance.

Traditionally, the selection of movement models to investigate motor system functioning has been biased away from dynamic, multijoint, functional actions prevalent in sports because of the view that experimental rigor can be better maintained in laboratory studies of simple movements (Davids, Button, Araújo,

© Marty Sniderman/Corbis

Complex systems in nature are composed of many parts that are free to interact with each other. Many examples abound in nature, as exemplified by schools of fish.

Renshaw, & Hristovski, 2006). Consequently, many traditional theories were conceived to explain a small group of related actions (Newell, 1989). For example, open-loop theories are best suited to fast, ballistic movements; closed-loop theory deals with slow, precise movements; and schema theory was devised to explain the learning of discrete movements. Traditional approaches to skill acquisition have not offered a unified theory of learning (Anson et al., 2005).

Historically, there has been an overemphasis on the amount of change in performance outcomes without sufficient analysis of the dynamic properties of change in movement coordination (Newell, 2003). This criticism may be partly attributed to the lack of sophisticated measuring devices for examining coordination (e.g., three-dimensional motion analysis systems). Another concern is that much skill acquisition research has been conducted only over short, intense practice periods (e.g., a number of days). There are few examples in the research literature of motor learning experiments performed over longer periods of practice, as experienced in real life (e.g., the months and years of practice involved in many work and sport environments), and conclusions are likely to be based on the relatively transient effects of practice rather than the permanent consequences of learning.

Implications for Movement Practitioners

Surprisingly, the links between skill acquisition theories and practice have not always been exploited to the extent that one might expect (Fairweather, 1999; Newell & Rovegno, 1990). Nevertheless, many movement practitioners such as therapists, teachers, and coaches have implicitly adopted the learner model developed by traditional theories. In this section, we will discuss some of the key implications behind translating accepted theoretical approaches into practice.

Amount of Practice

Because movement practitioners often have a limited amount of time to work with learners, it is interesting to consider how much practice learners require in order to achieve different levels of expertise. Unfortunately, due to practical difficulties of recruiting participants and monitoring progress over time, researchers have conducted very few long-term studies of motor learning. Notable exceptions include Snoddy (1926) and Crossman (1959). Analysis of expert performers' practice activities are perhaps the most illuminating. Some studies have reported that a minimum of 10 years of practice is necessary to reach exceptional performance levels. Ericsson, Krampe, and Tesch-Römer (1993), who studied musicians, suggested that cumulative hours spent engaging in deliberate practice were monotonically and positively related to performance level. It was argued that, within certain physical limits, the more hours you spend in deliberate practice, the more likely you are to develop a high level of expertise in a particular performance context. In terms of negotiating Fitts' (1964) three stages of learning, researchers have remained silent on the required practice duration. In summary, the traditional take-home message for practice seems to be that more is best as researchers have concentrated on studying the amount of time needed to acquire a high level of expertise.

Practice Variability

For dynamic tasks such as negotiating a cluttered environment or a busy street, an amputee would need to practice walking in different conditions to feel comfortable with a prosthesis.

Consider an amputee learning to walk with a new prosthesis or a new 10-pin bowler trying to perform a strike. Do such learners benefit from variations in practice conditions, or should they concentrate on simple repetitions designed to produce a constant movement pattern? The answer largely depends on how much variability in conditions the learner might experience in performance situations. In stable, predictable conditions such as in bowling, traditional approaches would recommend a good deal of trial-to-trial repetition of relevant skills such as foot placement, ball release, and follow-through to consolidate the motor program responsible for that action. For dynamic tasks such as negotiating a cluttered environment or a busy street, the amputee would need to practice walking in different conditions to feel comfortable with a prosthesis. As discussed in this chapter's Spotlight on Research, Schmidt's schema theory (1975) recommends practice variations in the key parameters that influence the production of GMPs, such as movement amplitude, force, or time. In a later article, Schmidt (1985) pointed out that researchers and practitioners should seek practice activities that preserve the invariant aspects of a learner's coordination (e.g., relative timing).

The results of research that consider variability of practice have been quite equivocal (see van Rossum, 1990). It seems that a number of factors mediate the potential benefits of variable practice conditions. For example, younger, inexperienced learners seem to benefit more from variable practice conditions than older learners (possibly suggesting how discovery learning may benefit that group). On the whole, the learning of ballistic and complex tasks also seems to respond well to variable practice (for a review, see Lee, Chamberlin, & Hodges, 2001). Because movements cannot be stereotypically repeated in an identical manner (Newell et al., 2006), the role of repetition in practice has come under scrutiny. It seems that requiring learners to adapt their movements under variable task constraints has considerable merit in helping them learn how to interact with complex environments.

Practice Organization

Firefighters and people who fish need to learn how to tie different types of knots for quite different purposes in their working environments. Should they learn to tie these knots in a blocked fashion (one knot at a time), or should they practice different knots within the same practice session (randomized practice)? Researchers' experiments in the area of practice organization have led to a well-known research phenomenon called the **contextual interference effect** (see Brady, 1998). Practice organization that is blocked seems to lead to better performance during acquisition of the skill; however, random practice organization benefits the learning (i.e., retention and transfer) of a skill. This effect seems to be most potent when different GMPs are randomly assorted during the practice (Schmidt, 2003). In addition, although the contextual interference effect has received considerable support in the literature, modifying variables such as skill complexity and skill level need to be taken into account (Ollis, Button, & Fairweather, 2005).

Surprisingly, adding random variability in the form of irrelevant movement components when practicing a target movement leads to better performance and learning than when practicing specific movement patterns alone (see Button, Davids, & Schöllhorn, 2006). This effect was evident in studies where soccer players practiced shooting at the goal with the addition of superfluous hopping movements or jumps (Schöllhorn et al., 2006). Traditional theorists argue that random practice seems to emphasize enhanced cognitive processing during practice, which in turn leads to more effective motor learning.

Part-Task Practice

Swimming instructors often ask their students to perform different elements of a stroke in isolation (e.g., leg kicks, arm pulls, and breathing) before fitting them all together to produce the whole pattern at a later stage of practice. Is this strategy consistent with theoretical modeling? Performing complex motor

Swimming instructors often ask their students to perform different elements of a stroke in isolation before fitting them all together at a later stage.

skills represents a considerable information-processing burden, particularly for early learners (Wulf & Shea, 2002), so movement practitioners have been advised to seek strategies that reduce the cognitive load, at least early in learning. In the swimming example, the instructor's implicit assumption is that learning one part of the task, such as the leg kick, will transfer positively to learning the whole task.

However, research has revealed once more that the nature of the task influences the value of this common practical strategy. In particular, tasks that have highly interdependent parts or complex coordination requirements (e.g., snowboarding jumps) do not always benefit greatly from part-task practice. Part-task practice can take different forms, such as segmentation, where sequences of movements are practiced separately, or fractionation, as in the swimming example. In general, due to an individual's potential to learn chunks of a movement more effectively, traditional theories support the concept of part-task practice.

Instructions and Feedback

Ask any teacher about the importance of giving prepractice instructions to students, and it is likely you will receive an enthusiastic response. From a traditional perspective, instructions facilitate the skill acquisition process by specifying an optimal movement pattern to the learner, thereby strengthening the representation of the desired action. Verbal feedback also is thought to be particularly useful because it helps learners understand when or why they made mistakes. The frequency of verbal input should gradually decrease over time so that learners can begin to rely on their own sensory systems to gauge their progress.

It is difficult to determine from past research how detailed instructions need to be to optimize skill acquisition. Once more, the information-processing approach suggests that early learners benefit from a limited number of simple instructions, whereas advanced learners are better equipped to deal with more detailed instructions. Practitioners also can use instructions to help focus the learner's attention on certain aspects of the task. In this regard, Wulf and colleagues (e.g., Wulf, McConnel, Gartner, & Schwarz, 2002; Wulf, McNevin & Shea, 2001) recommend using external-focus instructions that direct learners to the external consequences of their movement patterns rather than the internal processes of producing the required movement. For example, when learning to ride a bicycle, an external focus of attention might be the orientation and direction of the front wheel as the rider moves through the environment, whereas an internal focus might be what the legs and hands are doing with the pedals and handlebars. Instructions delivered as movement analogies have also been shown to be positive in reducing the learner's processing load (Liao & Masters, 2001).

Demonstrations of Technique

Providing a visual demonstration of the required technique is another way to present augmented information to the learner (Ashford et al., 2006). Many practitioners believe that a demonstration provides a visual model that the learner may more easily interpret than verbal commands. Further, many researchers encourage practitioners to use demonstrations early in learning to assist the coding of new information into a cognitive representation of a skill (Bandura, 1977). Although demonstrations have been shown to promote task consistency during learning, there is some concern that reproducing a particular movement pattern should not be viewed as achieving the task goal (Lee et al., 2001). In addition, there is still uncertainty over whether learners benefit from watching other learners or whether practitioners themselves should provide the demonstration (Magill, 2006). Horn and Williams (2004) suggested that the nature of the task dictates prescriptive advice regarding modeling (see table 1.1). For example, the learning of outcome-defined tasks, such as repairing a car engine or cooking a meal, benefits from expert models alternated frequently with practice, whereas process-defined tasks, such as a

TABLE 1.1 Research-Based Prescriptive Advice

	Type of task	Description	Examples	Advice	Research support
Increasingly outcome driven ↑ **Increasingly process-driven** ↓	Outcome-defined	The outcome of the action defines performance The process used to achieve the outcome is irrelevant	Computer tracking and game tasks, mechanical assembly, perceptual anticipation	Use multiple demonstrations for perceptual anticipation Make the strategy salient Alternate demonstration with practice Emphasize the action of objects rather than the model.	Weeks (1992); Weeks and Choi (1992) Burwitz (1975) Blandin et al. (1994) Hodges and Franks (2002)
	Outcome-dominated	The process or technique contributes to achieving the outcome, but outcome dominates the assessment of task performance	Higher cognitive: Semaphore and manual alphabet, movement sequence activities Lower cognitive: Weight lifting; performing complex motor skills for successful outcomes	Demonstrations before practice Encourage mental rehearsal Increase cognitive engagement by alternating demo and practice Lower cognitive Include learning models Provide model's KR	Bandura and Jeffrey (1973) Weeks et al. (1996) McCullagh and Caird (1990) Herbert and Landin (1994)
	Process-dominated	Outcomes contribute, but process dominates the assessment of performance outcomes	Performing complex actions such as kicking, throwing, or hitting with outcomes, but emphasizing technique	Minimize early intrinsic KR to induce rapid improvements in form Use demonstration retrospectively as a reference of correctness	Horn et al. (2002 and in press) Richardson and Lee (1999)
	Process-defined	The process defines performance Technique is the measured outcome, or no outcome is included	Diving, trampolining, gymnastics Performing techniques such as kicking, throwing, or hitting in absence of object or target	Guide learners' attention to key elements of the demonstration with verbal guidance Use slow motion to enhance relative motion	Champenoy and Janelle (1999) Scully and Carnegie (1998); Fehres and Olivier (1986)

Reprinted, by permission, from R. Horn and A.M. Williams, 2004, Observational learning: Is it time we took another look? In *Skill acquisition in sport: Research theory and practice,* edited by A.M. Williams and N. Hodges (Abingdon, UK: Routledge), 175-206.

gymnastics routine, may require slow-motion demonstrations combined with verbal guidance.

Summary

The scientific study of natural phenomena has always been influenced by the sociological and cultural influences of the time (Newell & Slifkin, 1998). In the study of human movement, theorists have been heavily influenced by the prevalent technology of the latter half of the 20th century, the so-called electronic and digital ages. Traditionally, information-processing approaches to motor learning and control have dominated sport science, kinesiology, and motor behavior, emphasizing the development of representations and plans for movement production (Rose & Christina, 2005). From this approach, the main goal has been to study the human brain, conceptualized as a capacity-limited, computational device into which raw sensory information is channeled and then processed with the help of stored representations of the world (e.g., Adams, 1971; Schmidt, 1975).

Traditional theories view symbolic movement plans as the major influence on how we control and learn actions. The increased efficiency and effectiveness of our movement representations help us to optimize and adaptively control our movements. A goal of cognitive neuroscience research has been to locate representations within the CNS, and practice is the process by which we increase the sophistication of these CNS-stored representations of the world and of our movements. Practitioners and physical therapists in many training and rehabilitation programs have implicitly adopted this popular view of the human performer. The traditional approach to motor learning and control has led to many advances in knowledge and has been described and evaluated in several important texts such as Schmidt and Lee (2005) and Magill (2006).

SELF-TEST QUESTIONS

1. Name some of the key research contributors to the development of skill acquisition theories. What features of skill acquisition did their work emphasize?

2. What common features do traditional models of skill acquisition share?

3. Apply Schmidt's schema theory to a movement skill of your choice. How should the skill be taught to a novice learner to optimize skill acquisition?

4. Compile a list of recommendations to be given to a movement practitioner. What considerations should be made concerning the task, the learner, and the practice environment?

ADDITIONAL READING

1. Schmidt, R.A. (1975). A schema theory of discrete motor learning. *Psychological Review, 82*:4, 225-260.

2. Schmidt, R., & Wrisberg, C.A. (2004). *Motor learning and performance* (3rd ed.). Champaign, IL: Human Kinetics.

3. Summers, J. (2004). A historical perspective on skill acquisition. In M. Williams & N. Hodges (Eds.), *Skill acquisition in sport: Research, theory, and practice* (pp. 1-26). Abingdon, UK: Routledge, Taylor, and Francis.

4. Willingham, D.B. (1998). A neuropsychological theory of motor skill learning. *Psychological Review, 105*, 558-584.

5. Wolpert, D.M., Ghahramani, Z., & Flanagan, J.R. (2001). Perspectives and problems in motor learning. *Trends in Cognitive Sciences, 5*, 487-494.

CHAPTER 2

Physical Constraints on Coordination
Dynamical Systems Theory

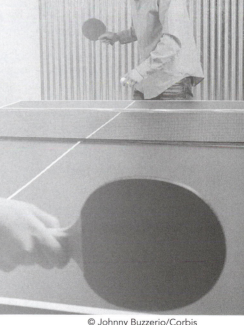

CHAPTER OUTLINE

© Johnny Buzzerio/Corbis

In this chapter we introduce concepts from dynamical systems theory as part of an alternative framework to the traditional theories of skill acquisition described in chapter 1. Dynamical systems theory provides a relevant model of understanding movement coordination and control in neurobiological systems. This approach views the learner as a complex, biological system composed of many independent but interacting subsystems. In many complex structures, the dynamical interaction between components can actually enhance the intrinsic system organization. These interactions can produce rich order within the system through a process known as *self-organization.* Self-organization processes exemplify the coordination tendencies that are inherent in many complex systems and are influenced by many constraints that act on the system.

We begin our analysis by defining complex systems and explaining how the human performer is a complex system. Then we describe how the process of skill acquisition takes place via the self-organizing properties of the human movement system. We explain how, during motor performance and learning, self-organizing properties are subjected to a range of constraints that shape the emergence of coordinated action. Self-organization under constraints is a major process that can be exploited during skill acquisition when practitioners create task constraints that encourage learners' exploratory behavior. In this respect, movement variability may play a functional role in helping learners explore the relevance of potential coordination solutions.

Complex Systems: A Definition

Dynamical systems theory emphasizes the need to understand natural phenomena as a system with many interacting component parts (e.g., Clarke & Crossland, 1985). A systems perspective provides an excellent rationale for studying human behavior because

> structures and configurations of things should be considered as a whole, rather than examined piece by piece. In a highly complex system like the human mind or human body all the parts affect each other in an intricate way, and studying them individually often disrupts their usual interactions so much that an isolated unit may behave quite differently from the way that it would behave in its normal context. (Clarke and Crossland, 1985, p. 16)

What do we mean by the term **complex system?** The word *complex* comes from the Latin word *complexus,* meaning "interwoven," and describes a network of related, interacting parts. So, complex systems are highly integrated systems that are made up of many interacting parts, each of which is capable of affecting other parts.

Characteristics of Complex Systems

Complex systems are fairly common in daily life. For example, the weather, the traffic flow in a large city, an ant colony, your favorite sport team, and even your own body are all phenomena that exhibit complexity. These systems share several fundamental attributes, including the following:

- Many independent and variable degrees of freedom (dfs). In the physical sciences, the term *degrees of freedom* typically refers to the independent components of a system that can fit together in many different ways. For example, performers in a dance troupe, workers in a commercial organization, and players on a sport team could be considered as independent dfs of a larger entity. Complexity is characterized by the number of potential configurations available to the independent parts of such a system. For example, the members of a dance troupe can take part in a number of different performance routines, which require different members to take on different roles. Larger dance troupes are capable of more diverse and complex routines, whereas the capacity for diversity and complexity in smaller troupes is less (see Newell & Vaillancourt, 2001).

- Many different levels in the system. Examples include the neural, hormonal, biomechanical, and psychological levels in the human body.

- The potential for nonlinearity of behavior (because the component parts can interact in many different ways). Examples include the unpredictable peaks and valleys in the financial market or the performance highs and lows of an athlete or sport team.

- The capacity for stable and unstable patterned relationships among system parts to occur through system self-organization (parts spontaneously adjusting and adapting to each other).

- The ability of subsystem components to limit or influence the behavior of other subsystems (see Gleick, 1987; Kaplan & Glass, 1995; Kauffman, 1993, 1995; Waldrop, 1992; Yates, 1979).

Complex Systems as Dynamical Systems

When we examine the microcomponents of a complex system, we observe constant interactions and fluctuations. The interactions among the individual parts of the system appear random, and there is the potential for much disorder within the whole system. For example, think of molecules of water in a stream, neurons in the nervous system, or individual blood cells in the human body. These microcomponents could potentially interact in unpredictable ways and thus result in system disorder, such as when the flow of water molecules becomes unpredictable after turbulence or when neurons in the cortex are induced by strobe lighting to fire at random, causing a seizure in people with epilepsy. However, analysis at the macroscopic (large-scale) level reveals surprisingly ordered patterns of behavior (Kauffman, 1993, 1995). At this level of analysis, complex systems exhibit coordination tendencies since individual components are capable of linking together to move in and out of functional and coherent patterns or synergies (Haken, 1996; Kelso & Engström, 2006).

A key to understanding the behavior of complex systems concerns how coordination occurs among the vast numbers of component parts. Dynamical systems theory embraces this challenge by deriving nonlinear mathematical descriptions to characterize the order that emerges within complex systems. Van Gelder and Port (1995) offer a liberal definition of a dynamical system as "any state-determined system with a numerical phase space and a rule of evolution (including differential equations and discrete maps) specifying trajectories in this space" (p. 9). The **numerical phase space** refers to all the hypothetical states of organization into which a dynamical system can evolve. In biological movement systems, these states correspond to patterns of coordination.

Because they are relatively open systems, dynamical systems can adopt different states of organization and harness surrounding energy sources to form stable patterns of organization. In nature, open systems are capable of receiving and outputting energy into the flows surrounding them, which means that they are sensitive to changes in their surroundings. The stable and functional patterns of organization exhibited by open systems are called **attractors.** For example, in a physical system formed by billions of molecules of water in a stream, an attractor is a stable region of system state space where the resulting force vector (that is, the direction and magnitude of any interacting forces on system flow) converges to a minimum (e.g., as in a vortex).

This situation results in a stable state of organization for any system, suggesting that a large perturbing force will be required to destabilize the particular order of the system at that time (e.g., an eddy or a strong current acting on a vortex) (Kugler, Shaw, Vincente, & Kinsella-Shaw, 1990). In neurobiological systems, attractors represent coordination tendencies among system components and are roughly synonymous with functional coordination patterns in the repertoire of a movement system. A good example of coordination tendencies is locomotion in humans when a runner's legs coordinate into an antiphase pattern (when one leg is in the stance phase supporting the body, the other leg is in flight phase, allowing gravity to accelerate the runner's center of mass in a series of controlled falls).

Constraints on Complex Systems

In complex systems, states of order emerge under constraints. This idea has been imported into human movement science from physics and biology, where scientists have been engaged in studying the emergence of movement behaviors under constraints (e.g., Kelso, 1995; Kugler, 1986; Kugler & Turvey, 1987). Newell (1986) proposed the idea of constraints as boundaries or features that limit the motion of the minute parts of a system. In other words, **constraints** are the numerous variables that define the phase space of a complex system.

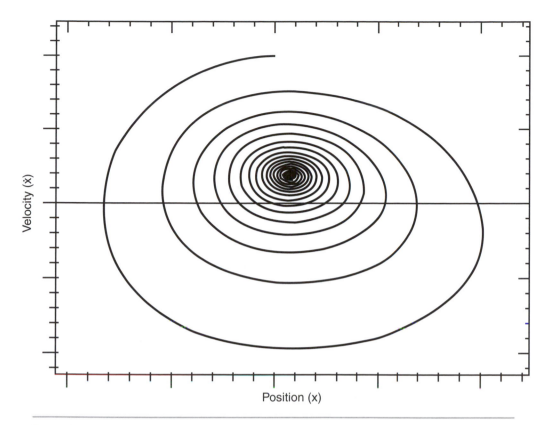

Figure 2.1 Constraints define the phase space of a complex system and both limit and enable the different behavioral trajectories that the system can adopt.

Constraints both limit and enable the number of behavioral trajectories that the system can adopt (see figure 2.1). It seems that complex systems are able to exploit the constraints that surround them in order to allow functional patterns of behavior to emerge in specific contexts. For example, a colony of millions of insects avoids random behavior by exploiting the informational constraint afforded by pheromones that they secrete into the earth to guide their concerted nest-building activity (Kugler & Turvey, 1987). Immediately, we can see how this process of emergent behavior is helpful if we want to adapt our movements to ever-changing performance contexts or to alterations in the skeletomuscular system as a result of aging or injury (Davids, Button, Araújo, Renshaw, & Hristovski, 2006).

Physical and Informational Constraints

Constraints can be either physical or informational. Physical constraints can be structural or functional in the human movement system. For example, the size and grip strength of a child's hands are structural physical constraints that influence how that child can pick up and manipulate an object such as a

The size and grip strength of a child's hands are structural physical constraints that influence how that child can pick up a toy.

toy train or a large ball during play. Functional physical constraints include processes such as reactions and perceptual abilities, which support movement performance. Informational constraints, on the other hand, are the various forms of energy flowing through the system, such as the pheromones for insects, light reflected from a toy train, or sound waves that a child perceives when a ball bounces across the floor. Young children explore haptic (touch) informational constraints as they pick up and play with objects in their environment. Informational constraints help to shape requisite movement responses and support the coordination of actions with respect to dynamic environments.

Self-Organization and Constraints

As noted earlier, complex open systems are capable of exchanging energy with the environment. A good example of a natural complex open system is a weather system, whose behavior is generally difficult to predict more than a few days in advance. Weather systems can contain differing amounts of energy due to air flows that vary in pressure and movement of water molecules from the oceans to clouds and back again. Achieving and maintaining stability is a challenge for open complex systems because of their potential for interacting with the environment. The problem with a weather system is that a tiny change in the energy flows that surround it can cause large-scale fluctuations in system output on one occasion and have minor effects at other times because the energy that exists within the system is never constant.

Given the longstanding laws of nonlinear thermodynamics, which predict a tendency toward entropy or disorder in nature, how can we explain the surprising amount of order that exists at a macroscopic level in many complex systems? To answer that question, we need to consider how open systems in nature can harness energy created by the interaction of their components at the local (microscopic) level to sustain order of the system at the macroscopic level. The capacity of an open complex system to exchange energy and matter with its environment provides it with natural tendencies to settle into attractors or stable patterns of organization; that is, it can take advantage of the physical process that we referred to earlier as **self-organization.**

To recap, biological systems, such as flocks of birds, an insect colony, or schools of fish, seem to have evolved the capacity to use environmental energy to sustain functional periods of stability that benefit the whole system (for a very good example in an ant colony see Gordon, 2007). These systems are able

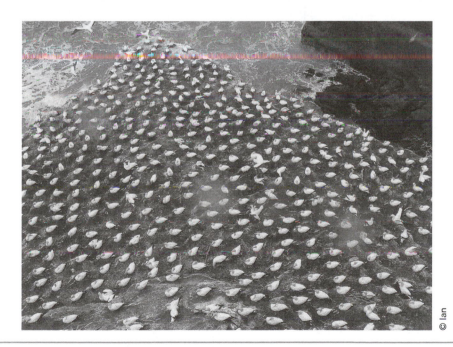

© Ian

Self-organizing order in biological systems is exemplified by nesting gannets in Muriwai National Park, west of Auckland, New Zealand. Although the nesting order appears regimented, this functional behavior emerges because it protects against possible predators during nesting season. Outside of the nesting season, these birds have a tendency to be argumentative and do not maintain such close proximity.

to seek and settle into functional attractors because they have a propensity for pattern formation (e.g., Prigogine & Stengers, 1984). In birds and fish, this spontaneous coordination tendency is manifested as flocking behavior. For example, in the case of flying birds, a V-like flocking pattern is common because it benefits the navigation of the whole flock without one bird acting as the controlling agent to direct the flight path. Similarly, sea birds adopt highly patterned nesting arrangements (about the length of one bird between nests) during the mating season without the need for a principal bird to dictate spacing. Fish swim randomly as they go about important daily activities such as feeding or mating, but they coalesce into highly synchronized schools when a predator appears.

All of these examples show that the openness of a system to surrounding energy flows is useful because energy is a source of information that acts as a constraint on the system. This informational constraint benefits the system by supporting functional and stable behavior patterns for relatively short periods of time. This form of dynamic stability, known as *metastability* (Kelso & Engström, 2006), is useful in complex, fluctuating environments. We will explore the influence of informational constraints in more detail in chapter 3.

In the study of open systems, scientists have been interested in the phase transitions that can emerge spontaneously in complex systems. **Phase transitions** are movements of the microcomponents of a system into and out of different states of organization. In weather systems, for example, the dynamics among system components typically lead to no large-scale changes in system behavior. There is merely a lot of underlying fluctuation that mildly affects system stability. However, critical changes in the energy arrays surrounding the system, such as a rise in atmospheric pressure within a weather system, can alter system stability and lead to macroscopic changes and reorganization into a different state (thunderstorms in tropical regions). Phase transitions form the basis of self-organization in complex systems, and examples of such pattern formations have been observed in open biological, physical, and chemical systems, such as when randomly moving fish gather into a synchronized school as a predator approaches.

Emergent Behavior in Human Movement

Self-organization is a powerful process that can help us adapt our movement coordination patterns to changing environmental circumstances, such as performing tennis strokes on different surfaces or driving in changing traffic conditions. How do we harness this natural process? To begin, self-organization in complex systems is not a completely blind process in which any random pattern can result. Typically, a dynamical system takes on few states of organization, and research has shown that we are not very good at producing random patterns of movement behavior. For example, Newell, Deutsch, Sosnoff, and Mayer-Kress (2006) have argued that producing random finger oscillations is a difficult task for humans and that the capacity to generate unstructured output is poorer in the larger movement effector systems, such as the legs and arms. Even when individuals are able to practice random movements over 5 days, little improvement can be observed (Newell, Deutsch, & Morrison, 2000), providing evidence for considerable structural and functional constraint on the dynamical dfs of the human motor system (Newell & Vaillancourt, 2001).

These findings support observations that natural dynamical systems tend to inhabit only certain parts of the total landscape of all possible states that a system can hypothetically adopt (i.e., the state space) (Kauffman, 1993, 1995). The type of order that emerges in the behavior of a system depends a great deal on existing environmental conditions and the constraints that shape the behavior (see Spotlight on Research).

Spotlight on Research

FROM HUMBLE BEGINNINGS TO THE HKB MODEL

When Scott Kelso published his series of studies (1981, 1984) examining changes in coordination between rhythmic finger movements, he may not have predicted how significant his ideas would become in the human movement sciences. In his original work, Kelso examined the spontaneous coordination dynamics emerging from the relative oscillations of several research participants' left and right index fingers during rhythmic movements. Surprisingly, each participant exhibited a spontaneous switch of coordination patterns as the frequency of finger movements was constrained by the beat of a metronome (i.e., a gradual increase from 1.25 to 3.5 hertz).

It was consistently shown that the relative phasing between each finger demonstrated stability in the coordination dynamics of the system at only two isolated attractor regions: fingers oscillating either in-phase (fingers moving toward the midline of the body together) or antiphase (one finger moving toward the body's midline while the other finger moves away from the midline) (see figure 2.2). The relative phase of any two oscillating systems (e.g., each leg used in walking) is the phase lag in one system's cycle of movement compared with the other. When the study participants began oscillating in the antiphase pattern, they eventually switched to an in-phase pattern as metronome frequency increased. The sudden phase transitions from one state of coordination to the other were not brought about by some intentional change prescribed by the participant, but through the self-organizing properties of the motor system.

Haken, Kelso, and Bunz (1985) proposed a mathematical model—the HKB model—that formally demonstrated how the movement behavior observed in the finger-waggling paradigm could emerge as the potential function of the movement system changed. The model demonstrated that scaling of a control parameter (e.g., metronomic beat frequency) could lead to a reduction in stability of the order parameter (e.g., relative

(CONTINUED)

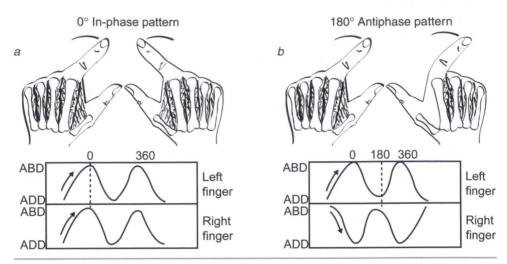

Figure 2.2 In the movements performed in Kelso's (1981, 1984) original experiments, *(a)* we can observe the 0° in-phase pattern, and *(b)* we can observe the 180° antiphase pattern. These patterns are thought to be intrinsically stable in rhythmic, bimanual movements. (ABD = abduction movements; ADD = adduction.)

Reprinted, by permission, from S.A. Wallace, 1996, Dynamic pattern perspective of rhythmic movement: An introduction. In *Advances in motor learning and control,* edited by H.N. Zelaznik (Champaign, IL: Human Kinetics), 170.

phase of finger movements). This behavior resulted from an alteration in the potential energy of the system, which Haken and colleagues modeled as two stable movement patterns. As a control parameter changes, the attractor landscape is deformed and system behavior switches from the least stable organization (antiphase) to the most stable (in-phase). In more dynamic environments where random forces are present, the degree of system stability is associated with the degree of fluctuations the movement system exhibits (Haken, 1996; Schöner, Haken, & Kelso, 1987).

The HKB model also had something interesting to note about other important features of the dynamical movement system, such as the relationship between attractor stability and the relaxation time, which is the speed at which the system would return to an attractor (stable motor patterning) following an external perturbation. Relaxation time has been used to test the stability of attractors in a variety of situations (e.g., Court, Bennett, Williams, & Davids, 2002, 2005; Scholz & Kelso, 1989). Since the innovative work of Haken, Kelso, and Bunz, researchers have found similar coordination tendencies, such as transitions, multistability, and sensitivity to frequency and amplitude, with a whole host of rhythmic movements. Although it seems that different rhythmic tasks may have different potential functions and, hence, different attractor regimes, the same self-organizational principles hold. From relatively simple beginnings, a new paradigm for studying motor behavior was born.

APPLICATION

Recreate Kelso's original paradigm. Oscillate your fingers in an antiphase fashion, slowly increase the speed, and explore the self-organization tendencies of your own movement system. List some of the control parameters that could affect when transitions might occur.

The exercise in the Spotlight on Research application is not just a frivolous party trick; it is of some significance when studying movement coordination. Consider, for example, how a skier's body position might self-organize to produce a perfectly timed turn on the ski trail. Because of the demanding nature of the ski trail, the skier's actions might not be determined in advance. Instead, both internal constraints such as the skier's anatomical organization and external constraints such as visual information and the contact of the skis with the snow influence the emergence of the skier's precise movement patterns on the

© Eyewire/Photodisc/Getty Images

Both internal and external constraints shape the emergence of the skier's precise movement patterns on the trail. A change in environmental conditions also could significantly affect the existing patterns of movement coordination.

trail (e.g., Bernstein, 1967; Warren, 1990). A change in environmental conditions, such as the gradient of the slope, the wind direction, or a patch of ice, could significantly affect the existing patterns of movement coordination. For instance, a steep slope would typically force a novice skier to adopt a pattern of traversing from side to side on the trail. By shifting the weight distribution over the inside ski and changing the alignment of the skis, the skier does not generate excessive downhill speed. This strategy provides a task-specific solution without a significant loss in postural stability.

Constraints and Movement Coordination

The implication of the ideas we've discussed so far is that perceptions, memories, intentions, plans, and actions may not be best conceived of as entities stored in the CNS. Rather, they may be better understood as self-organizing, macroscopic patterns formed by the interaction of the many system components and key constraints in the environment (Kelso, 1995; Kugler & Turvey, 1987). For example, the system components could be neurons in the brain firing together to form ideas, memories, or plans, or they might involve groups of muscles spanning several joints to form coordination patterns. Constraints

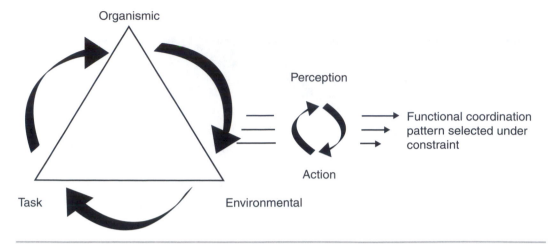

Figure 2.3 Three classes of constraints—organismic, environmental, and task—provide a coherent framework for understanding how coordination patterns emerge during goal-directed behavior.

are central to the self-organization process in human movement systems. A dynamical systems interpretation emphasizes environmental and physical constraints as well as individual constraints such as one's cognitions, memories, and intentions (Williams, Davids, & Williams, 1999).

According to Newell (1986), constraints can be classified into three categories: organismic, environmental, and task. These categories provide a coherent framework for understanding how coordination patterns emerge during goal-directed behavior (see figure 2.3).

Organismic Constraints

Organismic constraints refer to a person's characteristics, such as genes, height, weight, muscle–fat ratio, connective strength of synapses in the brain, cognitions, motivations, and emotions. Customary thought patterns, levels of practice, or visual defects can act as organismic constraints to shape the way a person approaches a particular performance goal. Such unique characteristics represent resources that are brought to bear on the task problem or limitations that can lead to individual-specific adaptations. A crucial distinction between many biological organisms and humans is that humans can use internal energy sources to intentionally constrain their actions to achieve goals or desired outcomes. That is, human behavior is not deterministic but can be intentionally driven (Kugler et al., 1990).

Environmental Constraints

Environmental constraints are global, physical variables in nature, such as ambient light, temperature, or altitude. On Earth, gravity is a key environmental constraint on movement coordination for all tasks, as our example of a skier traversing a steep mountain slope showed. Considering our skier once more, we can use the visual flow presented by a ski mogul to regulate the torques generated across the hip and knee joints. Larger mounds of snow require the skier to flex the hips and knees in order to absorb the reaction imparted to the legs, and ambient temperature can affect the skier's muscle properties. Additionally, some environmental constraints are social rather than physical, including family support, peer groups, societal expectations, values, and cultural norms (Haywood & Getchell, 2005).

Task Constraints

Task constraints are usually more specific to performance contexts than environmental constraints are and include task goals, specific rules associated with an activity, activity-related implements or tools, surfaces, ground areas, and pitches and boundary markings such as nets, line markings, and posts. Even with apparently stable activities, such as playing a musical instrument or swinging a golf club, motor behavior can fluctuate because the task constraints may vary from performance to performance. For example, musicians have to adapt to playing in different settings (e.g., small concert rooms, large auditoriums, outdoor venues), each with distinctive acoustics, sound systems, and stage layouts. They may even have to adapt to performing with different instruments on occasions, which may affect the nuances of performance.

© Jim Whitmer

Although playing a musical instrument is considered a highly stable activity, the musician's motor behavior may fluctuate because the task constraints can vary from performance to performance.

Being able to vary motor performance according to the different contexts of action is an integral part of skill acquisition, and adaptive learning allows people to cope with novel task constraints as performance conditions change. To encourage flexibility and adaptability in patients, physical therapists often manipulate task constraints. For example, a therapist might encourage a wheelchair patient to negotiate a busy and cluttered enclosed area in an attempt to improve the patient's control and maneuvering of the wheelchair. Such practices also encourage the patient to explore alternative coordination solutions and hence optimize techniques in daily motor skills.

Interacting Constraints

During goal-directed activity, the interaction of organismic, environmental, and task constraints on the neuromuscular system results in the emergence of different states of coordination that become optimized with practice and experience. For example, how a climbing instructor scales a rocky outcrop is a consequence of many constraints at any one time, including the climber's genes, physical endurance levels, and injury status; the nature of the climbing surface; and the climber's overall goals such as getting to the top as quickly as possible or demonstrating a safe path to students.

Because the three classes of constraints can interact, it is sometimes difficult to distinguish among them. For example, environmental constraints include surrounding energy flows (e.g., ambient light), whereas the specific nature of information sources is a key task constraint for learners (e.g., light reflected off the walls and floor of a swimming pool). In both examples the surrounding energy flows are the same, but the different task constraints lead to specific information sources being useful under varying performance contexts.

Another key idea from the study of nonlinear systems is that constraints on behavior are by no means permanent (Guerin & Kunkle, 2004). Research has taught us that constraints on motor performance are often temporary, and during performer–performer or performer–environment interactions, they can strengthen or decay on different timescales. For example, we can consider an infant's developing body as a slowly decaying constraint on its walking capability as the muscle-to-fat ratio of the lower limbs alters over time. However, if the mother calls out to her infant with a toy, this new constraint might have a temporary but irresistible emergent influence on the infant's coordination. The consequence for the behavior of emerging or decaying constraints is an increase or decrease in the self-organizing entropy of the system. This is an important point to consider in skill acquisition, and it is of particular importance when designing practice and rehabilitation environments, as we note in chapter 5. Practitioners should expect that the constraints on each individual are dynamic, interacting, and may be changing over time, as a result of influences such as development, learning, aging, and experience.

Coordination Processes in Human Movement Systems

Understanding how order emerges among the dfs of complex, dynamical systems is the fundamental problem for researchers of skill acquisition. During the 1980s and 1990s, when theoreticians introduced dynamical systems theory to the study of human movement coordination, they immediately recognized the links between their theories and the insights of Russian physiologist, Nikolai Bernstein. This timely interaction of ideas stimulated interest in the role of constraints on motor control and skill acquisition.

Bernstein and the Degrees of Freedom Problem

How do humans coordinate the activity of all the movement subsystems such as postural control, transport, and object manipulation? Russian movement physiologist Nikolai Bernstein (1967) reminded us that studying the processes of movement coordination is necessary to help us understand this question. He was concerned with how the many microcomponents of the human movement system—muscles, joints, and limb segments—are coordinated during the performance of complex tasks. For example, gymnasts bringing together parts of their lower and upper body while somersaulting, drivers using their foot and both hands to steer a car by braking and moving the wheel, and dancers coordinating arms and legs during a pas de deux neatly illustrate this coordination problem.

Understanding how the learner employs and constrains the large number of relevant motor system dfs during actions like reaching and grasping has, as mentioned in chapter 1, become known as Bernstein's (1967) degrees of freedom problem. Bernstein's definition of acquiring movement coordination neatly captures the fundamental issue in a dynamical systems interpretation of human movement. The acquisition of coordination is viewed as "the process of mastering redundant degrees of freedom of the moving organ, in other words its conversion to a controllable system" (p. 127).

Bernstein (1967) proposed that learners initially form specific functional muscle–joint linkages or synergies to manage the large number of dfs that are controlled in the human movement system. He suggested that such functional groupings compress the physical components of the movement system and specify how the relevant dfs for an action become mutually dependent. Synergies among motor system components help learners discover and assemble the relevant couplings between limbs (e.g., coordinating the braking action of a foot with the steering action of both hands when turning a car) to cope with the abundance of dfs (Mitra, Amazeen, & Turvey, 1998). In this way, fluctuations in the number of dfs used over repetitions of a task are managed by constraining variability in their implementation to a small subspace of the total number available (Scholz, Schöner & Latash, 2000; Todorov & Jordan,

2002). For example, when learning to drive a car, learners could potentially use either foot to depress the brake pedal and use a variety of shoulder, elbow, or wrist movements to turn the steering wheel. These limb segments constitute a considerable number of different motor system dfs that might be used to achieve the movement goal. With practice, eventually this large number of dfs is reduced to a smaller subset that is easier to manage and regulate (i.e., the wrists and right foot).

According to Bernstein (1967), the initial coordination patterns for tasks such as casting a fishing rod or maintaining balance on a surfboard begin as fixed, rigid linkages between body parts. This early learning strategy helps people cope with the extreme abundance of dfs in the motor system. The assembly of a functional coordination solution is beyond the learner's capacity and so the problem of controlling the movement system is managed by "dysfunctionally, suboptimally or overly" constraining the available motor system dfs (Broderick & Newell, 1999, p. 166). A common, but by no means universal, observation is that learners reduce the active regulation of individual mechanical dfs at the motor system periphery to a minimum. With learning and experience, the fixed characteristic of coordination is progressively altered as movement system dfs are released and allowed to reform into different configurations or synergies for specific purposes. Typically, as a result of extended practice, the initially strong couplings between muscles and joints are gradually unfixed and formed into task-specific coordinative structures

© Stockbyte

According to Bernstein (1967), the initial coordination patterns for tasks such as maintaining balance on a surfboard begin as fixed, rigid linkages between body parts.

so that internal and external forces can be better exploited to increase movement economy and efficiency (Bernstein, 1967; Newell, 1991). For example, the stiff upright stance adopted by the rigid coupling of hip, knee, and ankle joints in a novice surfer gradually becomes loosened with practice. Eventually there is a greater reliance on a coupling between only a few key dfs, such as the knee joints, for producing appropriate muscle torques to guide the board and harness the energetic impulses from currents and waves to create rapid transitions in the water.

Interestingly, it may be necessary for people recovering from injury or illness to temporarily reshape learned movement patterns with their reconfigured or altered dfs (e.g., walking on crutches with a broken leg, grasping an object after a finger amputation). The coordination patterns that arise early in relearning a skill have been given different names, such as *task-specific devices* (e.g., Bingham, 1988), *information–movement couplings* (Bootsma & van Wieringen, 1990; Davids, Kingsbury, Bennett, & Handford, 2001; Savelsbergh & van der Kamp, 2000), and *coordinative structures* (Schmidt & Fitzpatrick, 1996; Turvey, 1990).

Coordinative Structures in Action: Kicking a Soccer Ball

Coordinative structures harness the coordination tendencies that exist in neurobiological systems. They are designed for a specific purpose or activity, such as when groups of muscles are temporarily assembled into coherent units to achieve specific task goals, like throwing a Frisbee or hammering a nail. Quality perceptual information is necessary for assembling coordinative structures because the details of their organization are not completely predetermined and are tuned by the constraints of each activity. The assembly of coordinative structures is a dynamical process that depends on relevant sources of perceptual information related to a performer's key properties (e.g., proprioceptive information from muscles and joints) and the environment (e.g., vision of a target or surface). With practice, coordinative structures become more flexible and emerge from the rigidly fixed configurations that learners use early on to manage the multitude of motor system dfs. With each task goal, coordinative structures are assembled anew and may slightly vary each time the performer constructs an action in a dynamic environment.

For example, soccer players learn to adapt their coordinative structure for kicking a ball so that they can use it under changing conditions. These conditions may include sidefoot passes, goal chips, or shots; pitches that vary in dimensions; changing weather conditions; and motor system fatigue. This characteristic of skill-based differences can be observed in qualitative form in figure 2.4, which depicts the kicking skills of a novice soccer player and an experienced soccer player. These images qualitatively show that skill-based differences in coordination characteristics remain obvious throughout the kick,

Figure 2.4 Skill-based differences in coordination characteristics remain obvious throughout the kick where the expert kicker *(a)* shows greater hip extension and knee flexion than the novice kicker *(b)*.

from the preparation phase to the follow-through phase, where the expert kicker shows greater hip extension and knee flexion than the novice kicker.

Anderson and Sidaway's (1994) detailed analysis of soccer players confirms these differences. They found that novice kickers did not show the same coordination patterns associated with expert kickers. The rigidness of novice movement and the flexible nature of expert kicking are depicted in figure 2.5. Notice that before practice, the joint range of motion (ROM) for knee flexion and extension during kicking by novices is smaller in magnitude than for the experts (see the curve with open squares). Smaller ranges of joint ROM could signify greater rigidity of movement. After practicing 10 weeks at 15 minutes per week, the novice coordination pattern (figure 2.5a) begins to resemble that of the experts (figure 2.5b).

During the performance of motor tasks, the CNS typically can select from a large number of dfs for regulating movements (see Latash, 2000). Hasan and

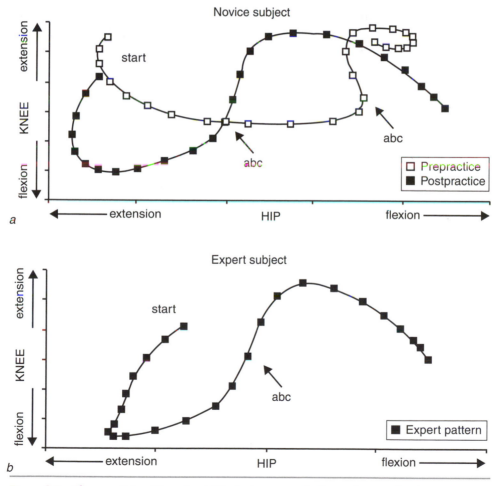

Figure 2.5 After practicing 10 weeks at 15 minutes per week, the novice coordination pattern (curve with black square) (a) begins to resemble that of the experts (b).

Reprinted with permission from *Research Quarterly for Exercise and Sport*, Vol. 65, No. 2, 93-99, Copyright 1994 by the American Alliance for Health, Physical Education, Recreation and Dance, 1900 Association Drive, Reston, VA 20191.

Thomas (1999) have referred to this abundance of dfs as "an embarrassment of riches" (p. 380) for the human CNS, and it has even been proposed that many dfs become redundant in some actions because they do not actively contribute to the regulation of an action.

It is important to understand the relationship between the controllability of the motor system and the flexibility of movement coordination. On the one hand, the abundance of motor system dfs can provide the opportunity for much-needed flexibility in adapting movement patterns to dynamic environments. On the other hand, the CNS has the problem of controlling the behavior of the motor system dfs in dynamic environments, which it achieves through the assembly of functional coordinative structures. By being open to information from the environment, physical constraints on motor system dfs can be adapted to function within each unique performance situation. In other words, movement coordination is controlled with respect to environmental events, surfaces, and objects during performance of many activities. This quality of the movement system invokes a second definition of coordination, which is discussed in chapter 3. We conclude this chapter by examining how dynamical movement systems use variability in coordination patterns to satisfy constraints.

Functional Role of Variability in Movement Systems

Because movement behavior emerges from the assembly of the many dfs of the movement system, it follows that practitioners need to understand the constraints on action. The large number of dfs in neurobiological systems naturally affords variability and adaptation in human movement. A large body of research shows that learners can achieve task outcomes by using different patterns of coordination (Davids, Bennett, & Newell, 2006). In the literature on movement science, this idea is informed by the concept of **degeneracy,** which refers to the capability of structurally distinct parts of complex neurobiological systems to achieve different outcomes in varying contexts. It is exemplified by the networks that exist at different levels of neurobiological systems, including the molecular, genetic, and musculoskeletal levels (Davids et al., 2007).

In neurobiological systems, degeneracy provides the capacity for the variability of actions required to instantaneously negotiate information-rich, dynamic environments (Edelman & Gally, 2001). For example, it is now well established that motor equivalence, or the ability of different patterns of neuromuscular activity to achieve specific movement outcomes, can provide the degenerate human movement system with the capacity to contextually adjust actions in dynamic environments. Degeneracy of human movement systems therefore provides the capacity to trade off specificity and diversity of actions under changing task constraints (Edelman & Gally, 2001).

We can consider intraindividual variability as functional because it permits great flexibility in adapting to a nonstationary environment (see Newell & Corcos, 1993). This is the sort of movement variability that skilled cross country athletes exhibit when slight alterations in running style can compensate for uneven terrain, different surfaces, and weather conditions. Additionally, variation in the way a person applies force in movements such as gait may help to prevent injury to the skeletomuscular system caused by constant repetition of a specific motor pattern (Hamill, Haddad, Heiderscheit, van Emmerik, & Li, 2006). As we noted earlier, movement between stable attractor states actually relies on the inherent instabilities (at a microscopic level) within any open complex system. Movement systems exhibit these instabilities in the form of critical fluctuations, or temporary losses in stability (Schöner et al., 1987). This prominent feature provides both theorists and movement practitioners with a way of predicting when a transition from one coordination pattern to another may be about to occur. By plotting the variability of a relevant order parameter as a control parameter changes, one should see increased within-individual variability before a transition followed by decreased variability as the movement system settles into a new stable state (Haken et al., 1985). Some examples from sport and motor impairments are useful to demonstrate how variability might be considered functional.

Key Concept

In the engineering sciences, an instability may be a sign of a dangerous malfunction in a system that needs to be repaired. After all, one would not voluntarily walk across an unstable bridge over a river. However, don't be fooled into thinking that instability in neurobiological systems is always a sign of weakness and poor functioning. Kelso (1992) recognized the important relationship between stability and instability in the complex, dynamical movement system, referring to instability as a "fundamental generator of change in open systems" (p. 261). Instabilities allow performers to adapt movements over different timescales to events such as injuries and illnesses or novel task circumstances. Without instabilities, athletes would not be able to adapt to changing constraints during performance and practice. In later chapters, we'll explore what instability implies for movement practitioners.

Variability Under Dynamic Task Constraints

Have you ever wondered how elite table tennis players cope with the severe time constraints of the sport? Tyldesley and Whiting (1975) suggested that players developed consistent techniques through extensive practice. Although within-individual levels of consistency have sometimes been reported as being very high in skilled performers (e.g., Schmidt, 1985), the distribution of variability within each trial repetition can vary. For example, during the forehand drive, skilled players typically show more variation in the trajectory of the paddle at the beginning of the drive. This is reduced to a minimal amount at the movement endpoint: the point of paddle–ball contact (e.g., Bootsma & van Wieringen, 1990). In a dynamic sport like table tennis, a higher level of variability at the movement starting point is exactly what a player needs when selecting a shot from a repertoire of strokes. The higher level of variability at the movement initiation allows the player to adapt to the different locations of the ball when the opponent returns it. This feature might also reflect an attempt to disguise the type of shot the player is about to play. Too little variability at the beginning of the movement would not allow a player to adopt some of the different start positions with the paddle, and this characteristic is typically exhibited by static learners with a limited repertoire of shots.

The skilled players studied by Bootsma and van Wieringen (1990) demonstrated a gradual reduction in variability during the stroke as the movement progressed. This observation led to the concept of funnel-shaped control to describe the shape of the reduction of variability as the stroke progressed (Davids, Handford, & Williams, 1994; see figure 2.6). Bootsma and van Wieringen viewed this reduction as a functional response by the skilled players because the point at which one does not want too much variability is when the ball contacts the paddle. Too much variability in spatial displacement of the paddle at this point of the movement would make ball control extremely difficult, and it is more a feature of novice and intermediate performance (Tyldesley & Whiting, 1975).

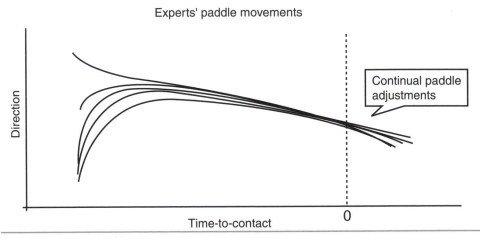

Figure 2.6 Studying the movements of skilled players, Bootsma and van Wieringen (1990) observed a gradual reduction in variability during the stroke as the movement progressed. This observation led to the concept of funnel-shaped control to describe the shape of the reduction.

From R.J. Bootsma and P.C.W. van Wieringen, "Timing an attacking forehand drive in table tennis," *Journal of Experimental Psychology: Human Perception and Performance* Volume 16, pp. 21-29, 1990, Copyright © American Psychological Association. Reprinted with permission.

These findings emphasize how differing amounts of variability can occur in different parts of the movement system. In some parts of the system, higher levels of variability can actually reflect the performer's subconscious compensatory measures. Typically, this compensatory mechanism is only found in skilled performers who are able to vary key microcomponents of a coordinative structure in order to stabilize a desired outcome of the system. If one microcomponent of the coordinative structure is perturbed by forces and subject to variation, the other components of the system adjust their relationship in order to maintain stability of the system (and outcome) (Scholz et al., 2000).

Variability Under Static Task Constraints

Functional variability is not simply a phenomenon of dynamic contexts, it has also been observed under more static task constraints. For example, in studying the performance of skilled and unskilled pistol shooters, Arutyunyan, Gurfinkel, and Mirskii (1968) reported different levels of variability in each joint of the upper arm in the skilled performers, which contributed to their successful achievement of the task (see also Scholz et al., 2000). Higher levels of variability in the shoulder and elbow joints complemented each other to allow the wrist to maintain a stable position. As with the table tennis forehand drive, the point of contact of the hand with the pistol was the point at which the magnitude of intratrial variability was lowest. The same high levels of variability were not seen in the shoulder and elbow joints of unskilled shooters. Consequently, the pistol position remained unstable and was more variable during shooting.

Conversely, recent research with patients who exhibit movement disorders such as Parkinson's disease reveals repetitive, stereotypic patterns with a striking degree of consistency (see van Emmerik & van Wegen, 2000). For example, children with spastic hemiplegic cerebral palsy exhibit reduced variability in coordination among the joints of affected limbs while walking (Jeng, Holt, Fetters, & Certo, 1996). In addition, people with tardive dyskinesia, a neurological disorder, display low levels of variability in the distribution of foot pressure applied to the surface of the ground during simple postural control tasks (Hamill et al., 2006). The striking implication from such research could be that many movement disorders might be attributed to a diminished capacity to exhibit functional movement variability.

Summary

In this chapter, we discussed how researchers have applied dynamical systems theory to the study of coordination in human movement systems. We outlined the significance of key ideas borrowed from mathematics, physics, and biology, such as complexity, self-organization processes, and constraints. Understanding coordination in dynamical movement systems represents an important scientific challenge for human movement specialists. Bernstein (1967) was the first to emphasize the need to understand coordination among motor system components. He argued that early in learning, people rigidly fix motor system dfs to cope with the redundant number available. Later in learning, synergies (i.e., coordinative structures) are imposed to functionally group motor system dfs to ensure that movements are adapted to changing circumstances of performance.

From a dynamical systems view, coordination is a property that emerges from each individual movement system in response to the constraints that need to be satisfied. Newell's (1986) model of interacting constraints highlights how dynamical movement systems can take advantage of inherent self-organization processes at different levels of the human body. Newell's model identifies the main categories of constraints—organismic, environmental, and task—that shape the coordination patterns emerging during performance and, as we shall discover, skill acquisition.

Although variability often has been viewed as noise or error that must be eliminated, dynamical systems theory implies a new approach to understanding variability of motor output. Because each person is different and performance circumstances are constantly changing, variability of motor output plays a functional role in helping people adapt to constraints. Variability permits a flexible adaptation to the constraints of a dynamic environment, a useful characteristic in rich and diverse performance contexts. This idea is at the heart of the constraints-led approach to skill acquisition.

SELF-TEST QUESTIONS

1. Think of an example of a complex system in a sport, exercise, or rehabilitation setting. What characteristics does this system share with other complex systems such as the weather or the CNS?

2. In what way does the concept of self-organization under constraints differ from the traditional ideas of a hierarchical movement system?

3. Describe how the control of a complex multijoint movement, such as the front crawl in swimming, may be explained from the dynamical systems approach.

4. How would you explain to athletes that movement variability is a vital part of their development?

ADDITIONAL READING

1. Bernstein, N.A. (1996). On dexterity and its development. In M. Latash & M.T. Turvey (Eds.), *Dexterity and its development* (pp. 2-244). Mahwah, NJ: LEA.

2. Corbetta, D., & Vereijken, B. (1999). Understanding development and learning of motor coordination in sport. *International Journal of Sport Psychology, 30,* 507-530.

3. Davids, K., Glazier, P., Araújo, D., & Bartlett, R.M. (2003). Movement systems as dynamical systems: The role of functional variability and its implications for sports medicine. *Sports Medicine, 33,* 245-260.

4. Kauffman, S.A. (1995). *At home in the universe: The search for laws of complexity.* London: Viking.

5. Kelso, J.A.S. (1995). *Dynamic patterns: The self-organization of brain and behaviour.* London: MIT Press.

CHAPTER 3

Informational Constraints on Coordination

An Ecological Perspective

CHAPTER OUTLINE

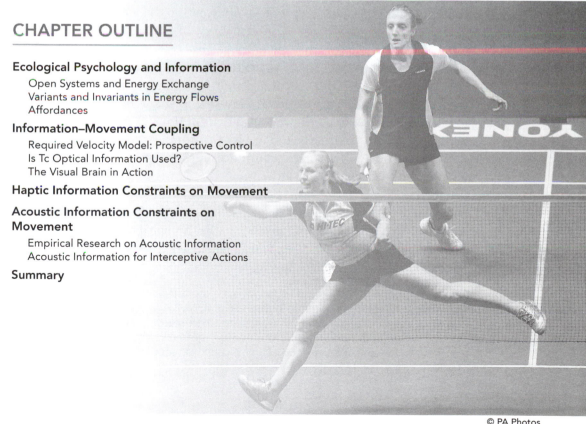

A constraints-led approach to skill acquisition is concerned with two overarching issues. In chapter 2 we discussed the first issue—Bernstein's (1967) insights regarding the physical constraints on motor system dfs. The second issue concerns how neurobiological systems coordinate actions with respect to important environmental events, objects, and surfaces, and it is the basis for James Gibson's (1979) research. This chapter focuses on the informational constraints on skill acquisition from the perspective of ecological psychology. Because healthy humans typically place significant emphasis on vision while learning to coordinate actions with their environment, our initial focus in this chapter will be on visual information. In later sections we will discuss the role of other informational constraints such as haptic (touch) and acoustic (sound) flow during skill acquisition.

Ecological Psychology and Information

Interceptive actions require coordination between the relevant parts of the movement system and between the relevant system components and the object or surface to be intercepted. For example, how does a child learn to pick up a toy? What information does a surgeon use when making a delicate incision during an operation? When coordinating their movements with respect to their environment, people need precise information to locate objects, obstacles, or surfaces in space (*where* information) at a specific instant in time (*when* information) (Davids, Savelsbergh, Bennett, & van der Kamp, 2002). Savelsbergh and Bootsma (1994) indicated that three task constraints need to be satisfied for successful coordination of movements with environmental events. Performers need to (1) ensure that they contact an object or surface in the environment at an appropriate moment in time, (2) ensure contact at the intended velocity and force, and (3) ensure contact at an intended spatial orientation. To satisfy these task constraints, performers need access to quality information to support their actions.

Michaels and Beek (1995) proposed how Gibson's (1979) insights in ecological psychology emphasized the "circular relations" (p. 261) existing between the systems for perception and action in the human body. The biological significance of this approach is captured neatly by the comments of Kugler and Turvey (1987):

> Ecological Science, in its broadest sense, is a multidisciplinary approach to the study of living systems, their environments and the reciprocity that has evolved between the two. . . . Ecological Psychology . . . [emphasizes] the study of information transactions between living systems and their environments, especially as they pertain to perceiving situations of significance to planning and executing of purposes activated in an environment. (p. xii)

Open Systems and Energy Exchange

To understand how information constrains behavior, we need to return to the concept of an open system, which we discussed briefly in chapter 2. Open systems are common in nature. Many biological organisms are open systems because they have variable amounts of energy moving among their components at any given moment (see figure 3.1). Whenever forces are applied within an open system, there are usually changes to system organization because internal energy within the system (e.g., as a result of the mechanics of limb movements) interacts with the available forces in the environment (e.g., reactive forces, gravity, friction, air resistance) (Kugler, Kelso, & Turvey, 1982).

For example, it is this openness that skilled ice-skaters are able to exploit as they use the momentum created by applying muscle forces of the lower legs and arms in a jump and spin (internal source of energy), with additional force available from the low

Figure 3.1 Because many biological organisms have variable amounts of energy moving among their components at any given moment, they are considered open systems.

coefficient of friction offered by the icy surface of the rink (external source). On the one hand, this combination allows skilled skaters to be more energy efficient and to generate more vertical and rotational forces. On the other hand, novice skaters are unable to control the additional forces available from the low coefficient of friction of the ice, and the changes to their movement patterns can be more abrupt and unintended.

The point is that complex, living organisms have onboard sources of energy (e.g., stored in muscle) that allow them to be self-sustaining and adaptive. With experience, they can also learn to exploit a range of surrounding environmental energy flows that act as a form of information to guide the system more efficiently (Kugler & Turvey, 1987).

This is good news for those of us who want to save energy, and particularly for athletes and professionals with physically demanding jobs. With task practice, they can become increasingly efficient in using their internal energy sources while also becoming skilled at exploiting freely available energy from forces such as gravity and friction, as evidenced by the skilled movements of acrobats and high-wire artists (e.g., see Sparrow, 2000). In accordance with Bernstein's (1967) ideas, therefore, coordination and control of movement do not occur in a vacuum and do not result from muscular force alone. A hallmark of increasing expertise in many physical activities is energy conservation, signaled by the capacity to exploit available reactive forces as a source of energy to be harnessed during action.

There is another way in which skill acquisition results in increasing expertise in exploiting the energy available in the environment. Skilled performers are able to exploit surrounding energy flows, such as optical energy in the form of light reflected off objects and surfaces, to use as information to constrain their actions (Gibson, 1979). We can begin to understand how energy can constrain actions by considering two important concepts in ecological psychology (Gibson, 1979): the relationship between variants and invariants in energy flows, and affordances for action.

Key Concept

Open systems are able to exchange energy and matter with their environment. For this reason the behavior of open systems in nature should be studied with reference to the specific environments in which they are located (Gordon, 2007). An important implication of this idea is that coordination in open movement systems is best analyzed in the midst of the stream of action (Reed, 1988). Most actions do not occur in a vacuum but take place in a dynamic context in which the surrounding energy flows provide many opportunities for exploitation of available forces to support perception and action. Movement scientists should thus beware of creating artificial and overly static movement tasks. Instead, the study of perception and action should take place in realistic environments provided by natural activities in work, sport, and other performance settings.

Variants and Invariants in Energy Flows

We are completely surrounded by energy. Light and sound waves and electrical activity in the nervous system all constitute significant forms of energy that we are equipped to detect. When we move, we affect the energy around us in many important ways. The energy flows generated from our movements can be both **invariant** (constant) and **variant** (changing). Surfaces, objects, and textures in the environment reflect light and in doing so provide structure for moving observers. For example, when some element of the superficial structure in the informational array changes as the performer moves relative to surfaces, objects, or events, the energy flow is considered variant. However, there is also an underlying essential structure that is invariant despite the changes in the superficial structure.

According to Gibson (1979), when a person moves, the essential structure of the ambient optical array, which underlies its superficial structure, is revealed. The essential structure of the optic array consists of invariant features of the visual environment that provide information for action. Information in the form of invariants is revealed to moving individuals because, although the superficial form of the environment might differ, the underlying essential form remains consistent and therefore provides information for performers.

An example will help us understand these ideas, and later we will examine tau, an optical invariant that has received a great deal of research attention. But it is also helpful to look at an example from golf. In figure 3.2, the golfer is exploring the invariant structure of a putting green as he moves around the ball and hole to study a required putt. The invariant structure of each putting green includes the information sources that are always available, regardless of whether one is playing on Pebble Beach (United States), Royal Lytham and St. Annes (United Kingdom), or a local golf course. Experienced golfers know that as they move between the ball and the hole, important characteristics such as the cut of the grass and subtle contours of the putting surface become more apparent (Button & Pepping, 2002). Movements of the performer reveal these invariant information sources for action.

The information from the relative motion between a performer and environmental objects and surfaces can be directly perceived in the structure of the optic array. A perceiver's visual system can pick up the alterations to the optic structure and the invariant structure can be immediately revealed for supporting action. This is why Gibson (1979) refers to these invariants as being *high order*. Given these theoretical ideas, it is not surprising that much research time and effort has been devoted to identifying those invariants

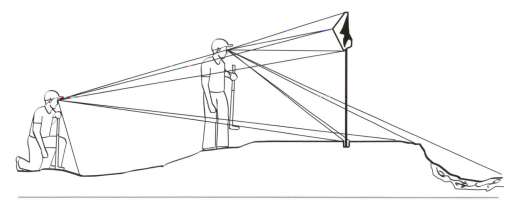

Figure 3.2 The golfer explores the invariant structure of a putting green as he moves around the ball and hole to study a required putt. Experienced golfers know that as they move between the ball and the hole, important characteristics of the putting green become more apparent.

that can specify actions. One of the most closely studied invariants in the informational array is an optic variable known as tau. Since its conceptualization by the experimental psychologist David Lee three decades ago, it has generated a significant amount of research and debate in the literature.

Research on the optic invariant tau has shown that, when a nondeforming object such as a ball moves toward an observer, the contours of the ball form a solid visual angle (see figure 3.3). This optic flow is perceived over time as a nested hierarchy of solid angles that expands symmetrically on the observer's retina. The optical information specified on the retina by the relative rate of expansion of the visual solid angle enclosed by these contours is called **tau.** Tau provides the individual with information about the remaining time to contact (Tc) between the point of observation and an approaching object (Lee, 1976).

Assuming that an approaching object has a constant velocity and is traveling toward the point of observation, there are considerable advantages of being able to perceive Tc. For instance, the individual does not need to indirectly process ambiguous cues on distance, object size, and velocity and perform mental calculations to compute the object's time of arrival. These cues from an approaching object are part of the superficial structure of the ambient array that differs between performance contexts. Not needing to rely on indirect processing of superficial structure is particularly beneficial in dynamic activities such as driving on an expressway, playing tennis, or skating rapidly on an ice rink. In these activities, performers have little time to react and may not have the time to calculate the time of arrival of an object or surface while interpreting events in the environment.

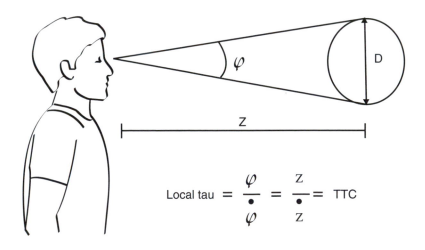

$$\text{Local tau} = \frac{\varphi}{\overset{\bullet}{\varphi}} = \frac{z}{\overset{\bullet}{z}} = \text{TTC}$$

Figure 3.3 Tau provides information about the remaining Tc between the point of observation and an approaching object.

GRASPING TAU

Savelsbergh, Whiting, and Bootsma (1991) attempted to determine whether the timing of an interceptive action was consistent with the use of first-order Tc information. Unlike previous research that inferred the use of tau, Savelsbergh and colleagues used a clever method to manipulate the relative rate of retinal expansion (tau) of the image of an approaching object. Under conditions of binocular viewing (experiment 1) and monocular viewing (experiment 2), participants were required to catch balls that approached on an inverted parabolic trajectory attached to a pendulum. They used three balls with different diameters: a large (7.5-centimeter) and small (5.5-centimeter) ball with a constant diameter, and a gradually deflating ball that changed in diameter from 7.5 to 5.5 centimeters during approach. To create the deflating ball without the participants' knowledge, the researchers encased a small ball with a balloon that was mechanically deflated with a vacuum pump. Although seemingly artificial, this is precisely the sort of controlled setting that scientists need when they want to identify specific invariant sources of information through experimental manipulation.

In the experiment, the relative rate of expansion of the deflating ball did not correspond to the movement pattern generated by a nondeflating ball approaching with a constant velocity. In effect, the relative rate of expansion of a deflating ball specified a longer Tc than a nondeflating ball. Logically, if tau regulated timing of the one-handed catch, then key aspects in the interceptive movement should occur later for the deflating ball compared with the large and small balls of constant diameter. In addition, the researchers observed no expected differences in the participants' response to the large and small balls of constant diameter because tau (the invariant) is independent of object size (the variant). There were also no expected differences for binocular and monocular viewing conditions because tau, which is specified in monocular geometry of the structure of light reflected from the ball's surface onto the retina, was available in both conditions.

The experiment showed that participants opened the hand to a wider aperture for the large and deflating balls compared with the small ball, but they took longer to grasp the deflating and small balls compared with the large ball. In effect, they treated the deflating ball as a large ball in the early part of the movement response and then as a small ball during the latter part of the response. Whereas peak velocity of the grasp was achieved simultaneously for the small and large balls, it was achieved significantly later for the deflating ball (see table 3.1). Savelsbergh and colleagues (1991) concluded that data on the timing of the events in the grasp were "consistent with the subjects' use of relative expansion information" (p. 321). An interesting finding from the study was that participants were not aware of any physical changes to the ball in its deflating condition.

In recent years, the "Grasping Tau" paper has received a significant amount of scrutiny, perhaps because it was the first study that sought direct evidence for using the relative rate of expansion in guiding the timing of an interceptive action. The most important criticisms relate to the need for quantitative predictions regarding the magnitude of the effect of the altered relative rate of expansion on the timing of the grasp, the need for

(CONTINUED)

TABLE 3.1   *Kinematic Characteristics of One-Handed Catching From the "Grasping Tau" Study*

	Ball		
	Large	Small	Deflating
Initiation time[ns]	1,575 (68)	1,580 (65)	1,585 (67)
Movement time[*]	140 (51)	154 (48)	153 (51)
Time of catch[***]	1,716 (39)	1,738 (36)	1,739 (36)
Time of peak closing velocity[*]	41 (10)	42 (11)	36 (14)

Note: All values are in milliseconds; standard deviations are in parentheses; ns = not significant; *p = 0.06; ***p<0.001

The perceived contour of approaching balls that were deflating was altered, with a consequent effect on the grasping action.

Data from Savelsbergh et al. (1991).

justifying the relevance of the dependent variables chosen for analysis, and the difference in magnitude of effect between the monocular and binocular viewing conditions.

APPLICATION

Due to demonstrable effects of other variables such as approach velocity, object size, and background structure, there is now little agreement that tau alone is used to time judgments (Michaels & Beek, 1995). Researchers have used the psychophysical paradigm to demonstrate whether humans are sensitive to tau and whether they use it to judge Tc with approaching objects. This paradigm includes prediction motion (PM) tasks that require a person to make a simple response that coincides with the time at which a previously visible, moving target will arrive at a contact point given that its motion before disappearance remains constant. Also popular within this paradigm have been relative judgment (RJ) tasks, in which people are required to make judgments regarding which of two or more approaching objects will arrive first at a specified contact point. For excellent analyses of the weaknesses of classical psychophysical methods in the study of real-world vision, see Tresilian (1995) and also Harris and Jenkin (1998).

QUESTION

Explain the key differences between the classical psychophysical methodology used for studying timing behavior (including PM and RJ tasks) and the experimental constraints of the experiment (involving an interceptive action) described in "Grasping Tau" by Savelsbergh and colleagues (1991). Wait until you read the section on information–movement coupling later in this chapter before formulating your explanation.

Affordances

The experiment by Savelsbergh and colleagues (1991, see Spotlight on Research) was a useful attempt in the challenging task of isolating optic invariants for study. Using a basic interceptive timing task, the experiment tried to show how different informational constraints could afford different coordination patterns. How invariants act as **affordances** for movements is another major idea from James Gibson (1979) that contributes to our understanding of perception and action. Gibson proposed that humans perceive invariants as affordances for action; that is, neurobiological systems perceive information by what it offers, invites, or demands in terms of an action. For example, surfaces in the environment afford different actions from different people in relation to distinct physical properties, such as limb lengths. In order to negotiate these surfaces with functional actions, individuals need to perceive properties of the surfaces as affordances for action. For instance, does the surface afford stepping on with the feet or climbing on with the legs and arms (in the case of a young child), given key physical properties of the person?

Affordances are, therefore, both objective (a surface invites an action) and subjective (the specific action depends on critical values of limb lengths of each person). For Gibson (1979), affordance was a central concept of ecological psychology, which captured the complementary relationship of an animal with its environment. He pointed out a fundamental criticism in indirect theories of perception, stating that "psychologists assume that objects are composed of their qualities . . . what we perceive when we look at objects are their affordances, not their qualities" (p. 134).

Example of Affordance: An Approaching Ball

Let's consider more closely how the invariant optic flow specified by an approaching ball may invite an interceptive action such as hitting, catching, or avoidance. As noted previously, the affordance is at the same time objective, perhaps being

© Photographer: John Terence Turner from Getty Images

The change in local flow that an approaching squash ball creates may enable the player to intercept the ball by volleying it with the racket rather than driving it.

constrained by rules or social conventions, and subjective, inviting a specific action that depends on perception from a person's environmental location and biomechanical characteristics (Fitch & Turvey, 1978). For instance, the change in local flow created by an approaching squash ball may enable the player to intercept the ball by volleying it with the racket, but not to drive it. Given a different type of local flow, information may be provided that results in avoidance behavior such as moving out of the way to avoid being hit.

The differences between the optic structures stipulate a different affordance for the player (i.e., objective affordance). However, the same changes in local flow can afford different actions depending on the state of the individual. For example, toward the end of a hard, 5-set game of squash, the affordances for one athlete may be to let the ball pass because it cannot be reached given the current level of fatigue in the muscular system (subjective affordance). There is no physical standard prescribing affordances for each player. Each individual's frame of reference for perceiving and moving will reveal the affordance in each situation. In this respect, affordances can provide a useful theoretical framework for understanding intra- and interindividual levels of decision making and movement variability, a concept revisited in chapter 5. (For a discussion of affordances that builds on Gibson's ideas but is not synonymous with Gibsonian theory, see Scarantino [2003]).

Tuning in to the Affordances of Invariant Information   Now we can consider Gibson's (1979) notions of invariants and affordances to understand how decision making and movement performance may occur. According to Gibson, much information to support actions is consistently and directly available for pickup in the environment as a consequence of the rich information available from the sensory organs. In the theory of direct perception, the learner in squash is not burdened with the task of developing symbolic memory structures through training, observational modeling, and competitive performance; rather, the perceptual systems become progressively more attuned to the invariant information available in environments through direct experience in practice and performance contexts. With task-specific experience, the information that the learner picks up becomes more subtle, elaborate, and precise.

Therefore, one important element of skill acquisition is the process of becoming better attuned to the affordances of invariant information perceived in specific movement contexts. The awareness of affordances that many experts achieve can be subtle in many high-level performance contexts. For example, anecdotal evidence from professional basketball shows how skilled ball handlers become attuned to information on the movements of teammates who are directly behind them. Do they grow eyes in the back of their heads? Not quite. To pick up this sophisticated form of information, they simply learn to detect the pursuit eye movements of the opposition forwards in front of them.

A common misconception in the literature is that adhering to the theory of direct perception eliminates the role of cognitive processes in action. However, Gibson (1979) did not deny the existence of cognitive processes such as reminiscence, expectation, dreaming, and imagery. He also did not suggest that memory played no role in perception. Rather, his view could be interpreted as suggesting that the performer–environment relationship was the appropriate scale of analysis for examining the interacting roles of perception, action, and cognition in supporting behavior. Gibson focused less on the role of internalized, mental processes, preferring instead to emphasize key ideas such as informational invariants and affordances in the direct coupling of information and movement.

Eyes in the back of the head: Opponents' eye movements afford perception of a teammate's motion.

Information–Movement Coupling

Earlier we discussed how a golfer moves to create changes in optic flow that will provide information for action. This strategy exemplifies a central tenet of Gibson's (1979) ideas: that movement generates information which, in turn, supports further movements, leading to a cyclical relationship between perception and movement. Gibson summarized this position, saying that "we must perceive in order to move, but we must also move in order to perceive" (p. 223). According to ecological psychologists (e.g., Michaels & Carello, 1981), using information to support movement requires a law of control that continually relates the individual's present state to the state of the environment. In other words, a law of control relates the kinetic property of a movement to the kinematic property of the perceptual flow (Warren, 1988).

Because an interdependency between the perception of information and the generation of movement has evolved in neurobiological systems, it has been suggested that these processes should not be studied separately (Michaels & Carello, 1981). This has important implications for the organization of practice environments and for the design of research experiments. Only in practice contexts where perception and action processes are coupled within realistic environments will we observe the smartness of evolutionary-designed perceptual mechanisms (see Davids, Button, Araújo, Renshaw, & Hristovski, 2006; Runeson, 1977). In this context, *smartness* refers to the dedicated function for which a perceptual mechanism has evolved. This view of tight couplings emerging between perceptual and action systems provides a number of interesting implications for movement practitioners, as we shall explore in part II. In order to clarify these implications for the design of skill acquisition procedures, we need to understand the functionally designed coupling of perception and action processes.

Early research on balancing in children and adults supported the notion of the tight coupling between the optic array and the individual (Lee & Lishman, 1975). In a purpose-built room with a fixed floor and moveable walls, researchers induced postural sway by moving the walls slowly forward or backward. The direction of the participants' sway depended on the direction in which the walls moved (see figure 3.4). Although participants were unaware that the walls were moving, they "unconsciously and unavoidably" (p. 162) corrected posture to compensate for what they perceived as forward or backward ego-motion (motion of the "self" through space) signified by the optic flow. The amount of wall movement was closely related to the amount of postural sway the subjects exhibited, and in some cases young children even fell over. These findings showed why we need to understand perception and action as functionally intertwined. Since that early work, the ideas have been devel-

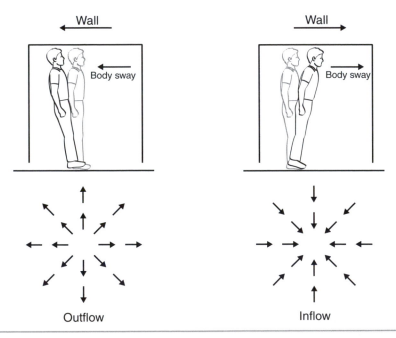

Figure 3.4 Unaware that the walls were moving, subjects in the swinging-room experiment unconsciously corrected posture to compensate for what they perceived as forward or backward ego-motion signified by the optic flow.

oped to such an extent that modeling now exemplifies a prospective control strategy for continuously regulating action through information. We highlight this development next by discussing the required velocity model.

Required Velocity Model: Prospective Control

Savelsbergh and colleagues' (1991) classic experiment stimulated a body of research that examined whether tau is the only optical invariant used for interceptive actions (see Williams, Davids, & Williams, 1999). In follow-up work, van der Kamp (1999) (1) included an inflating ball in addition to the small, large, and deflating balls; (2) directly compared monocular and binocular viewing conditions; (3) had an object approaching on a rectilinear trajectory with two different constant velocities (1.0 meter per second and 2.0 meters per second); and (4) reconstructed the relative rate of expansion as a function of the actual Tc in order to quantitatively compare differences between conditions.

Results showed that manipulating ball diameter during approach was partially consistent with the use of tau. Compared with the balls with a constant diameter, the timing of the catch (described by variables for moment of grasp onset, moment of hand closure, and peak closing velocity) was delayed for the deflating ball. Timing of the catch occurred earlier for the inflating ball. No effects of object size, viewing, or approach velocity were observed when comparing the two constant-diameter balls. However, if the relative rate of expansion was the sole information source that the catchers used, the magnitude of the observed effects of the deflating and inflating ball on timing of the catch was three to four times less than the magnitude of predicted effects. Therefore, although the results were in the expected direction, indicating that participants may have been using tau, they were not consistent with the *sole* use of tau. The implication is that some other information sources also must have been involved.

Bootsma and Peper examined other potential sources of visual information for the regulation of interceptive actions (e.g., Bootsma, 1998; Bootsma, Fayt, Zaal, & Laurent, 1997; Peper, Bootsma, Mestre, & Bakker, 1994; but see also Schöner, 1994). According to their required velocity model, catching a ball requires an individual to control the hands. This is the difference between the catching hand's current position relative to the ball and the acceleration of the hand needed to intercept the moving ball, based on an optically specified velocity differential (see the equation on page 68 from Peper, Bootsma, Mestre, & Bakker, 1994). Their model specifies how a person can use information continuously to control the hand's acceleration and match the required velocity to intercept a projectile. For example, the current hand velocity at a given instant *t* can be increased or decreased for the hand to move at the required velocity needed to catch a ball. To explain performance of interceptive actions, predictive strategies traditionally have been designated in performer information-processing models. In these models the target's future location and the required kinematics of the limbs are both estimated in advance of the movement (e.g., Jeannerod, 1981).

As shown in the following equation, the required velocity can be expressed as the ratio of the current lateral distance between the hand and the ball's projection plane onto the hand-movement axis to the first-order Tc between the ball and the hand-movement axis (see figure 3.5). Factors on the right-hand side of the equation (i.e., the velocity differential) can be optically specified by monocular and binocular variables (see Laurent, Montagne, & Durey, 1996).

$$\ddot{X}_h = \alpha \dot{X}_{h\,req} - \beta \dot{X}_h$$

$$\text{with } \dot{X}_{h\,req} = \frac{X_h - X_b}{Tc_1}$$

where $\ddot{X}_h$, $\dot{X}_{h\,req}$, and $\dot{X}_h$ are the hand's current acceleration, current required velocity, and current velocity, respectively, and α and β are constants, and where X_h, X_b, and Tc_1 are the hand's current position, the projection of the ball's current position on the hand-movement axis, and the first-order Tc between the ball and the hand-movement axis.

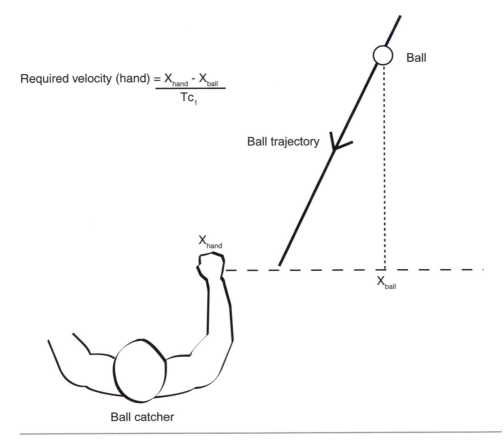

Figure 3.5 The required velocity model states that catching a ball requires a performer to control the hand's acceleration based on an optically specified velocity differential.

Access to the spatiotemporal properties of the interception point with the moving object, which is required if using a predictive control strategy, is never necessary with the required velocity model. Rather, by modulating limb acceleration with optical information to achieve and maintain the required velocity, the limb will move to the right place at the right time to catch the approaching ball. Therefore, the required velocity model is a welcome advance over previous work that had been restricted to understanding only the timing of interceptive actions.

Montagne and colleagues recently reported some direct evidence for the use of prospective control (e.g., Montagne, Fraisse, Ripoll, & Laurent, 2000; Montagne, Laurent, Durey, & Bootsma, 1999). In one experiment designed to observe the influence on hand acceleration, Montagne and colleagues (1999) manipulated the current lateral distances between the ball and hand. Subjects were required to catch a ball that approached the same point of interception from different starting points. Montagne and colleagues hypothesized that the kinematics of the catching action would be the same if a predictive strategy were used because all trajectories converged to the same point, with the same Tc, and with the same required hand displacement (for conditions x and y). However, if a prospective strategy were used, they assumed that different kinematics would result, as evident in the hand's percentage of movement reversals or changes of the hand's initial direction. Specifically, they predicted that when the hand was positioned at the point of interception, subjects would start by moving their hand to fill in the lateral distance (to the left for an outward angle, to the right for an inward angle). This initial movement would be followed by a change in direction in order to catch the ball (causing a movement reversal). As predicted, they found significant differences in the kinematics of the catching action when initial hand location and ball trajectory were varied. Subjects demonstrated a significant number of movement reversals for the balls that approached on an inward or outward trajectory rather than a straight pathway (approximately 60% of all trials). Further, it was shown that they started moving their hand at the required velocity approximately 300 milliseconds before catching the ball.

Is Tc Optical Information Used?

Research has shown that given certain boundary conditions, first-order Tc between an approaching object and interception point can be specified from invariants in the optic array and may be used to enable precise timing behavior. An underlying assumption of this work is that first-order Tc is used to continually guide the unfolding movement. Support for using a particular source of optic information is often sought by searching for constant timing of key aspects of the movement under conditions in which the information is experimentally manipulated (i.e., approach velocity, object size, monocular and binocular viewing).

Drawing on the finding that movement typically occurs earlier and slower as the duration of Tc increases, Tresilian (1999) has also proposed that a more flexible strategy for using Tc information needs to be considered. Rather than initiating movement at constant values of Tc, Tresilian suggests that although movement may be regulated using Tc, the adopted value will vary with the constraints of execution and internal factors. There are subtle variations that might affect a basic action constrained by an individual's immediate needs, intentions, or emotions at the time of performance (e.g., when you really need to catch an object, such as a valuable glass ornament, compared with when you merely need to stop it from passing you, such as casually intercepting a child's plastic toy rolling by on the floor). Depending on these constraints, aspects of a movement can be "initiated earlier or later, depending on whether this would facilitate performance" (p. 516). These explanations seem to capture how task and organismic constraints can affect how people acquire and use information to support motor skills.

If one incorrectly assigns the kinematic property of the perceptual flow (i.e., Tc), attempts to discover the laws of control or strategies that relate information to movement may be fraught with difficulty. Consequently, it is necessary to consider the specific constraints of the experimental task under scrutiny. Tresilian (1999) has suggested that an important factor in determining the use of Tc information is the time window for successful performance (i.e., necessary temporal precision). Tasks with a margin of error in the range of 2 to 25 milliseconds (e.g., one-handed catching, table tennis, cricket batting) require precise information about the impending contact and therefore are likely to be regulated by Tc information. However, tasks with a less precise time window (e.g., gait or a tumble turn in swimming), which often have relatively long movement times (i.e., >500 milliseconds) and target-viewing times, (i.e., >300 milliseconds) are not necessarily regulated using Tc. Finally, tasks that do not impose a precise time window for successful performance (e.g., avoidance behavior) and that can be initiated very early and still be successful may not require the use of Tc.

In summary, many of the research findings on visual information for interceptive actions are consistent with performers perceiving information from the invariants and variants in the optic array and using it to guide their interaction with their environment. They can pick up these invariants as affordances for action that interact with key properties of each individual's movement system, such as limb length. Coupling perceptual systems with movement systems can occur from an early age and can be enhanced with practice. It also can be shaped by specific needs, intentions, and emotional circumstances of performance.

The Visual Brain in Action

Evidence of the strength of the developed couplings between perceptual and movement systems comes from studies in behavioral neurosciences. These studies also clarify how the intentional constraints of each person interact

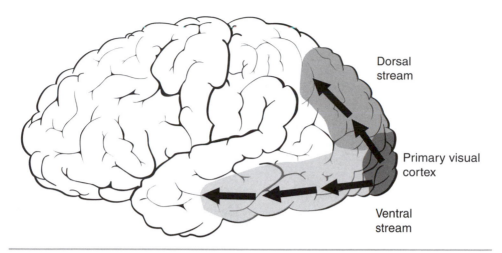

Figure 3.6 In the two visual systems, information is carried via the lateral geniculate nucleus to the V1. From the V1, the ventral stream projects to the inferotemporal cortex and the dorsal stream projects to the posterior parietal cortex.

with informational constraints on action. Because we need different types of visual information to support the rich diversity of tasks we perform, our brains are composed of numerous functional divisions (see Harris & Jenkin, 1998). Probably the most widely known of these functional divisions is that of the two visual systems (Milner & Goodale, 1995), where the functional division is between perception for action (i.e., object-directed action) and perception for recognition (i.e., object perception). According to this scheme, information is carried via the lateral geniculate nucleus to the primary visual cortex (V1), from which the ventral stream projects to the inferotemporal cortex and the dorsal stream projects to the posterior parietal cortex (see figure 3.6). A further connection to the posterior parietal cortex has been identified from the pulvinar via the superior colliculus.

Milner and Goodale (1995) have drawn from research on vertebrates, primates, brain-impaired human patients, and pictorial illusion studies to produce a comprehensive argument for a more diverse role of the visual system. Probably the most convincing evidence in favor of the two visual systems emanates from research on brain-impaired patients. Goodale, Milner, Jackobson, and Carey (1991) and Milner and colleagues (1991) described the case of a human patient, DF, who suffered brain damage predominantly to the occipital area, specifically V2, V3, and V4. They noted that patient DF had many deficits in visual perception, including discriminating between geometric shapes and recognizing letters and numbers. Disorders such as these have been described as *visual form agnosia* or *blindsight*. However, when it came to actually performing movement tasks such as grasping objects, patient DF did not suffer from the same difficulties. Milner and Goodale (1995) suggested that

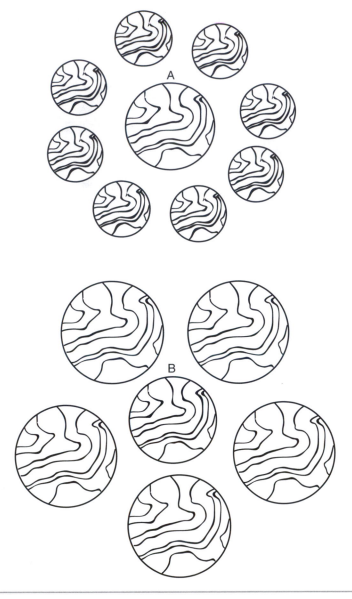

Figure 3.7 In the Ebbinghaus illusion, circles A and B are the same size, but circle B appears to be smaller.

this apparent paradox occurred because the damaged ventral pathway was not able to support object perception but the intact dorsal pathway was able to process the necessary information to support action.

Research examining the effect of pictorial illusions such as the Ebbinghaus illusion (e.g., Aglioti et al., 1995) and the Müller-Lyer illusion (e.g. Gentilucci, Chieffi, Daprati, Saetti, & Toni, 1996) has also been interpreted as supporting the functional division of the two visual systems. For example, in experiments using the Ebbinghaus illusion, participants are required to perceive the size of two central disks, each of which is surrounded by a circle of disks (see figure 3.7). When the size of the surrounding disks is manipulated, participants typically misperceive the size of the central disks. However, even though their perceptual judgment is fooled, their grip aperture remains scaled to the actual size of the central disk. These results suggest that, although the process of object perception is deceived by the illusion, processes of object-directed action remain unaffected (Aglioti et al., 1995; Haffenden & Goodale, 1998; Hanisch, Konczak, & Dohle, 2001; Pavani, Boscagli, Benvenuti, Rabuffetti, & Farnè, 1999).

Decety and Grèzes (1999) have found that the functional division between ventral and dorsal streams tends not to be observed (i.e., both areas are active) when no constraints are placed on performance of a perceptual task. Under specific task constraints such as perception for action or perception for recognition, however, the distinction becomes more apparent. Therefore, according to the two visual systems, the nature of the visual information we use depends on what we intend to do with the information. For example, the ventral stream dominates the attainment of perceptual information when we perform a perceptual recognition task, but the dorsal stream is predominant when we perform a coordinated movement coupled with a source of information (e.g., an interceptive action). The implication of these findings is that the performance of many psychomotor tasks that require a judgment about the intending moment of contact may depend on visual information picked up through the ventral stream. However, real-world interceptive actions that require tight coupling of a movement to an object or event in the environment are likely to depend on visual information picked up through the dorsal stream.

So far we have focused on how invariants are detected in the optic flow that surrounds a person. However, there are additional energy flows that support actions. For example, a driver may use acoustic information from the constant revving of the engine to guide the pressure change needed on the accelerator pedal. A pedestrian may use acoustic information from the ringing bell on an approaching bicycle to perceive information on its approach trajectory. A tennis player may pick up and shake a racket to check how it feels before taking to the court. In the remainder of this chapter we examine the role of haptic (touch) and acoustic information.

Haptic Information Constraints on Movement

A small but significant field of research has examined the role of haptic information in constraining movements. When a person holds an implement such as a pen, paintbrush, or baseball bat, information regarding its shape, size, texture, and structure is haptically provided when muscles, ligaments, tendons, and skin are stretched or compressed. Using this perceptual system, a blind person walking along a street and sweeping a cane in order to prospectively regulate gait can generate haptic flow. Gibson (1979) proposed that haptic information is most useful in its dynamic form when people actively generate complex sources of information through manipulation and touch. Numerous experiments by Gibson and colleagues have found many parallels between the systems for acquiring information from the optic and haptic flows, supporting the power of perception through the latter (Gibson, 1979). Indeed, the prevalence of manipulative movements in daily life led Turvey, Burton, Amazeen, Butwill, and Carello (1998) to argue that "the role of dynamic touch in the control of manipulatory activity may be both more continuous and fundamental than that of vision" (p. 35).

People can also acquire haptic information about the mass of an implement through active manipulation. For example, an athlete typically does not hold an implement such as a racket, bat, club, or stick in a static manner, but tends to wield it (Beak, Davids, & Bennett, 2002). The athlete twists and turns the implement in different directions to gain information about its significant properties. A wielded object has a resistance to rotation in different directions that is defined by **moment of inertia.** Moment of inertia is a product of the mass of an implement and the radius of rotation (i.e., $I = mr^2$) and can be invariant for different combinations of these variables. Solomon and Turvey (1988) have shown that the perception of the spatial characteristics of handheld rods is not affected by the density of the rods, the direction of wielding relative to body coordinates, or the rate of wielding. Rather, without vision of the rod during wielding, perceived reaching distance was specified

Athletes typically twist and turn their equipment in different directions to gain information about its significant properties.

by a haptic invariant, the principal moment of inertia of the hand–rod system about the axis of rotation (see also Beak et al., 2002; Carello, Thuot, & Turvey, 2000; Turvey, 1996).

In a sport like golf, such evidence suggests a much more important role for taking a practice swing rather than simply rehearsing an upcoming movement. In this way people can attune themselves to the characteristics of the implements they are using when playing with unfamiliar equipment or switching between clubs. Numerous examples exist in sport to suggest how athletes might gain haptic information from an object, such as juggling a soccer ball before taking a free kick, wielding a javelin before throwing, and manipulating a pole before vaulting. As Button and Pepping (2002) suggested, more research is needed to examine practice strategies that sensitize learners to haptic information.

Acoustic Information Constraints on Movement

Evidence suggests that acoustic information flows in humans can regulate many functional movements (Button, 2002; Button & Davids, 2004; Lee, 1990). Indeed, Keele and Summers (1976) suggested many years ago that in regard to the temporal organization of movements, the acoustic perceptual system might be superior to the visual system. For example, percussionists must learn to time and sequence complex bimanual movements with acoustic information in order to play effectively. In sport, there is an abundance of anecdotal evidence highlighting the role of acoustic information as a constraint on the coordination of discrete movement tasks. For example, the runner's reaction to the starting gun is a crucial element of sprinting since the difference between winning or losing can be just a few milliseconds.

The role of acoustic information is not limited to initiating movements; it can also be used in decision-making processes such as stroke selection in racket sports. In table tennis, for example, the particular sound of paddle–ball contact can give the experienced player important information about the speed and spin of the approaching ball. In volleyball, many coaches believe that information about an opposing setter's intentions to produce a short overhead or a long set to an outside hitter can be obtained from acoustic information during ball–finger contact. Some swimmers now train with minipacers placed by their ear to regulate the rhythm of a stroke.

Empirical Research on Acoustic Information

Although there is a large amount of anecdotal evidence, there have been few empirical attempts to investigate how acoustic information acts as a constraint

To play effectively, percussionists use acoustic information to time and sequence complex bimanual movements.

during skill acquisition. Some evidence has shown that acoustic information may be obtained from a bouncing ball in perception of its elastic properties (e.g., Warren, Kim, & Husney, 1987). Typically research has examined the role of acoustic information in coordinating and timing actions in relation to environmental events. For example, Shaw, McGowan, and Turvey (1991) modeled an acoustic variable that specifies Tc with an approaching object, given certain boundary conditions. They pointed out that early research on acoustic information focused on the localization of static sound sources rather than attempting to ascertain how actions could be acoustically guided. They identified the latter task under the framework of ecological acoustics and considered the convergence between a performer and an acoustic source. Their data supported the idea that the intensity of sound can be used to locomote directly toward a target in the environment, especially if the time difference between the person and the acoustic source is minimal.

Schiff and Oldak (1990) and Rosenblum, Carello, and Pastore (1987) also have revealed experimental support for the use of the acoustic array to support actions. Schiff and Oldak found that sighted individuals were able to make reasonable judgments about the time to pass of approaching objects using audition alone. Congenitally blind participants were more accurate than sighted participants in their acoustic judgments and matched the accuracy of sighted participants who used visual judgments. Moreover, Rosenblum and colleagues found that the rising change in intensity of an acoustic information source was the most effective invariant for specifying the time to arrival of a looming object.

Acoustic Information for Interceptive Actions

These findings show the importance of acoustic information for making judgments about approaching objects. In everyday activities, we generally integrate acoustic and optical information forms to respond to environmental events (e.g., Netelenbos & Savelsbergh, 2003). Acoustic perception is not possible or is at best limited for deaf people. One study by Savelsbergh, Netelenbos, and Whiting (1991) examined differences in catching ability between deaf and hearing children. They found that deaf children could satisfy the task constraints of one-handed catching as well as hearing children. However, they had problems catching balls approaching from their periphery or from outside their field of view. In addition, deaf children showed later initiation times of a catching movement after ball release from a ball machine. However, no differences were observed in overall movement times between the deaf and hearing children. Deaf children showed some compensation in the coordination of the hand transport and grasp phases. This was likely due to the lack of acoustic information about projectile release, causing a functional reorganization of the movement pattern. Other work by Kalkavan and Fazey (1994) found that in the absence of vision, experienced catchers could successfully perform interceptive actions provided that ongoing acoustic information from ball flight was available.

Cobner and Cardiff (1980) examined whether acoustic perception contributed to the performance of a forehand stroke in table tennis. They removed acoustic information by asking novice players to play while wearing headphones emitting white noise. There were significant decrements in performance accuracy during those trial blocks in which acoustic information was removed. Verbal self-report data from the participants suggested that the "general timing of the shots tended to deteriorate when sound cues were not present" (p. 71). However, in all these studies, including Savelsbergh, Netelenbos, and Whiting (1991), a detailed kinematic analysis of the temporal coordination of the interceptive actions was absent.

Some studies have attempted to undertake this task. For example, Holder (1998) examined coordination of the table tennis forehand drive in skilled participants by manipulating acoustic information from a feeder's bat. He found that accuracy of shot placement decreased in the nonacoustic condition. Intraindividual analyses showed that variability in the time to peak wrist velocity increased when acoustic information was perturbed, as estimated by an increase in the magnitude of standard deviations. A ball-catching study by Button (2002) examined whether perturbation of acoustic informational constraints at the point of ball projection (i.e., the sound of a ball-projection machine) would lead to adjustments by the ball catchers. Acoustic information from the projection machine was present in a control condition but was eliminated in an experimental (nonacoustic) condition where participants wore foam earplugs and headphones emitting white noise.

The similarity of the number of successful catches under both conditions was a striking feature of the data. A comparison between the two conditions for all participants revealed that 12 out of 160 trials (7.5%) were dropped in the acoustic condition whereas only 6 trials (3.25%) were dropped in the nonacoustic condition. For the nonacoustic condition, maximum opening velocity (MOV) of the hand generally increased (345 millimeters per second) compared with the acoustic condition (260 millimeters per second). Another group effect revealed an increased maximum closing velocity (MCV) of the hand, also in the nonacoustic condition (366 versus 269 millimeters per second). The times at which MOV and MCV of the hand were attained before ball contact also were compared in both conditions. This comparison revealed that MCV occurred earlier in the nonacoustic condition (0.17 seconds before hand–ball contact, compared with 0.12 seconds). The time of MOV also occurred earlier in the nonacoustic condition (0.37 seconds before hand–ball contact, compared with 0.32 seconds).

The observed reorganization of motor patterns by the skilled ball catchers confirmed that acoustic information from the ball machine at the point of projection, together with the visual information of the ball, also contributed to perception of timing information. In that study, acoustic information provided potential timing information about 100 milliseconds before ball flight. The most consistent finding was that participants generally initiated movements later in the nonacoustic condition. The adjustments in both MCV and MOV under nonacoustic informational constraints seem to be due to the increase in movement initiation time. Because acoustic information at release was the only constraint manipulated in the experimental setting, it is feasible that participants were using it to time the initiation of movement.

Summary

According to ecological psychology, changes to the energy in surrounding perceptual arrays that are generated following self or object motion can provide information that humans directly perceive to regulate action (e.g., see Gibson, 1979; Kugler & Turvey, 1987; Turvey, 1990). This conceptualization of the cyclical relationship between perception and movement stands in stark contrast to the traditional mediated view of perception advanced in the information-processing approach (see chapter 1). A consequence of an ecological interpretation is that perception and movement should not be viewed as separate processes to be studied independently. In an effort to establish laws of control for this cyclical relationship, ecological research has examined the nature of the information that regulates movement (i.e., *what* information), rather than the minimal amount of information necessary to successfully complete a task (typical of a psychophysical approach). Depending on the nature of the task constraints, it seems that there are various informational variables that humans may use. Task constraints, such as the time window for task performance, and the nature of the required response, such as rapid movement or verbal or manual judgment, determine the strategy people use and hence the information they use to support action.

The examples from research on interceptive actions that we have presented here show that humans are adept at acquiring different types of information and harnessing these sources to coordinate the dfs of the motor system.

SELF-TEST QUESTIONS

1. List some of the informational flows available to ice hockey players as they skate with the puck.

2. Explain why information is conceived of as rich and meaningful in ecological psychology.

3. How would the concept of affordances help to explain interindividual differences in coordination?

4. How and why would a person rehabilitating from an ankle sprain need to move to perceive information?

5. Discuss why an interceptive action such as hammering a nail is unlikely to be performed using optical tau alone.

6. Devise an experiment to test Milner and Goodale's (1995) model of two visual systems. (Tip: Think of a task in which perception for action or for recognition can be performed independently).

ADDITIONAL READING

1. Gibson, J.J. (1979). The ecological approach to visual perception. Boston: Houghton Mifflin.

2. Michaels, C.F., Withagen, R., Jacobs, D.M., Zaal, F.T.J.M., & Bongers, R.M. (2001). Information, perception, and action: A reply to commentators. *Ecological Psychology, 13*(3), 227-244.

3. Milner, A.D., & Goodale, M.A. (1995). *The visual brain in action.* Oxford: Oxford University Press.

4. Scarantino, A. (2003). Affordances explained. *Philosophy of Science, 70,* 949-961.

5. Tresilian, J.R. (1999). Analysis of recent empirical challenges to an account of interceptive timing. *Perception & Psychophysics, 61*(3), 515-528.

CHAPTER 4

Redefining Learning
A Constraints-Led Approach

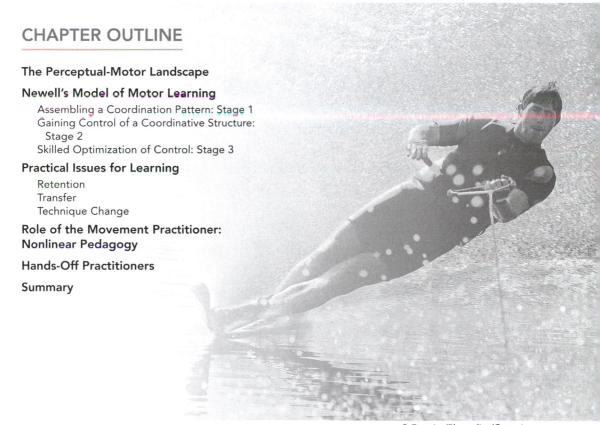

© Eyewire/Photodisc/Getty Images

CHAPTER OUTLINE

The Perceptual-Motor Landscape

Newell's Model of Motor Learning
Assembling a Coordination Pattern: Stage 1
Gaining Control of a Coordinative Structure:
    Stage 2
Skilled Optimization of Control: Stage 3

Practical Issues for Learning
Retention
Transfer
Technique Change

**Role of the Movement Practitioner:
Nonlinear Pedagogy**

Hands-Off Practitioners

Summary

In chapters 2 and 3, we discussed the key principles of dynamical systems theory and ecological psychology. A generally held view among researchers on skill acquisition is that, compared with the development of theoretical and mathematical models of movement coordination, these alternative theories have not yet placed enough emphasis on understanding learning processes. For example, Summers (1998) proposed that the ecological perspective "lacked a comprehensive theory of learning and development" and that there was a need for "a rigorous program of research" (p. 12) on these processes (see also Walter, 1998). Although there is still a need for more research on learning and development from a constraints-led standpoint, some useful work on these processes is beginning to emerge.

In this chapter, we will analyze motor learning under the umbrella of the constraints-led approach and examine the implications of this framework for the role of movement practitioners. Our discussion may be useful for coaches, physical education specialists, teachers, physiotherapists, kinesiologists, and sport scientists. These professionals may have distinct objectives, but each shares the goal of enabling people to acquire coordination and movement control. Coming from the perspective of ecological psychology and dynamical systems theory, we intend to show how knowledge of the constraints that each individual needs to satisfy can help build a better understanding of key practical issues such as

- an objective structuring of learning and rehabilitation environments, including the design of practice tasks and the role of artificial aids;
- the nature and frequency of presenting augmented information to learners;
- the scaling of practice equipment according to individual needs; and
- developing a principled model of the learner and a rationale for the practitioner's role.

The Perceptual-Motor Landscape

How do long-term changes to the organization of movement systems occur as a result of learning and practice? From a constraints-led perspective, we can characterize skill acquisition as a learner (a dynamical movement system) searching for stable and functional states of coordination or attractors during goal-directed activity. Different learning phases are the creation of temporary states of coordination that resist constraints with the potential to perturb the stability of the system. In many complex performance environments such as work and sport, people typically need to develop a repertoire of movement attractors (stable states of coordination) to satisfy the constraints of unpredictable contexts. We can consider this repertoire of attractors as a kind of **perceptual-motor landscape** in which performers need to coordinate their actions with their environment in order to perform skills effectively. For example, a perceptual-motor landscape for a gymnast might include various jumps, turns, landings, and balances involved in floor exercises. For a child learning to ride a bicycle, the landscape might include movement attractors for steering the handlebars, pedaling the wheels, and controlling the force of braking.

The landscape of attractors is a useful metaphor for describing an individual's intrinsic dynamics. Its layout is constrained by genetic endowment, developmental status, past learning experiences, and social influences; that is, each person's landscape is continually shaped by the interaction of genes, perceptions, and intentions, as well as physical constraints, surrounding information, and system dynamics (Muchisky, Gershkoff-Cole, Cole, & Thelen, 1996; Thelen & Smith, 1994). Because these performance constraints are not static, the landscape is undulating and ever changing: a truly dynamic and open system. As a learner's constraints change over time, the topology of the landscape alters to reflect the effects of development and new experiences as well as the acquisition of new skills (see figure 4.1).

Using a constraints-led approach, we can think of learning as adapting to changing constraints across different timescales related to development and life experiences (e.g., Newell, Liu, & Mayer-Kress, 2001). Behavior emerges under constraints during self-organization, and motor learning is viewed as a personal struggle to implement change. Each learner has to seek and assemble a unique movement solution that will help satisfy particular task constraints (Goldfield, 2000; Haywood, & Getchell, 2001; Rosengren, Savelsbergh, & van der Kamp, 2003). This process occurs when people learn to coordinate their movements with respect to the objects, surfaces, and other people in a range of environments. The purpose of practice is to seek, explore, discover, assemble, and stabilize functional and reliable movement patterns (McDonald, Oliver, & Newell, 1995; Newell, 1986; Williams, Davids, & Williams, 1999).

Once a learner has specified a functional task goal through intentions, a process of continual exploration eventually results in the emergence of an approximate solution to the task. The emergence of a more refined solution to the task goal strengthens the connections among body parts as a specific coordinative structure (Williams et al., 1999). The successful or functional coordination pattern gains increasing stability as practice progresses, helping the individual adapt to the changing constraints of the task and environment. At the same time, the learner discards less successful patterns stimulated during the search process because they are less functional. From this perspective, we can consider practice processes during skill acquisition as the selection of functional behaviors under constraint (Thelen, 1995).

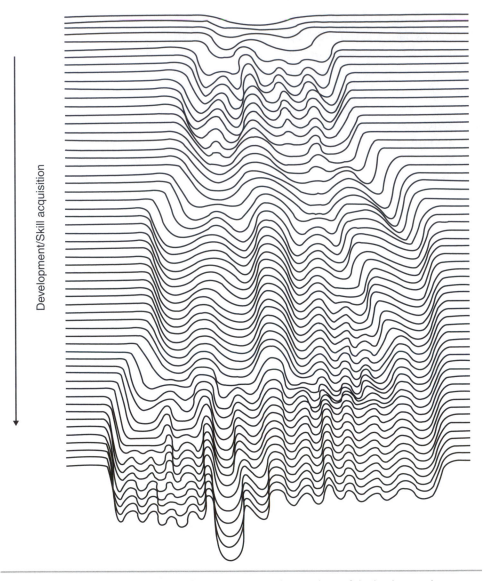

Figure 4.1 As a learner's constraints change over time, the topology of the landscape alters to reflect the effects of development and new experiences as well as the acquisition of new skills.

Reprinted from *Advances in infancy research*, C. Rovee-Collier and L.P. Lipsitt, p. 130, Copyright 1996 with permission from Elsevier.

Key Concept

Using the constraints-led approach, we can redefine motor learning as an ongoing dynamic process involving a search for and stabilization of specific, functional movement patterns across the perceptual-motor landscape as each individual adapts to a variety of changing constraints.

Newell's Model of Motor Learning

Let's consider the three stages that learners go through to find adaptive behaviors. How can we characterize the differences between performers at different skill levels? Newell (1985) formulated a model based on Bernstein's (1967) insights on the mechanical dfs of the body. This model provides a good framework for understanding the relationship between coordination and control, and it is useful for understanding how motor system dfs can reorganize over time as people adapt to changing constraints. In this section, we will study the overarm volleyball serve as a vehicle for understanding Newell's model.

Assembling a Coordination Pattern: Stage 1

The first stage of Newell's (1985) model concerns the assembly of a suitable coordination pattern from the large number of available motor system dfs. As noted in chapter 2, to create a coordinative structure, the learner initially attempts to establish basic relationships among the key components of the dynamical movement system. In other words, the learner assembles the appropriate relative motions among relevant body parts such as legs, hips, trunk, and arms. For example, a novice volleyball player needs to explore the perceptual-motor landscape that is created by interactions with important objects (the volleyball held in the non-serving hand), surfaces (the court), obstacles (the net), and strategic goals (serving the ball over the net and into a specific area of the opponents' court). In the absence

A volleyball player attempts to coordinate an action in which the ball is thrown into the air and struck with the hand. Through practice, a basic coordination pattern may emerge from the available motor system components.

of intervention from a practitioner, learners may explore many different areas of the landscape as they seek a relatively stable movement pattern to achieve the task goal.

A volleyball player attempts to coordinate an action in which the ball is thrown into the air and struck with the hitting hand. Through practice, a basic coordination pattern may emerge from the available motor system components, particularly the throwing arm, the hitting arm, and the legs. Early in learning, this basic pattern may emerge and disappear quite suddenly as the learner tries to coordinate throwing, hitting, and stepping subcomponents of the movement into a successful serving action. Gradually, a reasonably successful coordination pattern begins to appear regularly during practice. Under the specific task constraints of the volleyball serve, the attractor (composed of the throwing, hitting, and stepping subcomponents) becomes more stable.

As a volleyball player develops and acquires other movement patterns during practice, a range of attractors or functional coordination patterns is gradually formed into a larger landscape to serve the performance of related skills such as spikes, digs, and serves. We can view the formation of this landscape as a continual struggle between the performer's existing intrinsic dynamics and the task demands (see chapter 2). If the intrinsic and required task dynamics are complementary, an existing attractor (coordination pattern) may simply require readjusting key variables such as forces, timings, and movement durations to support performance of a new movement, and the attractor landscape will be altered in a relatively minor way.

Positive transfer occurs when a functional coordination pattern (attractor) that already exists in the landscape is functionally adapted for another task, rather like a multipurpose tool. A good example of this process occurs when a tennis player's basic overarm movement pattern (attractor) for serving a tennis ball can be refined to support the action of overarm serving in volleyball. A close match between motor system intrinsic dynamics and those of the task may exist in many vocations with similar task demands that require similar tools and equipment. Examples include a mechanic and an engineer, or a joiner and a carpenter.

Typically, a more continual adaptation occurs as an existing attractor is destabilized during a struggle with a nearby attractor in the landscape and is absorbed into the new, more functional system organization. Alternatively, very early in learning, or when more mature adults try to take up new activities, completely new attractor states may develop, thereby increasing the number of stable states and causing abrupt shifts in movement patterns (Zanone & Kelso, 1994). Thus, if a novice volleyball player is a young child who has not played tennis and has done very little overarm throwing, the child needs to construct a new attractor in the rather empty perceptual-motor landscape. In the absence of much experience and learning, a person's intrinsic dynamics may be influenced by genetic transmission and developmental processes.

However, after a short period of life experience, a learner's intrinsic dynamics typically contain at least the trace of a suitable attractor that can be adapted. This is particularly true for older children and young adults. After all, most complex movement routines involve some elements of fundamental movement patterns that are explored early in infancy, including grasping, gripping, hitting, intercepting, stepping, postural control, balance, and locomotion. All of these fundamental movement patterns can be refined for specific integration into complex actions. Liu, Mayer-Kress, and Newell (2006) have pointed out that at this stage of learning, practitioners are more likely to see sudden transitions in movement patterns such as jumps, skips, or regressions in performance as they explore ways to reorganize motor system dfs in trying to solve the motor problem.

Once a reasonably successful solution to the search problem has been discovered in the coordination stage, it is not uncommon for learners to try to couple multiple dfs in an attempt to reduce the control problem to a smaller number of larger coordinative structures (or subspaces of the total number of dfs). The learner, who desperately needs some consistency, might seize upon a basic but fixed motor pattern. This is exactly what Bernstein (1967) predicted should happen as a performer attempts to compress the abundance of motor system dfs into more manageable components. Volleyball serving can occur successfully as long as the learner is not required to move too much, little strategic variation is required, and the performance context does not change.

Gaining Control of a Coordinative Structure: Stage 2

The second stage of Newell's (1985) model is the control stage. Once the relationships among body parts and the basic coordination of the serving action have been established, the individual is faced with the challenge of gaining a tighter fit between the assembled coordinative structure and the performance environment. For example, volleyball players are required to perform on a variety of courts that vary in key dimensions such as ceiling height, floor surface, proximity to walls, and ambient lighting. At a more advanced stage, players need to explore the coordinative structure for serving in order to function adaptively in many relatively unique situations. During this exploration, players probe an assembled movement pattern by varying the values for important parameters of the coordinative structure in relation to environmental demands. In chapter 2, we noted that variability in the movement system is unavoidable and omnipresent, which means that the task of exploring a coordinative structure over repeated practice trials is relatively easy. For this reason, many theorists advocate that movement variability can play a functional role in helping humans adapt to novel surroundings and learn new skills (Davids, Bennett, & Newell, 2006). According to Liu and colleagues (2006), this stage of learning is typically characterized by subtle, refined variations in movement patterning as attractor stability is probed to strengthen its adaptability in different circumstances.

Even at a more advanced stage of learning, the process of practice is an attempt to improve the functionality of behavior by discovering motor patterns that are functional under different conditions. Exploring the perceptual-motor landscape leads to generating and acquiring perceptual feedback, a process that directly tunes a coordinative structure until the learner attains desired kinematic outcomes and satisfies the set of task constraints (Fitch, Tuller, & Turvey, 1982). In volleyball serving, players can use information, such as the mass of the ball and the position of opposing players, to tune their basic patterns of coordination. In learning to ride a bicycle, a child can pick up haptic information from the stiffness of the handlebars and the rate of change in direction of the front wheel to tune the coordinative structure for steering. Perceptual search is necessary for acquiring these information sources, and as we explained in chapter 3, Gibson (1979) argued that exploratory behavior in practice is important for revealing relevant information sources to guide actions.

During the control stage, exploration and search processes are facilitated if previously assembled coordinative structures are flexible enough to be progressively released and are allowed to reform into slightly different configurations over practice trials. In the case of a novice volleyball player, both coordinative structures regulating the movement of the arms and legs eventually are reconstructed into one larger unit. The control stage is characterized by the reconfiguration of motor system dfs so that coordinative structures become more open to being reconstrained by an environmental information source or by the performer's intention.

The requirement for adaptive behavior in many human movement contexts is enhanced by the **metastability** of the movement system (Kelso, 1981). *Metastability* refers to a dynamic form of stability in neurobiological systems in which system parts adhere together specifically to achieve functional movement goals while maintaining their own separate identities and flexibility of operation (Kelso & Engström, 2006). In other words, metastable movement systems do not have fixed coordination patterns that are somehow stored in their memories or physical structure. Instead, they exhibit coordination tendencies as parts come together long enough to form a functional movement pattern that can achieve a performance goal under specific environmental circumstances.

By exploiting movement system metastability tendencies, the advanced learner gradually copes with subtle variations in performance conditions caused by unplanned changes, such as trajectory of the ball toss, competitive stress, and fatigue. Depending on the tactical requirements of a game, an advanced learner can vary movements intentionally. For example, a short ball toss can be allied to a power strike, or a long toss can be accompanied with less forceful ball–hand contact. Perceptual information generated by environmental movement becomes critical as the player attempts to control the newly released dfs. As learners become increasingly tuned to the perceptual consequences associated with stable attractor regions, greater control over dfs is temporarily surrendered to environmental information such as optic or acoustic variables.

This process is exemplified by coordination of the ball toss by skilled volleyball players with and without a striking action. Figure 4.2 shows how the ball toss is adapted for striking. When not required to strike the ball, the toss is configured in a different way. As described in chapter 3, various information sources acting as constraints facilitate the self-organization of task-specific coordinative structures. This is what is implied by the formation of a strong information–movement coupling, which can be tuned to operate in different contexts.

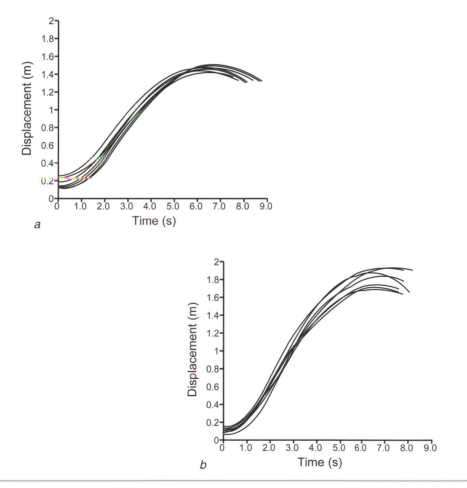

Figure 4.2 Time-displacement profiles for ball placement during (a) serving conditions (placement and hitting the ball) and (b) ball placement–only conditions for one representative subject. Displacement data on the y-axis are calibrated in meters.

Spotlight on Research

FREE(Z)ING COORDINATIVE STRUCTURES

The work of Vereijken, van Emmerik, Whiting, and Newell (1992) provided an initial impetus to investigate motor system reorganization with learning. Evidence on how learners cope with motor system dfs during skill acquisition was provided from their research on learning to perform gross body movements on a ski simulator (see figure 4.3).

Figure 4.3 Evidence for how learners cope with motor system dfs during skill acquisition has come from research conducted on a ski simulator.

Journal of Motor Behavior, vol. 24, issue 1, pp. 135-137, 1992. Reprinted with permission of the Helen Dwight Reid Educational Foundation. Published by Heldref Publications, 1319 Eighteenth St., NW, Washington, DC 20036-1802. http://www.heldref.org. Copyright © 1992.

By making whole-body movements that force energy into the system, which is formed by the platform, springs, and tracks of the simulator, the skier's aim is to produce slalom-like movements of the platform on the tracks. Successful movements on the ski simulator are characterized by movements of great amplitude, in which the platform moves to the outer edges of the tracks; an increasing frequency of slalom-like movements; and a fluency in which initial jerkiness is reduced.

ARTICLE

The research team asked five novice skiers to learn to produce slalom-like movements over 7 days. During this period, 140 trials lasting 60 seconds each were undertaken. The researchers gave no specific task instructions and recorded the amplitude and frequency of movements by using joint markers on the ski platform and the joints of the upper and lower body.

The authors argued that if joints were not actively involved in task performance, the variability around the mean of recorded joint angles (in degrees) would be low, as would the ranges of the angular motion of the joints. Moreover, relationships between joints would be high as learners constructed strong couplings between key joints. The data showed that, early in learning, the variability around the mean of joint angles over the period of the movement (estimated by the SD around the mean) was low. The range of angular motion of the joints was also low and the values for cross-correlations between joints were high. These are exactly the type of findings that one would expect if learners were freezing dfs in order to control a multiple-df action. However, there was evidence that learners were attempting to unfreeze these strong couplings in order to permit joints to become more actively engaged in the movement.

With practice, the magnitude of the angles for the hip, knee, and ankle increased, and there was a decrease in the cross-correlations between the hip and knee and the hip and ankle. The rapidity of learning effects on coordination is underscored by the fact that the biggest change in the SD of mean joint angles occurred between trials 1 and 8 of the total number of trials (*n* = 140) (see figure 4.4). The SD of the knee joint demonstrated the biggest increase over trials, which suggested that the knee joint was most influential in learners gaining control of the slalom movement during practice.

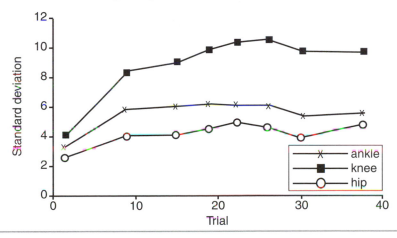

Figure 4.4 The biggest change in the SD of mean joint angles occurred between trials 1 and 8 of the total number of trials (*n* = 140).

Journal of Motor Behavior, vol. 24, issue 1, pp. 135-137, 1992. Reprinted with permission of the Helen Dwight Reid Educational Foundation. Published by Heldref Publications, 1319 Eighteenth St., NW, Washington, DC 20036-1802. http://www.heldref.org. Copyright © 1992.

APPLICATION

Think of situations in which performers free or release dfs to satisfy temporary task constraints. For example, what coordination patterns would you expect from a beginning skier who has to negotiate a steep black run? How do advanced skiers deal with the constraints of a bumpy mogul field or deep, powdery snow?

Bernstein's (1967) insights on motor learning were extremely helpful in understanding how learners cope with muscles, joints, and segments of the body during practice of a multiarticular action. However, as an understanding of concepts from dynamical systems theory and ecological psychology has emerged over the years, it has become apparent that Bernstein only captured part of the skill acquisition process.

Some researchers have reconsidered Bernstein's (1967) original insights into changes to motor system dfs as a result of learning. According to Newell and colleagues (2001), the transition from the coordination stage to the control stage is not a linear and permanent process, as some translations of Bernstein's original writings imply. More recently, it has become clear that motor system dfs become reorganized depending on a range of constraints acting on the system at any one time as learners exploit metastability tendencies in the movement system (see Chow et al., 2006; Liu et al., 2006; Newell, Liu, & Mayer-Kress, 2005). Even highly skilled performers may switch back to the coordination stage and exhibit rigid movements (typically characteristic of novices) if this is deemed a functional pattern for satisfying the task constraints under specific performance circumstances (see data on the volleyball serve by Temprado, 2002).

Newell and Vaillancourt (2001) argued that Bernstein's original conceptualization of the change process in motor systems was probably too narrow in that it failed to recognize that motor system reorganization can result in an increasing and decreasing number of mechanical dfs due to the changing nature of the constraints that need to be satisfied. Sometimes a reduction in the motor system dfs used in coordination patterns can be functional for expert athletes performing under particular task constraints. There are situations where motor problems become more challenging due to an inordinate emphasis on precision or due to unreliable environmental information such as poor lighting during a cricket or tennis match, a slippery walking or driving surface, or performing in front of a critical audience.

In such intense practice contexts and in competition, fluctuations in emotional states such as anxiety and arousal can lead to diminished accuracy of information detection (Bootsma, Bakker, van Snippenberg, & Tdlohreg, 1992). For example, Weinberg and Hunt (1976) reported a reduction of sequential muscle activity in favor of an energy-expensive, inhibitive cocontraction of agonist muscles and antagonist muscles in highly anxious throwers. We can interpret observed increases in muscle tension as efforts to refreeze dfs and to reorganize coordinative structures in an attempt to regain control. Further, due to natural processes such as aging, illness, or disease, changes to the organization of motor system dfs can result in an increase or a decrease in the number used in a particular coordination solution.

Research on soccer kicking has neatly illustrated how learners can adopt different approaches to using motor system dfs to satisfy the task goals of kicking a ball over a height barrier while varying the force control over different distances. Chow and colleagues (2007) found that some learners increased and decreased involvement of motor system dfs over practice in a nonsequential way as they searched for a functional chipping action in soccer.

Berthouze and Lungarella (2004) have even gone as far as suggesting that a strategy of alternately freezing and freeing motor system dfs might be the most successful way to acquire movement coordination. This idea requires evaluation in further research, but regardless, evidence suggests that increasing or decreasing motor system df involvement depends on the constraints of the task and the person's natural state at any one moment (Newell, Broderick, Deutsch, & Slifkin, 2003).

Skilled Optimization of Control: Stage 3

The final stage of Newell's (1985) model refers to the skilled optimization of a coordinative structure that the performer has gradually made more flexible and open to exploit environmental information sources, thus enhancing efficiency and control. At this performance level, players become adept at exploiting forces from the movement to ensure flexible and efficient actions. For example, experimenting with control of the volleyball serve can help to optimize performance. As players seek an optimal solution to the challenge of serving under different task constraints, they can alter the force, duration, and amplitude of the movement pattern.

Newell's use of the term *optimal* suggests that energy efficiency is a significant factor that governs the emergence of a movement pattern during performance. According to Newell (1985), energy efficiency is "an a priori organizing principle of coordination and control" (p. 304). Skill, or optimal organization, arises when the components of a coordinative structure are quantitatively scaled so that performers are able to use the reactive forces of the limbs during movement. Passive, inertial, and mechanical properties of limb movements are fully exploited in a skilled movement, which is characterized by smoothness and fluidity. At this stage, coordinative structures become stable as additional dfs are released. This stabilization increases the number of controllable parameters open to constraint by environmental information and results in more flexible movement (Bernstein, 1967).

In the expert volleyball serve, for example, this increased fluency may allow performers to take advantage of elastic energy released by the tendons during muscle stretch–shortening cycles not previously stimulated. Hence, as a result of reflex involvement, the acceleration phase of the hitting hand and arm may be increased and may be combined with torso rotation to generate power in the serving action. With optimization, the serving movement now becomes highly energy efficient. This is why observers often describe the execution of actions by elite athletes as effortless. Additional characteristics of optimal skilled performance levels include instantaneous adaptations to sudden and minute environmental changes (Newell, 1996).

Even at the stage of optimal skill performance, discovery learning plays an important role as people search for creative task solutions or patterns that are even more energy efficient. At all stages of learning, performers are searching for the most functional solutions for satisfying the constraints placed upon them. These features of skilled movement behavior are discussed further in the Spotlight on Research and in chapter 5.

Practical Issues for Learning

It is helpful to reconsider some important practical considerations that arise from the preceding discussion of the constraints-led approach to motor learning. In this section, we will examine the implications of these theoretical ideas for practical problems that confront most practitioners involved in skill acquisition: retention, transfer, and technique alteration.

Retention

Retention refers to the fact that given the right practice conditions, humans can usually retain some essence of a movement pattern regardless of the type of task they perform (Newell, 1996). This is because there may be a trace of an attractor well that has previously formed in the learner's intrinsic dynamics and can provide a modicum of stability for action (see chapter 2). Recall that an attractor well is a stable region of a dynamical system that is resistant to external perturbations. For example, in human movement systems, the attractor well might be the stable patterning between limbs that characterizes a swimming stroke or perhaps the coordination of the upper and lower body that allows us to ride a bike after many years without practice. This characteristic of motor learning is particularly important in rehabilitation from injury or illness.

In theories of cognitive learning, the inability to retain a skill is attributed to the poor retrieval or the degradation (forgetting) of information for the relevant motor program over time (Schmidt & Lee, 2005). From the constraints-led approach, skills are not forgotten due to a degraded representation; rather, the intrinsic dynamics become unstable due to the lack of practice and performance becomes more variable. It also is possible that the constraints that gave rise to previous motor skills may have changed significantly. For example, the learner's physical characteristics may differ as a result of aging or growth and development. Due to rapid changes in sport technology, such as material composition of equipment, the performance environment may be unfamiliar compared with the original acquisition period. Therefore, skills are more likely to be retained if they are originally acquired across a range of different constraints. Of course, other factors such as a reduced practice time, the duration of the retention period, and the activities undertaken during that time will also affect the stability of the original movement pattern. Since the original attractor is further weakened by the formation of other attractors, there is a decreased likelihood that the performer can reproduce this stable action in the future without extended practice.

Transfer

Transfer refers to the influence of previous practice or performance of a skill on the acquisition of a new skill (Magill, 2006). Practitioners often expect learners to transfer their practice performance into competitive situations. The essence of transfer is being able to adapt an existing movement pattern to a different set of ecological constraints. Attractors provide a stable base of support for actions, and an important consideration is how to establish an attractor for a new action in the presence of an old attractor.

From a constraints-led perspective, transfer is best considered in terms of the proximity of a new attractor in relation to an older one in the perceptual-motor landscape. Attractors compete and cooperate within the landscape, and positive transfer occurs when an existing attractor provides a basis for learning a new skill. If the new attractor shares elements with an old attractor, a practitioner might expect positive transfer; for example, the attractors for throwing a javelin and throwing a cricket ball are compatible. Negative

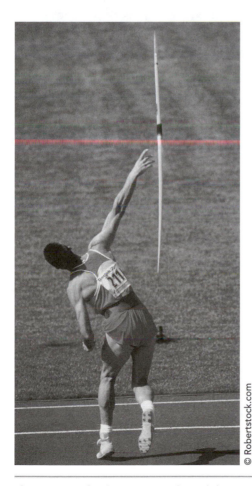

The attractors for throwing a javelin and throwing a cricket ball are compatible (the new attractor shares elements with the old attractor), so a practitioner might expect positive transfer.

transfer occurs when an existing attractor has too much influence in pulling the system away from the site of a new, emerging attractor in the landscape. For example, competing skills such as the alteration in weight distribution required for skiing and ice-skating could lead to performance decrements in the sport to which one is transferring an initial skill.

Technique Change

Would you suggest to Tiger Woods that he change his golf swing to improve his game? At what stage should you begin to teach young swimmers a new stroke? Practitioners must continually address questions such as these regardless of the performer's current ability. In these kinds of situations, practitioners tend to rely on a preconceived image of an idealized technique to determine whether a change is required. Research has shown, however, that even in highly stable skills such as rifle shooting or golf putting, common optimal coordination patterns do not exist (Ball, Best, & Wrigley, 2003; Brisson & Alain, 1996; Fairweather, Button, & Rae, 2002). This is because each time a skill is performed, it must be adapted to subtle differences in initial conditions (e.g., changes in body sway, physiological status, or psychological factors) and in the environment (e.g., a slight breeze, different temperatures, different surfaces). Given the multitude of constraints that can alter the behavioral manifestation of a movement skill, even elite performers need to display a significant amount of functional movement variability (Button, Macleod, Sanders, & Coleman, 2003; Davids, Glazier, Araújo, & Bartlett, 2003). This idea has strong implications for a learner model and suggests that the emphasis during learning should be on encouraging change and adaptation rather than achieving some hypothetical, idealized state.

The ability to evaluate technique qualitatively is perhaps the most important quality for practitioners to possess. This difficult skill demands an awareness of the broad biomechanical principles of movement and an understanding of whether the learner is exploiting these principles optimally (Sanders, 2000). In a practice drill for field hockey, for example, the practitioner should be able to explain why a pass was not performed accurately. Was the passer applying force (or torque) to the stick optimally, or was the ball too close to the body to achieve the optimal amount of torque (see figure 4.5)? Alternatively, a gymnastics coach must be able to spot when a somersault is executed poorly because the tuck position was not held for long enough. Only the ability to identify such details within the learner's movement patterns will allow the practitioner to time an intervention and use feedback effectively. Note that these observations of whether broad biomechanics principles are being adhered to during performance need to be couched in relative and not absolute terms. In this respect, it is vital for all practitioners to combine their

Biomechanical checklist

1. Does the mover have optimal stability when applying or receiving the force?
2. Is the mover using all the muscles that can make a contribution to the skill?
3. Is the mover applying force with the muscles in an appropriate sequence?
4. Is the mover applying the right amount of force over the appropriate time frame?
5. Is the mover applying the force in the correct direction?
6. Is the mover correctly applying torque and momentum transfer?
7. Is the mover manipulating linear or rotary inertia properly?

Figure 4.5 In a practice drill for field hockey, a practitioner should be able to explain why a pass was not performed accurately.

experience with a fundamental understanding of the principles of movement (Carr, 1997; Coleman, 1999).

Characteristics that practitioners might use to qualitatively identify performers who need to alter their technique include the following:

- Inability to adapt technique across different environmental constraints (poor transfer), such as a golfer who cannot adapt putting technique to different speeds of greens
- Inefficient use of energy, such as a wheelchair athlete who does not spend enough time in the push phase to generate force optimally

- Technique that does not persist over time (poor retention), such as a dancer who is unable to perform moves practiced a month ago
- High prevalence of injury, such as a rugby player whose tendency to mistime tackles has resulted in head injuries
- Uneconomic movement patterns, such as cyclists with an upright posture who become quickly fatigued due to the added demands of maintaining their body position and cycling against air resistance

Role of the Movement Practitioner: Nonlinear Pedagogy

Characterizing learners as nonlinear dynamical movement systems provides the basis for advocating a **nonlinear pedagogy** (Chow et al., 2006). This theoretical foundation views learning systems as nonlinear dynamical systems and holds that the observed properties of human movement systems form the basis of a principled pedagogical framework. Nonlinear pedagogy can provide practitioners with key principles to use in teaching situations, such as how to assess performance, how to structure practices, and how best to deliver instructions and provide feedback. A theoretical approach to practice provides the impetus for pedagogists to begin shaping the emergence of goal-directed behavior (Newell, 1986), thus enhancing perceptual-motor learning.

Nonlinear pedagogy advocates awareness by practitioners that a learner's coordination solutions are the products of self-organization and that periods of movement variability should be valued as part of the learning process. To encourage emergence of functionally relevant coordination solutions, it supports the manipulation of performer–environment interactions through altering relevant task, environmental, and performer constraints. As Newell and colleagues (2001) have pointed out, constraints to action exist on multiple timescales, and consequently, both motor learning and motor development are punctuated by nonlinear jumps of varying magnitudes to more mature motor patterns. Nonlinear pedagogists understand that constraints are temporary influences on performers and that practice should replicate the specific dynamics that might exist in a particular performance context such as a game or work activity. In other words, constraints may be emerging or decaying for each learner depending on the current status of the movement system and the nature of the task constraints that exist in the practice environment (see Chow et al., in press; Guerin & Kunkle, 2004).

In many ways, nonlinear pedagogy differs from traditional methods of teaching and coaching (Chow et al., 2006). In terms of skill development, the movement practitioner's role has traditionally been associated with tasks such as employing practice drills to perfect performance in relation to an idealized

TABLE 4.1 *Behavior Typically Associated With Effective Coaches*

Characteristic	Coaching behavior (Douge and Hastie, 1993)
Verbal feedback	Frequently provided Numerous prompts
Corrections	High levels of corrective cues Reinstruction of critical features
Questioning	Frequent use of questions and clarification
Instruction	Spend most of their time engaged in direct instruction
Structure of training environment	Manage training environment to achieve considerable order

motor pattern, evaluating technique, giving instruction and feedback, and carefully managing the learner's practice environment. For example, Curtner-Smith, Todorov, McCaughtry, and Lacon (2001) presented compelling evidence that physical education teachers spend up to 78% of their time engaging in such teaching strategies. A central theme emerging from nonlinear pedagogy is the importance of facilitating independent learning through search, discovery, and exploitation of constraints. These important learning processes seem to have been largely ignored within common pedagogical practices (see table 4.1). In chapter 10 of this book, we will use case studies from a variety of instructional situations to stimulate more thought about the practitioner's role during motor learning.

Hands-Off Practitioners

In the second part of this textbook, we advocate the concept of the hands-off practitioner, which embraces the constraints-led approach to skill acquisition and captures the methodological stance advocated for a nonlinear pedagogist. The hands-off concept does not imply a diminished role for the practitioner, but merely a different approach to motor skills acquisition. The hands-off practitioner is every bit as involved as the traditional coaching model seems to require; however, it will become obvious in the following chapters that the main strategies in nonlinear pedagogy are much more learner centered and key tasks are approached differently.

A useful analogy for the hands-off practitioner is that of a gardener. Plants differ in preferred growth conditions, such as soil composition and position in the garden, and gardeners do not dictate when a plant should flower. Instead, evidence shows that flowering is a result of emergent, self-organizing processes, and gardeners play an important role in creating the appropriate growing environment for each plant. When necessary, gardeners may intervene by watering the plant or relocating it to a larger pot, but the main business of growth and flowering is ultimately left to the plant, which has perceptual systems to sense informational constraints such as ambient temperature and light (Yanovsky & Kay, 2002). In a similar vein, significant tasks for the hands-off practitioner are to create a learning environment for the discovery of optimal solutions by manipulating constraints, interpreting movement variability, and nurturing learners in their search activities. There is no ideal motor pattern that suits every performer, so compared with more traditional instructional approaches, these hands-off methods allow greater opportunities for each learner to seek and identify appropriate movement patterns within practice.

Although each practitioner may have an individual teaching style (Lyle, 2002), one of the main benefits of the hands-off concept is that it can easily accommodate a wide range of individual teaching styles, including established techniques such as **Teaching Games for Understanding** (TGfU) (Chow et al., 2006).

TGfU has been the most prominent model of pedagogical practice in the teaching of games for the past 20 years (see chapter 5 for more information about TGfU). Bunker and Thorpe (1982), who first conceptualized TGfU, argued that traditional approaches to teaching games overemphasized the practice of skills in isolation, leading to poor decision-making ability and transfer of skills in the game context. TGfU was developed to allow people to learn the tactical aspects of games by playing modified versions of target games so that an understanding of tactics is the major focus rather than component motor skills.

Unlike some traditional approaches to teaching games, TGfU has a student-centered emphasis for learning tactics and skills in modified game contexts (e.g., Griffin, Butler, Lombardo, & Nastasi, 2003; Hopper, 2002). The modified games usually result in equipment, the playing area, or rules being adapted to constrain understanding of learners toward the targeted tactical concept. Although TGfU has generated interest among practitioners and has been promoted by physical education researchers as an effective method for teaching team sports, surprisingly little in the way of empirical evidence exists to support its effectiveness (Strean & Bengoechea, 2003). Clearly, the constraints-led approach has a strong theoretical basis that can support a principled understanding of how and why to modify game practice.

In pointing out how the principles of TGfU are harmonious with a constraints-led approach, we are not suggesting that all other pedagogical techniques are flawed. Instead, our goal in part II of this textbook is to develop a nonlinear pedagogical philosophy that is not context specific but may be adopted to underpin many relevant, existing instructional behaviors.

Summary

As we complete the theoretical overview section of this book, it may be useful to consider how some of this information relates to skill acquisition in the real world, which forms the basis of a nonlinear pedagogy. To prepare you for part II, here are some pedagogical implications of the constraints-led approach:

- Careful consideration is needed concerning how key task and personal constraints interact to influence performance and skill acquisition for each learner.

- Time spent in practice is one among many important constraints on attainment of excellence. Practitioners should not overemphasize quantity of time spent in practice because the power law of practice is just one of many different learning curves that describes how individual learners may change over time (Newell et al., 2001).

- Time spent in practice does not necessarily guarantee the acquisition of expertise. What athletes are challenged to do during practice is a more accurate index of skill acquisition than amount of time spent on the training field (Davids, 2000). The microstructure of practice needs to be monitored so that qualitative differences between practice sessions are understood.

- Sport scientists and practitioners need to work together to fully understand the nature of the personal, task, and environmental constraints acting on individual performers in different sports and physical activities.

- Practitioners could facilitate rapid development and skill acquisition by careful identification and manipulation of the major constraints on each learner during practice and training. Planned manipulations may cause behavior jumps or sudden transitions in skill level. This is akin to infants who skip motor milestones, exemplified by research observing the appearance or disappearance of stepping in infants. In this respect, behaviors may just be waiting in the wings to be brought out from each learner (Thelen & Smith, 1994).

- Individual differences need to be understood and valued more than ever. Variation could signal successful adaptation to unique constraints. For example, the history of sport is littered with successful athletes who have satisfied task constraints in unique ways. Learning could be viewed as a personal struggle to assemble a successful coordination solution to a given movement problem.

- The key unit of analysis from a constraints-led approach is the individual performer (Button, Davids, & Schöllhorn, 2006). Variability in movement performance needs to be carefully interpreted. Sometimes high levels of variability help in adapting to the environment, and on other occasions low levels help increase performance stability.

- Many activities involve complex movements. Although genetic variations may or may not limit certain capacities for a person (e.g., power or physical endurance), other strengths can be exploited for performance excellence.

- As technology develops and ethical guidelines are considered, genetic variations can be screened and exploited as constraints that provide an advantage for learners.

- To understand the complexity of sport performance and skill acquisition, practitioners and sport scientists need to recognize the limitations of monodisciplinary perspectives. Teams of scientists need to develop a multidisciplinary approach to analyzing constraints on the different functional levels of performance (e.g., cognitive, social, physiological, biomechanical).

SELF-TEST QUESTIONS

1. How does the constraints-led approach to skill acquisition differ from traditional approaches in its definition of learning?

2. Use the analogy of the perceptual-motor landscape to explain the following characteristics of learning: intrinsic dynamics, search, discovery, and efficiency.

3. Reflect on your own learning experiences for a movement activity you participate in and the current repertoire of skills you have available. Map out a hypothetical perceptual-motor landscape, labeling the valleys as attractors for stable actions that are well learned. Sketch out the peaks and the rugged terrain to depict the less stable skills that are more open to perturbations. List some of the influential constraints that help to configure the landscape.

4. How might young children learning to throw a ball organize the large number of dfs at their disposal?

5. Provide some examples of emergent movement behavior in experienced performers and inexperienced performers.

6. Explain how retention, transfer, and technique change can be indicative of the learning process from a constraints-led approach.

ADDITIONAL READING

1. Chow, J-Y., Davids, K., Button, C., Shuttleworth, R., Renshaw, I., & Araújo, D. (2006). Nonlinear pedagogy: A constraints-led framework to understanding emergence of game play and skills. *Nonlinear Dynamics, Psychology and Life Sciences, 10,* 71-103.

2. Muchisky, M., Gershkoff-Cole, L., Cole, E., & Thelen, E. (1996). The epigenetic landscape revisited: A dynamical interpretation. In C. Rovee-Collier & L.P. Lipsitt (Eds.), *Advances in Infancy Research* (pp. 121-160). Norwood, NJ: Ablex.

3. Newell, K.M. (1996). Change in movement and skill: Learning, retention and transfer. In M.L. Latash & M.T. Turvey (Eds.), *Dexterity and its development* (pp. 393-430). Mahwah, NJ: Erlbaum.

4. Newell, K.M., Liu, Y.-T., & Mayer-Kress, G. (2001). Time scales in motor learning and development. *Psychological Review, 108*(1), 57-82.

II
PART

Applying the Constraints-Led Approach

Part II highlights how we can use a constraints-led approach to describe and explain change in movement coordination that results from learning and development processes. Newell's (1986) model categorizes constraints into three different but interacting types related to the individual performer, task, and environment. The model considers the effect of identifying and manipulating key constraints under which skilled behavior emerges. An important role for coaches, teachers, and physical therapists is to understand the nature of the constraints that each person needs to satisfy when performing motor skills. During practice and rehabilitation activities, practitioners can enhance learning by manipulating the key constraints on each learner. This strategy forms the basis of nonlinear pedagogy.

   Each chapter in part II adopts specific concerns that practitioners can use to gauge their understanding of the theoretical ideas discussed in part I. In chapter 5, we discuss the creation of a perceptual-motor landscape as a part of the motor learning process from a dynamical systems perspective. We present a method for assessing stability and instability in a perceptual-motor landscape to check whether learning has occurred. Chapter 6 emphasizes how practitioners can understand individual differences as personal constraints, leading to variations in movement behavior. In chapter 7, we look at the implications of these ideas for the design of practice environments in which task constraints can be manipulated to guide learners' search for relevant movement solutions.

If motor learning is a process of searching a perceptual-motor landscape, then strategies to present feedback should reflect this process, as we note in chapters 8 and 9. In chapter 8, we evaluate the merits of instructions and feedback based on either movement dynamics or effects on the environment. Chapter 9 looks at the presentation of visual demonstrations as part of the observational learning process. Finally, chapter 10 provides six hypothetical case studies that illustrate how practitioners can adopt a constraints-led approach.

CHAPTER 5

Understanding the Dynamics of Skill Acquisition

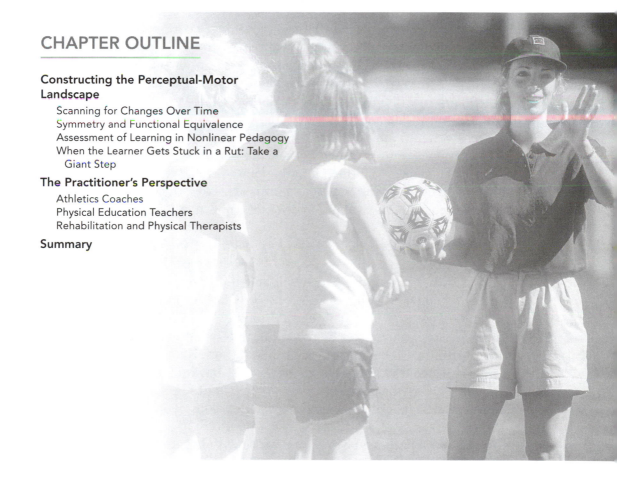

CHAPTER OUTLINE

In part I, we discussed the theoretical ideas of dynamical systems theory and ecological psychology and how practitioners can better understand learners. These theories underpin the constraints-led approach to motor learning and enable us to redefine skill acquisition as an ongoing dynamic process involving search and stabilization of appropriate movement patterns across the perceptual-motor landscape.

In this chapter, we will describe empirical research that supports Newell's (1985) model of motor learning to further illustrate the dynamics of skill acquisition (e.g., Zanone & Kelso, 1992, 1997). We also will discuss how to assess skill acquisition from a constraints-led approach, which is a critical concern in nonlinear pedagogy. Finally, we will consider in more detail how coaches, physical education teachers, and therapists can use the hands-off philosophy described in chapter 4.

Constructing the Perceptual-Motor Landscape

In chapter 2, we explained how human movement coordination results from the movement system settling into specific attractor states within the perceptual-motor landscape. This landscape or pattern of dynamic attractors must be gradually altered to allow the performer to combine these tasks simultaneously and in a functional manner. For example, novice jugglers may be able to catch and throw a ball independently but struggle to combine these elements initially, which indicates the adaptation that the perceptual-motor landscape must experience. For learning to occur, the performer must use the task to be learned as a specific form of information to remold the perceptual-motor landscape. In other words, "Once learning is achieved, the memorized pattern constitutes an attractor, a stable state of the (now modified) pattern dynamics" (Kelso, 1995, p. 163).

Before we consider empirical evidence, we must understand several key concepts. First, we need to understand the nature of the learning process, specifically that "the extent to which specific behavioral information cooperates or competes with spontaneous self-organizing tendencies determines the resulting patterns and their relative stability" (Kelso, 1995, p. 169). If the initial behavioral tendencies do not conform to what is required of the performer, learning will be more difficult than if there is a close match between the learner's intrinsic dynamics and the task's behavioral information. For this reason, it is clear that practitioners should expect to see great differences in the rates at which learners acquire movement skills over time (Newell, Liu, & Mayer-Kress, 2001). Consider a child who picks up a pencil to draw with the right hand. For this type of learner, writing is likely to take longer to learn with the left hand than with the right hand.

A second point is that the process of learning a new task involves not just one feature changing, but the whole attractor layout. As one attractor well is being carved out, nearby attractors can become less stable. Picture a child sitting comfortably on the surface of a trampoline. If a second child were to jump onto the trampoline near the first child, the deformation in the trampoline bed would perturb the first child's stability. We can expect a similar reaction from a fluid, interconnected, dynamical movement system. Therefore, when planning programs for skill acquisition, practitioners should take care to reduce the perturbing effects of constructing one attractor on the stability of existing attractors or skills. We will return to these design features of motor learning programs in chapters 7, 8, and 9.

Scanning for Changes Over Time

For theorists and practitioners of motor learning, it is important to find a way to monitor changes to the layout of the landscape. In research studies, one effective way of probing the entire

The fact that novice jugglers may be able to catch and throw a ball independently but struggle to combine these elements initially indicates the adaptation that the perceptual-motor landscape must experience.

perceptual-motor landscape during learning has been to use a **scanning procedure** (Yamanashi, Kawato, & Suzuki, 1980; Zanone & Kelso, 1992). This empirical technique requires the participant to intentionally vary an order parameter, such as relative phase, in steps. As the behavior of the order parameter is monitored, the observer is effectively scanning the perceptual-motor landscape for stable and unstable regions (differing in levels of variability of selected measures). This scanning technique can result in snapshots of the attractor layout as it is evolving, revealing the relative stability of regions over time (Button, Bennett, & Davids, 2001).

Zanone and Kelso (1992) used a scanning procedure to examine the dynamics of motor learning while participants were acquiring a bimanual coordination task. In 5 daily sessions, participants sat in front of a blackboard displaying a kind of visual metronome and were instructed to flex each finger in temporal coincidence with the onset of two lights. A typical session comprised 3 blocks of 5 learning trials in which participants practiced a new required relative phase (RP) of 90° between the fingers. On the metronome, the movement frequency was set at 1.75 hertz. Knowledge of results in the form of actual RP was provided after each trial. At the beginning and end of each daily session, as well as between training blocks, a scanning run was carried out where the RP was progressively increased from 0° to 180° by 12 discrete steps of 15°. To assess pattern stability over time, recall trials were administered 7 days later in which participants had to reproduce the 90° condition for 1 minute.

At the end of day 1, the RP variability was still lowest at 0° and 180°, increasing markedly at intermediate values. The low values of RP variability indicated regions of stability in the landscape. As expected, in-phase and anti-phase patterns were most stable, with the latter more variable than the former (see also Spotlight on Research, chapter 2). In addition, between-participant variability was smallest at these required phasings. By the end of day 5, however, RP variability was also low at 90°. Attraction toward the 90° region was evident by the negative slope of curves on either side of 90°, indicating a switch from bistable to tristable dynamics in the landscape (see figure 5.1).

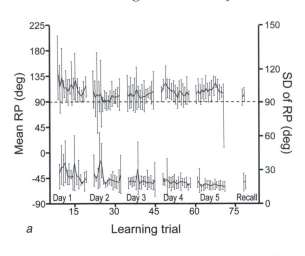

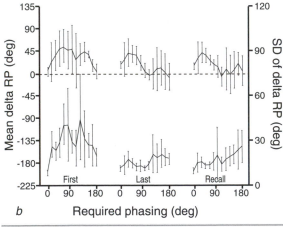

Recall data also suggested that this change to the perceptual-motor landscape was relatively permanent. Subsequent analysis on the 0° and 180° patterns revealed that the initial attractors became less stable (and less attractive) as the 90° phase was learned. As we noted in chapter 4, this latter finding clearly shows the metastability that characterizes the tendencies of a movement system that is changing with learning (see Kelso, 1981). Zanone and Kelso (1992) suggested that learning does not necessarily always require an abrupt phase transition (see also Nouritt et al., 2003) but may also occur more gradually as

Figure 5.1 Attraction toward the 90° region of the landscape is evidenced by low RP variability and the negative slope of curves either side of 90°, indicating a switch from bistable to tristable dynamics.

From P.G. Zanone and J.A.S. Kelso, "Evolution of behavioral attractors with learning: Nonequilibrium phase transitions," *Journal of Experimental Psychology: Human Perception and Performance* Volume 18, Issue 2, pp. 403-421, 1992, Copyright © American Psychological Association. Reprinted with permission.

"the distance in collective variable space between behavioral requirements and intrinsically preferred patterns appears to determine the nature of change" (p. 418). Finally, in the Zanone and Kelso study, the rate of learning for the 90° pattern differed among participants. Some people showed evidence of attraction to this pattern after just 2 days, whereas others needed up to 5 days. Of course, differences among learners are a feature that many coaches and teachers recognize, albeit one that is vaguely articulated. A dynamical systems interpretation of motor learning suggests that interindividual variability may be inherent to the learning process because learners begin with differences in intrinsic dynamics. As mentioned in chapter 4, compatibility between the to-be-learned task dynamics and a learner's intrinsic dynamics can determine the rate of motor learning.

In figure 5.2, we can observe how the shape of attractor wells changed during Zanone and Kelso's (1992) experiment. Figure 5.2a shows how the stability of relative phase fluctuates across the attractor layout, with antiphase and in-phase patterns exhibiting stable states (a bistable regime). As discussed previously, these states are thought to represent the intrinsic dynamics for this task in the absence of behavioral information. In figure 5.2b, the three lines show what happens to the landscape when 0°, 90°, or 180° patterns are learned (i.e., when specific parametric influences are added). Note that when 0° or 180° patterns are learned, the width of the associated attractor well has increased. This indicates that learning can enhance the attractiveness to the movement system of these states. However, when the 90° pattern is learned, the potential is deformed and the competition between behavioral information and intrinsic dynamics pulls the minima toward 90°. A new, wider attractor well has been created in which increased flexibility arises due to the influence of the underlying intrinsic dynamics. As learning continues at 90°, the shape of this attractor well narrows and deepens as the pattern

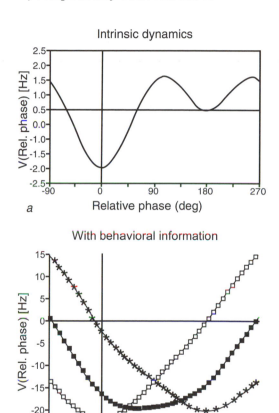

Figure 5.2 (a) The stability of relative phase fluctuates across the attractor layout, with antiphase and in-phase patterns exhibiting stable states. (b) The three lines show what happens to the landscape when 0°, 90°, or 180° patterns are learned.

From P.G. Zanone and J.A.S. Kelso, "Evolution of behavioral attractors with learning: Nonequilibrium phase transitions," *Journal of Experimental Psychology: Human Perception and Performance* Volume 18, Issue 2, pp. 403-421, 1992, Copyright © American Psychological Association. Reprinted with permission.

becomes memorized and increases in stability at the expense of the 0° and 180° patterns (see Wenderoth & Bock, 2001).

Symmetry and Functional Equivalence

In a later study, Zanone and Kelso (1997) again used a bimanual finger-waggling task to demonstrate two other interesting characteristics of learners seeking to stabilize a new motor pattern. First, they demonstrated that learners were able to produce symmetrical partners of the patterns that they were practicing. For example, when participants learned a 90° phasing (i.e., the left finger lagging the right by one-quarter of a cycle), they also could execute a 270° or 90° phasing pattern (i.e., the left finger leading the right by the same amount), even though they had never practiced the latter pattern. The authors suggested that practicing the 90° pattern gave rise to a new, stable pattern emerging in the perceptual-motor landscape at 270°. This remarkable finding showed that learning can result in global changes to the perceptual-motor landscape and can affect the stability of other movement patterns even when they are not the subject of specific practice.

A second result of Zanone and Kelso's 1997 study was that participants could perform the newly learned phase relationship in different ways. Although the task requirement was always met, the different solutions ranged from smooth, quasi-sinusoidal motion of both end effectors (fingers) to jagged, discontinuous movements. Zanone and Kelso interpreted these findings as the learners demonstrating functional equivalence, in which learning occurs at the abstract level of the coordination dynamics regardless of the end-effector (limb segment) used to bring about the end result. Kelso and Zanone (2002) later verified this concept by showing that regardless of whether participants practiced a bimanual phasing pattern with their arms or with their legs, they were able to transfer the learned pattern to a different end-effector system. These data indicate just how abstract and universal the learned coordination dynamics can be.

Assessment of Learning in Nonlinear Pedagogy

The scanning procedure described earlier would be difficult to implement in realistic learning environments without sophisticated measurement tools. However, regularly assessing a learner's progress is critical for the practitioner to help guide ongoing practice. Practitioners have typically associated movement variability with error and believed that minimizing performance errors would indicate improvement. However, in nonlinear pedagogy, practitioners view movement variability more positively. In the motor system, variability is omnipresent, unavoidable, and might even provide a useful signpost for exploratory behavior in learners; in fact, a change in constraints can act as a catalyst for a new movement pattern by helping to induce more variability in the learner. Zanone and Kelso (1992) argued that the movement system must experience critical fluctuations before it can relocate itself in a new attractor state. Further, in order to widen the attractor base that learners currently occupy, they must practice under a range of constraints.

Manipulating constraints is a natural way to learn skills and to assess skill development. In many respects, this is the basis of nonlinear pedagogy. For example, task constraints represent a direct route to changing behavior and might produce sudden transitions in technique at the beginning of practice. Later in practice the changes may be less abrupt and the pattern variability may reflect refinements and adaptations by learners (Liu et al., 2006).

It can often take longer to alter organismic or personal constraints, and we may expect to see slower and more permanent adaptations in coordination as a result of, for example, prolonged flexibility or endurance training. In terms of

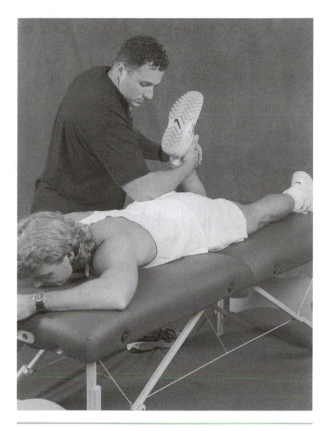

Practitioners should view movement variability more positively because it might provide a useful signpost for exploratory behavior in learners. A change in constraints can act as a catalyst for a new movement pattern by helping to induce more variability.

environmental constraints, cultural and social constraints also have a slower and more subtle impact on behavior, although it has been argued that these constraints emerge and decay more rapidly than some organismic constraints, such as effects of genetic constraints on population variation (Ehrlich, 2000). In a busy traffic environment, for instance, drivers need to adapt their actions quickly, but their driving style may not be rapidly affected by societal views of driving as dictated by changing cultural perspectives.

When considering how the perceptual-motor landscape changes over time, it is necessary to acknowledge the different timescales in which influential constraints operate. According to Newell (1986), constraints may be relatively time dependent or time independent; that is, "the rate with which constraints may change over time varies considerably with the level of analysis and parameter under consideration" (p. 347). Newell and colleagues (2001) have pointed out that "time scales in motor learning and development would include the influence of the time scales of phylogeny and ontogeny in motor learning and the related impact of culture and society on the development of human action.

This broader context serves to highlight and emphasize the central role that some scales play in the study of motor learning and development" (p. 64).

The issue of different constraints operating on different timescales has implications for the practitioner's judgment of the learner's rate of progress. When learning a new coordination pattern, more permanent behavioral changes take longer to appear than immediate adaptations to task constraints during practice. Therefore, practitioners should understand that some behaviors might represent transient adaptations to immediate task constraints imposed during practice, and these constraints interact with organismic constraints related to developmental status. Important constraints here include the effects of the specific equipment, location, and instructions that a learner experiences at a given state of development. Practitioners need to observe with care to ensure that emergent behavior under constraints is not due to transient effects but reflects a stable characteristic of each learner's current level of performance. Assessment of learning requires nonlinear pedagogists to be familiar with the influential constraints that shape behavior. In structuring an effective learning environment, these constraints should be manipulated to facilitate the learner's search for more effective coordination patterns. The following 4-step plan may help practitioners systematically approach assessment within their learning environments:

1. Identify significant constraints that limit behavior within each movement task that the practitioner is teaching (e.g., task, individual, environment).

2. Examine the reaction of a few learners at different developmental stages to subtle changes in the constraint, monitoring the learners' initial and short-term reaction.

3. Modify the degree and frequency of constraint changes to suit the individual learner.

4. Using movement variability as an indicator of attractor stability, continue to evaluate the learner's skill retention and transfer.

When the Learner Gets Stuck in a Rut: Take a Giant Step

Another concern practitioners often face is how to make experienced performers alter well-established coordination patterns. Despite long periods of repetitive practice, the learner may get stuck in a rut, showing little progress. Although practitioners sometimes call this a *performance plateauing effect*, the movement system actually has become temporarily trapped in a deep, stable attractor state that may not be as effective as other, nearby states. In figure 5.3, a pole-vaulter's performance level, indicated by the personal best height, has stopped improving despite further practice. In other words, some motor patterns can become too stable. In addition, the formation of the

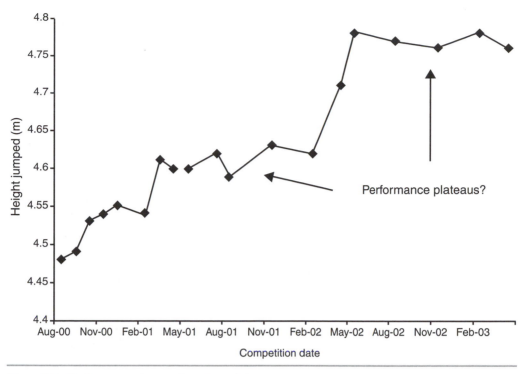

Figure 5.3 Performance plateau of a pole-vaulter.

established pattern has weakened the stability of nearby attractors, making it less likely that the learner can use an alternative coordination pattern. Could the plateau indicate that some change in coordination is needed to stimulate further improvement?

The practitioner can consider two potential approaches to this problem. For simplicity, we will use the example of a tennis player who relies heavily on a two-handed backhand stroke. Adopting a nonlinear pedagogical approach, how can a practitioner help the tennis player explore alternative shots on the backhand side? The first useful strategy involves gradually weakening the stability of the existing attractor state by trying to induce movement pattern variability. This is a counterintuitive notion since traditionally the aim of practice has been to make movement patterns more stable (and therefore less prone to error) over time. To achieve this aim, the practitioner should encourage the tennis player to keep practicing with the usual technique, but the practitioner must find ways to gradually alter potential control parameters such as ball speed or height of ball bounce to encourage more variability.

For example, during practice the tennis practitioner could use an adjustable ball machine or a range of new and used tennis balls to change the flight characteristics of the ball. In these situations the two-handed technique should become more variable as a function of the altered task constraints, and the player will begin to find it difficult to play a customary shot. For example, forcing the player to strike the ball earlier if it bounces too high, reducing the backlift of the racket for quicker returns, or taking one hand off the racket to release additional dfs may begin to destabilize an existing motor pattern and provide valuable exploratory practice time for the player. It may take some time for this approach to lead to long-term changes in behavior, but given the amount of time invested in stabilizing the original technique, this should come as no surprise.

An alternative approach to changing well-established techniques would be to perturb the system from an existing attractor toward a more functional movement pattern (Newell, 1996). In other words, the practitioner can try a more radical manipulation of constraints to push the performer out of the customary technique. Returning to the tennis player, the practitioner can immediately prevent the two-handed solution from emerging by artificially constraining the nondominant arm, such as by asking the player to hold a ball or a racket in the nondominant hand. Now the player will be quickly forced into practicing the one-handed shot as a consequence of the altered task constraints. This drill also could have the added benefit of helping the player develop balance during the shot by counteracting the position of the playing arm with the nondominant limb.

In each of these approaches, both the learner and practitioner should understand that there will be a temporary increase in errors as the new movement pattern evolves and the old attractor state is weakened. Although the transition into a new, shallow attractor state is quick in the second approach, it may take some time to develop the consistency associated with the two-handed shot. Adding variability to a movement pattern can thus benefit long-term changes in movement behavior. Neither the practitioner nor the learner should interpret this initial rise in movement variability as negative. Instead, sometimes you need to take two steps backward to move one giant step forward.

Photo courtesy of Matthew Dicks

A practitioner can prevent the two-handed solution from emerging by asking the tennis player to hold a ball or a racket in the nondominant hand.

The Practitioner's Perspective

Up to this point we have attempted to describe how skill acquisition occurs over time. Researchers have traditionally considered learning as an unobservable process indirectly assessed by relatively permanent behavioral changes (e.g., Schmidt & Lee, 2005), but a more informative unit of analysis is available in the learner's coordination dynamics. Practitioners can begin to recognize important signs within a learner's development that indicate how the learner is attempting to match task requirements to existing intrinsic dynamics. Movement variability can be viewed as the learner's attempts to search for more effective solutions to the task goal. We will now consider evidence concerning whether coaches, physical education teachers, and therapists are adopting these ideas.

Athletics Coaches

Athletics coaches have a complex, multifaceted role to play because they're often expected to act as trainer, teacher, friend, motivator, and disciplinarian all at once. Abraham and Collins (1998) distinguished between two traditional approaches that are typical within coach education, a review of which may be useful to enhance our understanding of nonlinear pedagogy. The first approach is **experiential coaching,** which draws upon the wealth of knowledge and experience that many coaches have developed during their participation in a specific sport or activity. Practitioners who adopt the experiential approach rely on their intuitive understanding of sport and the knowledge passed down by influential colleagues to inform their planning and organization within the learning environment (Potrac, Brewer, Jones, Armour, & Hoff, 2000).

However, although experiential knowledge has its advantages in this context (such as gaining the immediate attention of learners), it does not provide coaches with a theoretically based objective framework for understanding how they can help learners acquire skill. A model of how people actually learn is a significant element that is too often missing in coach education and training. Intuitive coaching also is likely to inhibit the communication of knowledge gleaned from motor learning research into the practical arena (Fairweather, 1999). Indeed, the wide range of journals, books, and magazines produced by and for practitioners is notable for the absence of a discussion of theoretical frameworks to underpin practical work (see also Lyle, 2002). In related professions such as sports medicine and physiotherapy, it is unlikely that experiential knowledge alone would be sufficient for a therapist working with an injured patient for the first time. For this reason, many professions have established accreditation procedures that document the amount of study, level of knowledge, and nature of the practice skills acquired by each person during training.

The second common educational approach that Abraham and Collins (1998) identified is **method coaching,** whereby practitioners learn to break down and teach specific movement skills in a mechanistic manner to piece together the correct technique. This is the dominant coaching method and has been influenced by the learner model advocated in the information-processing approach to motor learning (for examples, see Christina & Corcos, 1998; and Sharp, 1992). It is widely recognized that many sport practitioners either explicitly or implicitly use this popular learning model (Handford, Davids, Bennett, & Button, 1997; Schmidt & Wrisberg, 2004).

Given the theoretical influence of the information-processing approach on traditional coach education, it is not surprising that practitioners typically provide lots of verbal instructions to their athletes. In today's winning-oriented climate, coaches are often seduced into this manner of teaching. As a result of social pressure to be seen as a hands-on instructor, the temptation to provide advice whenever an athlete makes errors can prove to be too great (Sidaway & Hand, 1993). Further, when working with large groups of athletes, many coaches present the illusion of being in control by constantly barking out instructions. However, a major dilemma arises if athletes become overloaded with information or become too dependent on the coach's input during practice. Therefore, although method coaching seems to produce immediate and temporary performance benefits, it may not encourage independent problem solving or effective performance retention and transfer (Davids, Kingsbury, Bennett, & Handford, 2001). There is little value in instructing athletes to copy an idealized motor pattern that may not suit their individual intrinsic dynamics.

Many coaches become excellent practitioners despite shortcomings in their training or education. Such coaches are often excellent communicators.

Potrac and colleagues (2000) recently pointed out that a shift in the emphasis of coach education is now required, "from a mechanical mind/body approach to a sharper focus on the person, by illuminating the complex micro level interactions that represent the everyday and complex reality of the dynamic coaching process" (p. 195). Of course, there are many coaches who become excellent practitioners despite shortcomings in their training or education. These coaches are often excellent communicators, and they know when they need to talk to athletes and when they need to listen.

Physical Education Teachers

Two markedly different teaching approaches have been advocated for physical education teachers: traditional game teaching via a direct-command approach and the Teaching Games for Understanding (TGfU) method. Some similarities with the TGfU approach (Bunker & Thorpe, 1986) and nonlinear pedagogy that were described in the previous chapter should have become apparent, although the theoretical frameworks also differ in many key aspects.

TGfU and Nonlinear Pedagogy The focus of TGfU is to provide learning experiences for people to acquire tactical skills by playing modified versions of a target game. Because TGfU emphasizes the development of tactical understanding before movement techniques, it has been seen as an approach for redressing the balance toward understanding the *why* of games playing before the *how* (Hopper, 2002; Werner et al., 1996). To exemplify the focus on tactical awareness, Thorpe (1990) pointed out that "the basic philosophy of games for understanding is that a person can play games with limited techniques and, even with limited techniques be very competitive" (p. 90).

Traditional approaches emphasize acquiring techniques in isolation from the performance context before using these skills in a particular game (Turner & Martinek, 1999). In contrast, TGfU is student centered, with the learning of both tactics and skills occurring in modified game contexts (Griffin, Butler, Lombardo, & Nastasi, 2003; Hopper, 2002; Thorpe, 2001). In this sense, modified games are practiced to enhance understanding and awareness of learners in full-game contexts. Game appreciation is emphasized to enhance understanding of the rules and the nature of the game. Tactical awareness is also encouraged in order to challenge learners to solve problems posed in the game and to gain relevant knowledge for performance. This initial emphasis is followed by developing decision making, which leads to knowing what to do and how to do it in relation to specific tactical situations. Skill execution and performance are then assessed by observing the outcomes of decisions as they are executed by learners during actual game play (Turner & Martinek, 1999; Werner et al., 1996). To summarize, the key features of TGfU are its student-centered approach and its flexibility in manipulating constraints in modified games to teach tactical knowledge and, subsequently, skills related to tactical concepts (Griffin et al., 2003; Hopper, 2002).

Nonlinear Pedagogy as a Theoretical Framework for TGfU Although research on TGfU has been conducted over the last 20 years, questions still exist over its relative efficacy, including the following:

- Is the perceived need to differentiate skill development from tactical development valid when assessing the effectiveness of TGfU compared with traditional technique-based approaches?

- Is there a theoretical framework of adequate power for providing explanatory concepts and testable hypotheses to disambiguate expectations and predictions in empirical research related to TGfU?

- Is TGfU suitable for people at all stages of learning?

TGfU currently lacks a sound theoretical base for examining its efficacy as a pedagogical approach. In their review of TGfU, Griffin, Brooker, and Patton (2005) commented that its efficacy could be grounded in three possible theoretical frameworks, including achievement goal theory, information processing, and situated learning. In particular, many physical education researchers believe that the TGfU approach is generally aligned with the theoretical orientations of cognitivism and constructivism as well as situated learning (e.g., Kirk & MacPhail, 2002). However, McMorris (1998) made a critical observation when he noted that there have been few attempts to examine the relationship between research on TGfU and prominent theories of perceptual-motor learning. Thus, despite its popularity, few extensive theoretical rationales for TGfU have been provided in the literature that emphasize how goal-directed movement behavior emerges in a TGfU setting (however, see Turner & Martinek, 1999, for a rationale based on declarative and procedural knowledge).

This weakness has been remediated by the framework of nonlinear pedagogy, which harnesses the theoretical work on motor learning constraints to form a principled basis for teaching and learning. Evidence shows that manipulation of constraints by physical educators can lead to the production of successful motor patterns, decision-making behavior, and intentions that guide the achievement of task goals (see Chow et al., 2006; Chow et al., in press). This radically different conceptualization of movement variability fits well with pedagogical claims on the efficacy of a TGfU perspective. For example, den Duyn (1996) observed that, "One of the interesting aspects of the game sense approach is that incorrect technique is not necessarily seen as a 'bad thing' that must be immediately changed. Many athletes use unorthodox techniques that still achieve the right result (and often bamboozle their opponent)" (p. 7).

However, this is not to say that coaches and physical educators should allow free play and hope that learners complete a set task in whatever way the learners deem appropriate. The teacher must consider the constraints within the learning environment so that the students can use an appropriate response to achieve the desired learning outcome planned for the session. Task constraints are particularly important for the TGfU approach because they include the rules of the game, equipment used, boundary playing areas and markings, nets and goals, number of players involved, and information sources present in specific performance contexts. Clearly, pedagogists need to master the task constraints of specific sports and games since their manipulation could lead to the channeling of certain coordination patterns and decision-making behaviors (Araújo et al., 2004).

Modified games in the TGfU approach typically involve modification of task constraints to allow for appropriate progressions for tactical development. For example, instead of having a full-sided game in field hockey, manipulation of rules to allow a 3-versus-1 (3v1) situation may be presented to encourage ball possession for the team of three players. The use of modified equipment also is widely promoted in TGfU. Shorter rackets, bigger playing balls, and lighter projectiles are all possible manipulation of task constraints that make the modified game easier for learners to play. Manipulating task constraints and making modified games playable for all learners certainly meets Bunker and Thorpe's (1982) beliefs of developing a games-appreciation outcome for TGfU. The use of task constraints and informational constraints in TGfU allows learners to successfully couple their movements to critical information sources in specific contexts.

With learning, games players become better at detecting key information variables that specify movements from a myriad of noncritical variables. In addition, learners can attune their movements to essential information sources available through practice, thus establishing information–movement couplings that can regulate behavior (Jacobs & Michaels, 2002). For example, in a striking and batting game like baseball, where the tactical problem in a TGfU lesson could be stopping scoring, outfielders need to develop effective information–movement couplings by perceiving positional and timing information of ball flight and coupling that information with appropriate movements to make a successful catch. A good example of this idea was provided by Thorpe (2001), who illustrated how someone who is falling can still pass the basketball in a temporally constrained situation, thus demonstrating the interconnectedness of perception and movement in such dynamic sporting contexts.

Suitable task constraints can be manipulated to provide the necessary boundaries to encourage learners to execute a tactical move in a team game. For example, in teaching offensive play in volleyball, equipment constraints can be manipulated so that badminton nets that are much lower in height than actual volleyball nets can be used. In addition, specific instructional constraints can emphasize playing the ball toward an opponent by contacting the ball above the head, encouraging learners to set the ball up for an attack above the head. Other constraints that allow for a bounce between hits within the same team and tossing for service provide opportunities for greater success in the situational game. The task constraints in the lesson can guide learners to search for appropriate goal-directed movements to attempt to outplay their opponents. With the appropriate task constraints in place, learners will soon realize that for an attack hit to be played across to the opponents' court, the pass before the attack hit will have to be high. In turn, the learners will attempt to set the ball high, either by digging the ball or trying a volley set.

In this sense, goal-directed behavior emerges without the need to provide explicit, prescriptive instructions for executing an overhead set pass for a smash. Subsequently, skill development occurs after the question-and-answer session (which confirms the demonstration of the desired movement behavior and decision for setting up an attack). Task constraints can be manipulated further to provide tighter boundaries for learners to set up an attack with the modified instructions, to execute the set pass before the attack hit. Through attempting to satisfy constraints manipulated by the physical educator, learners will gradually acquire the appropriate decision-making skills to set up an attack and therefore solve the tactical problem for this particular TGfU lesson.

Regardless of the similarities between TGfU and nonlinear pedagogy, physical education teachers undoubtedly have a difficult job. Their classes typically comprise large groups of children (often up to 30) with a wide range of abilities and motivation levels, and they may only have a few hours of practice time a week. These factors should be taken into account when considering the feasibility of the nonlinear pedagogical approach at a practical level. Nevertheless, the implications of the model are clear.

In chapter 1, we suggested that traditional instructional methods have a tendency to focus on practice situations (or drills) that are isolated from the context of the game. For example, the technique approach to teaching the set in volleyball could require the player to practice setting a ball toward a target on a wall. Using this approach, the coach or teacher might observe the player closely to correct errors and provide verbal and visual feedback on factors such as correct hand and leg positions during the shot and how to follow through with the arms. The teacher gradually leads the player through many repetitions of basic skills before introducing complex tactics and conceptual knowledge (Vickers, Livingston, Umeris-Bohnert, & Holden, 1999). Undoubtedly, the technique approach is reasonably successful at inducing short-term performance gains among early learners in physical education (Rink, 2001), and teachers often mistakenly confuse such temporary improvements with long-term behavioral changes (learning).

The limitations of the technique approach are similar to those of method coaching. For example, the leap from simple practice drills to complex game situations is often too much for learners, resulting in poor transfer (Turner & Martinek, 1999). Indeed, habitual, acquired motor patterns are of limited value in many dynamic contexts where adaptability and anticipation are characteristics of success. Learners also can get quickly discouraged if they do not master such simple skills to the teacher's satisfaction. When working with large groups, providing detailed feedback to every player often is not possible, forcing teachers to provide the entire group with standardized instructions or demonstrations in a one-size-fits-all approach. Typically, this method favors the weaker players.

Returning to the volleyball example, players could engage in minidrills, such as setting to a partner, to allow them to realize the value of changing their technique within a subphase of the game. A by-product of the TGfU approach is that learners are placed in situations where they must discover appropriate, individualized solutions rather than simply trying to imitate a common movement pattern. Hellison and Templin (1991) noted that timely teacher intervention during the practice drills is crucial to the TGfU approach. For example, when a successful move has been made, the teacher may verbally reinforce that behavior. Alternatively, when a drill breaks down due to inappropriate techniques, the teacher must be on hand to question why the problem arose and to provide feedback.

Spotlight on Research

COMPARING TECHNIQUE VERSUS TGFU TEACHING METHODS

Turner and Martinek's (1999) research study comparing technique versus TGfU teaching describes the different approaches applied in field hockey lessons. In the lessons applying the technique approach, students were presented with a demonstration of a skill, a progression of static to more dynamic practice drills, and finally a brief game of hockey at the end of the lesson. The TGfU lessons, on the other hand, were designed to emphasize the tactical elements of game play. For example, minigames were immediately introduced to a matched group of students in a 2v2 format. The minigames progressed to more realistic full hockey game scenarios as the players improved. Finally, a control group that practiced softball was employed to ascertain whether either group exhibited a positive learning effect.

Following 15 lessons of 45 minutes each, all students were given a hockey skills test (i.e., the Henry-Friedel Field Hockey Test) and a knowledge test. Game performance was also videotaped and rated. The results indicated superior performance for the TGfU group on ball control, passing, decision making, and execution during game play. Not surprisingly, the technique group performed well in the skills test, outperforming the control group. However, the technique group did not perform significantly better than the TGfU group, and on several measures of game play, the technique group

(CONTINUED)

performed similarly to the control group, which was taught softball throughout the intervention! The authors suggested that "the players' skills may have fallen apart in the more complex game situations, because their initial skill learning took place under simple conditions" (p. 294). On the declarative and procedural knowledge tests about hockey, the TGfU group outperformed the control group but not the technique group. The authors suggested that the TGfU group's improvements resulted from the emphasis on learning why a certain tactic was necessary, learning how to appraise the relative benefits of tactics within game situations, practicing within conditioned games rather than oversimplified drills, and improving decision making and skill improvisation within the context of the game.

Turner and Martinek (1999) and others recommend the TGfU approach in physical education classes over teaching strategies that focus on technique instruction. They argue, "Excellent technical players may not necessarily be skillful, because they do not understand when and where to use their techniques . . . in the context of game situations" (Turner & Martinek, 1999, p. 45). Such higher level contextual understanding is difficult for practitioners to teach explicitly and hence is more effectively developed by the learner during practice. It has been suggested by Griffin, Mitchell, and Oslin (1997) that the TGfU approach is of particular value to young children (ages 5-11) whose fundamental skills are still developing. Griffin and colleagues (1997) also proposed a more advanced version of TGfU, called the *tactical approach,* in which sport-specific drills are encouraged for older children (ages 11-16). For further examples of how the TGfU approach has been adapted for practical teaching within a range of sports, see Griffin et al. (1997).

APPLICATION

How can an interpretation of TGfU from a constraints-led perspective inform design of a teaching program for children of different ages within one or more of the following team games: basketball, tennis, squash, ice hockey?

Rehabilitation and Physical Therapists

As more people are surviving previously fatal diseases or accidents and the population of physically active older adults continues to grow, there is an increasing demand for rehabilitation and physical therapists. Additionally, increasing numbers of older adults are participating in sport, physical activities, and exercise for longer periods, and recent years have witnessed a growth in masters or senior-level (over 35 years) competitions and events across the world. In addition, our improving awareness of movement-debilitating conditions, such as developmental coordination disorder (DCD) and tardive dyskinesia, among both children and adults has resulted in a higher profile for tertiary care and associated therapy methods. Movement therapists often have the relative luxury of working one on one with patients and also have objectives that differ from those of a coach or physical education teacher. Therefore, it's important to consider the instructional styles and teaching approaches that these professionals typically use.

Carr and Shepherd (1998) have argued that **facilitation approaches** have been popular in physical therapy for some time. The word *facilitation* refers to physical manipulation or a passive learning style in which the therapist manually guides the learner through a movement—not exactly a hands-off approach. However, Carr and Shepherd conceded that simply facilitating a certain movement pattern in therapy does not promote transfer or functional transfer into real-world activities outside the clinic. The problem appears to lie in the nature of movement tasks presented to the patient and the emphasis on their use during normal activities. Like the technique approach to games teaching, the facilitation approach emphasizes the replication of specific movement patterns and is based on traditional ideas of stimulus–response associations, rather than solving movement problems and adapting to changing structural constraints in the motor system as advocated by the constraints-led approach.

Recently, the literature on physical therapy has tended to look to disablement models as theoretical approaches to guide practitioners (Jette, 1994). A disablement framework relies on causal links being established between pathologies and disabilities (e.g., anterior cruciate ligament damage and lack of stability in the knee joint). Such approaches allow practitioners to focus their intervention strategies while maintaining functional validity in the motor tasks they're examining. Injury or disease rehabilitation often involves relearning a motor skill given the new structural constraints on the motor system. This may be difficult for the patient depending on the previous stability associated with a motor skill (such as walking or grasping). For example, given disease or injury to the hands and arms, it is clear that patients do not need to focus on relearning only one way of picking up an object; rather, they need to learn how to adapt their movements to satisfy the various constraints that act on them in any given situation.

Ironically, popular assessment tools in movement rehabilitation and developmental research, such as the Movement-ABC (Henderson, Sugden, & Barnette, 1992) and the Test of Gross Motor Development (TGMD-2) (Ulrich & Sanford, 2000), seem to contradict this philosophy by scoring patients on a battery of movement skills incorporating lists of ideal criteria corresponding to so-called normal movement patterns. This traditional approach reflects the influence of the "medical model," in which variations in movements are often viewed as deviations from the norm rather than as adaptive behaviors on the part of people who are seeking to satisfy the range of interacting constraints on them (Davids, Glazier, Araújo, & Bartlett, 2003). Viewing physical, perceptual, or cognitive differences in a positive or negative light is too judgmental of individual differences. Rather, in this book we argue that a physical, perceptual, or cognitive disability should be viewed as a constraint on the structure of the CNS or anatomy of an individual. In the constraints-led approach there are no negative connotations to this idea. The constraint would just make them different from an individual without the constraint, adding to the variation observed in the range of behavior in human beings. The idea that current clinical and medical practice does not recognize individual variation enough has begun to emerge in science (e.g., West, 2006). West (2006) proposed that science and medicine have tended to overemphasize the significance of an average value in observations of phenomena related to individual health. The science of complexity has questioned traditional assumptions in physiology, supported by innovative thinking in fractal physiology, which presupposes that understanding variability provides more insights into an individual's health than does measuring average values in system behavior. According to West (2006), it is important to understand that variability in system behaviors such as heart rate, breathing, and walking are much more susceptible to the early influence of disease than are averages.

It might seem that physiotherapists do not need to use a high level of verbal instructions and feedback as has been traditionally implied for practitioners (see chapter 1). However, an observational study of physiotherapists in the Netherlands by Niemeijer, Smits-Engelsman, Reynders, and Schoemaker (2003) indicated that although the therapists under study applied a range of teaching styles, they all gave instructions frequently. Interestingly, the authors inferred that giving lots of clues to the children enabled them to perform better in the training program. However, the authors did not consider the implications of these findings for skill retention and transfer. Additionally, due to the diversity of children with DCD who acted as participants, they did not consider the relative benefits of one teaching style over another. They concluded that the Neuromotor Task Training program that is taught to all pediatric therapists in the Netherlands represents a top-down (or cognitive) approach to treatment that is applied regardless of the children's initial motor performance level.

Summary

Motor skills practitioners play a valuable role in learners' development. Under the constraints-led approach, their role in nonlinear pedagogy emphasizes different aspects compared with elements emphasized in other theoretical approaches. Traditionally, practitioners have taught learners to consistently replicate a prescribed idealized technique toward which all learners should aspire. These strategies include high frequencies of evaluation and feedback, practice that focuses on basic skills removed from the performance context, and modeling with advanced performers. However, such practices may lead to poor retention and transfer of a technique that may not even be appropriate for the learner. Conversely, from the constraints-led approach in nonlinear pedagogy, it has been suggested that practitioners should adopt a hands-off role by allowing learners enough time and space to explore and discover appropriate movement solutions for themselves. The emphasis in nonlinear pedagogy is on monitoring, guiding, and facilitating the learner's progress. Striking a balance between insightful input and discovery learning is essential for optimal skills retention and transfer. Tools such as feedback, modeling, and hands-on instruction still exist within the constraints-led framework; however, knowing when to be hands-off is equally important.

In the early stages of learning, it is important that practitioners recognize initial movement tendencies and the subsequent implications for practice. For example, the greater the mismatch between a learner's current movement tendencies and those required by the task, the longer it may take for the learner to progress. We now know a lot more about how the practitioner can manipulate constraints to help limit or promote learning at different rates. Further, we have described how movement variability can be viewed positively as a medium or platform through which transitions from one action to another lead to the emergence of a more functional pattern. Practitioners can emphasize movement variability during practice to weaken stable states of coordination, which are mildly dysfunctional and which learners can use to seek alternative and more appropriate solutions.

The changing role of the practitioner does not mean that coaching, teaching, and physiotherapy are likely to become less important or any easier in the future. Indeed, supervising the learning or rehabilitation environment will always remain a challenging and time-consuming art. However, if practitioners can develop their understanding of the dynamics of skill acquisition, they are likely to become more effective at promoting long-term changes in behavior.

SELF-TEST QUESTIONS

1. Explain how to use coordination dynamics to describe the process of skill acquisition for a learner. (Tip: Try to use terms such as *intrinsic dynamics, perceptual-motor landscape, attractor, stability, symmetry,* and *functional equivalence*).

2. How might a practitioner assess the initial coordination tendencies of a novice skier?

3. Design two contrasting lesson plans for hockey, one adopting the technique approach and the other adopting the TGfU approach.

4. What alternative strategies in nonlinear pedagogy could you use to help a learner who has reached a performance plateau?

5. Capel (2000) suggests that there is a lack of conclusive evidence to support the use of alternative teaching approaches to the technique approach. With reference to the practical considerations of modern-day physical education, discuss why such evidence may take some time to surface.

ADDITIONAL READING

1. Capel, S. (2000). Approaches to teaching games. In S. Capel & S. Piotrowski (Eds.), *Issues in Physical Education* (pp. 81-98). Cornwall, UK: TJ International.

2. Chow et al. (in press). The Role of Nonlinear Pedagogy in Physical Education. *Review of Educational Research.*

3. Griffin, L.L., Mitchell, S.A., & Oslin, J.L. (1997). *Teaching sports concepts and skills: A tactical games approach.* Champaign, IL: Human Kinetics.

4. Newell, K.M., Liu, Y.-T., & Mayer-Kress, G. (2001). Time scales in motor learning and development. *Psychological Review, 108*(1), 57-82.

5. Zanone, P.G., & Kelso, J.A.S. (1997). Coordination dynamics of learning and transfer: Collective and component levels. *Journal of Experimental Psychology: Human Perception and Performance, 23*(5), 1454-1480.

CHAPTER 6

Dealing With Individual Differences
Implications for a Nonlinear Pedagogy

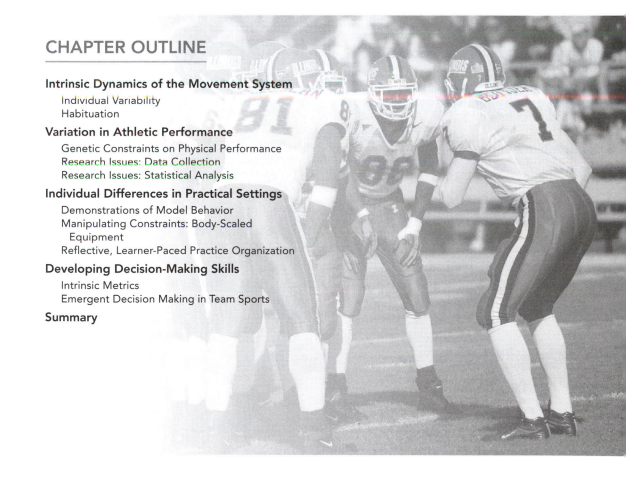

CHAPTER OUTLINE

The human motor system is blessed with more biomechanical dfs than it actually needs to achieve most everyday tasks. The body has more muscles, joints, and limb segments than necessary to accomplish tasks such as reaching and grasping, walking toward a target, or kicking a ball. As long as learners can coordinate and control a multitude of body parts, this abundance is a powerful aid to flexibility and creativity in movement. By studying detailed analyses of movement patterns that show subtle variations in trajectory and joint angles from one occasion to the next, we can observe the different ways in which we exploit the abundance of motor system dfs (e.g., Button, MacLeod, Sanders, & Coleman, 2003; Chow et al., 2006; Chow et al., in press). Müller and Sternad (2004) have proposed that a level of functional variability exists within the motor system to help it adapt and achieve its overall goals consistently. Consequently, the fact that people tend to find their own solutions to common motor problems in sport, at work, and at home should come as no surprise to those interested in adopting a constraints-led approach. In this chapter, we describe why an individual level of analysis is important and how research methods are changing to reflect this shift in emphasis. We also highlight the difficulties that practitioners face when they have to work with more than one learner simultaneously. Finally, we provide practical suggestions for teaching groups that complement the constraints-led approach in nonlinear pedagogy.

Intrinsic Dynamics of the Movement System

One persistent problem that researchers and practitioners must consider is how people are able to produce novel movements to suit the demands of dynamic contexts. In other words, why are novices sometimes able to produce task-specific coordinated movements as successfully as accomplished performers (a phenomenon commonly referred to as *beginner's luck)?* From a dynamical systems perspective, we can explain such phenomena in terms of the **intrinsic dynamics** of the movement system. Thelen (1995) defined this term as "the preferred states of the system given its current architecture and previous history of activity" (p. 76), or the set of movement capabilities that people bring with them when learning a new skill. Each person's intrinsic dynamics are unique and shaped by many constraints, including genetic factors, learning experiences, and environmental influences (Davids, Glazier, Araújo, & Bartlett, 2003). By knowing an individual's intrinsic dynamics, we can specify which aspect of the movement repertoire actually changes due to environmental, learned, or intentional influences (Zanone & Kelso, 1992).

Individual Variability

Due to individual differences in intrinsic dynamics, the conditions under which coordination changes occur are individual specific (Button, Bennett, & Davids,

2001). Ulrich, Ulrich, Angulo-Kinzler, and Chapman (1997) discovered this level of interindividual variability and noted that, at a very early age, infants already show preferences for individual phasing patterns when producing spontaneous kicking movements. Researchers claim that intrinsic dynamics represent the basic building blocks upon which humans construct functional movements. For novices, the behavioral requirements of a new task sometimes provide a close match with their preexisting intrinsic dynamics, leading to immediate and relatively successful performance. The close fit between task and intrinsic dynamics may explain precocial behavior in sport when some athletes perform incredibly well from an early age (see the examples in chapter 7). Conversely, problems arise for some learners when there is a conflict between the intrinsic dynamics they bring to a learning situation and the specific constraints of the task.

Spotlight on Research

THE PEDALO LOCOMOTION TASK

Recent developments in the research tools designed to analyze human movement have resulted in more study of motor skills involving multiple dfs. Chen, Liu, Mayer-Kress, and Newell (2005) used a novel pedalo locomotion task to monitor the rates at which four learners acquired this skill (see figure 6.1). While standing on the pedalo, or paddleboat, participants could move backward or forward by using their feet to pedal up and down. Although the task required the coordination of the torso and limbs, it could be learned relatively quickly. The participants practiced the pedalo task by orienting themselves to a specified location over 50 trials each day for 7 days.

The authors calculated the Cauchy variable—the difference in the average distance of two consecutive trials—for each participant over the course of practice trials. They discovered considerable fluctuations over practice trials and different rates of learning among individuals. Overall, however, each participant significantly reduced the movement pattern difference score (i.e., became more consistent). The majority of improvement in movement time occurred over the first 2 days.

The authors also used a statistical technique called *principal components analysis* to determine the number of independent components required to capture the structure of each learner's movement

(CONTINUED)

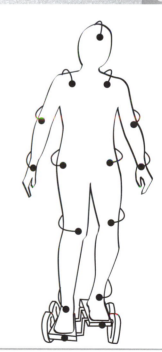

Figure 6.1 Pedalo locomotion task from Chen et al. (2005). The task involved a pedaling motion with the feet to move the paddleboat in the water.

Journal of Motor Behavior, vol. 37, issue 3, pp. 247-256, 2005. Reprinted with permission of the Helen Dwight Reid Educational Foundation. Published by Heldref Publications, 1319 Eighteenth St., NW, Washington, DC 20036-1802. http://www.heldref.org. Copyright © 2005.

patterns. The participants required between three and six components to accommodate 95% of the variance in the kinematic data. By day 7, each participant needed fewer components to capture the acquired movement patterns. For two participants, the upper-body variables were initially the strongest weighted components, with the lower-body variables having an increasingly smaller contribution. In contrast, the other two participants showed a relative increase in the importance of the lower body as a function of learning. The findings demonstrated that in the absence of explicit instructions or demonstrations, individual differences in coordination dynamics are a common consequence of learning. Different learners use a variety of methods to solve the specific coordination problem faced during task practice.

APPLICATION

The participants in this study demonstrated a significant convergence of the motions of the torso and limbs while practicing this multiarticular task. The consistency measure used in this study may be a useful quantitative assessment tool when a particular movement form is required, such as in dancing or gymnastics. The data also revealed that although improvements in performance outcome scores (movement time) had plateaued by the end of practice, participants were still searching and fine-tuning their coordination dynamics for more effective solutions. The fact that coordination changes were not necessarily related to changes in performance outcome is an important finding that warns against the sole use of outcome measures in research on skill acquisition (see also Button, Davids, & Schöllhorn, 2006).

Using ice-skating, dancing, rhythmic gymnastics, or synchronized swimming, consider how the findings of the pedalo study could help us understand individual differences in motor learning as a result of practice.

Habituation

Averaging scores over individuals and trial blocks ignores the fact that laws of learning should reflect both immediate responses and persistent changes in individuals over time. In practical terms, momentary effects on task performance may be due to developmental changes, fatigue, injury, task exploration, or habituation. **Habituation** refers to the need for a warm-up period before performance during which people can show poor movement timing and coordination while demonstrating more errors than usual. It occurs when a person practices for a long period (e.g., several weeks or months) and then takes a short break (e.g., several days) from the task. Habituation effects can be observed when a person recovers from a serious injury or illness and performs routine tasks like walking or riding a bicycle. Another example can be observed when professional athletes return to full training after a vacation or an injury. When returning, there is often a need to readjust or habituate to the task, and this need is skill dependent (experts need smaller habituation periods). Habituation effects are sometimes attributed to so-called rustiness. As people readjust to the task context, their initial performances can have a higher level of variability than normal.

In the short term, many examples of sport behavior reflect habituation to a specific context such as practice swings in golf and baseball, bouncing new balls when preparing to serve in tennis, or getting used to swimming in water of varying density (e.g., when triathletes perform in the ocean or in a pool). Task exploration can occur when people face unfamiliar task constraints in the form of a new performance goal or novel conditions (Gauthier, Martin, & Stark, 1986). The latter is a particular problem faced by touring professionals in sports such as motor racing and tennis where they must perform on different surfaces and circuits (e.g., tennis players who perform on clay courts in one continent before traveling to compete on grass courts in another part of the world). Kelso (1992) recognized the valuable role of movement variability in such circumstances when he argued that "without variability, in this sense, new forms of behavioral organization would be severely limited" (p. 261).

Variation in Athletic Performance

Some people are commonly described as naturals, which means that their genetic profile appears highly suited to the task at hand. A related question concerns why some people benefit more from training and practice than others. These observations raise questions about the contribution of genetic and environmental constraints to skill acquisition and performance. How these constraints shape variations in human performance is a question of increasing interest in movement science and sports medicine. This problem is a manifestation of the longstanding nature–nurture debate over the precise proportion of performance variation accounted for by genetic characteristics or environmental influences (e.g., Davids & Baker, in press). Much has been written about this particular dualism in science, and resolution has proved remarkably difficult over the years since it is clear that both nature and nurture can act as constraints on behavior (for excellent analyses, see Johnston & Edwards, 2002; Lewontin, 2000; Ridley, 2004).

Despite this controversy, there have been relatively few attempts to examine the nature of genetic constraints on variation in motor skill performance. One study by Fox, Hershberger, and Bouchard (1996) examined pursuit rotor tracking of monozygotic (n = 64 pairs) and dizygotic (n = 32 pairs) twins reared apart (MZA and DZA). Pursuit rotor tracking is a popular experimental task that requires a participant to trace a path along a shape, such as a star, circle, or square, at rapid speed. Fox and colleagues measured performance by time spent on target (expressed as a proportion of the perfect score: 20 seconds). The authors concluded, "Performance levels of the two groups are highly similar; both showing substantial improvement over the five trial blocks of the first day" (p. 356). Patterns of variability for both groups were similar: "With practice, there is improvement for some subjects more than others, hence increases in the within-group variability with stability being found by day 3. The differences between the variances of the MZA and DZA twins were not statistically significant" (p. 356). The influence of heritability (reflecting both genetic and environmental factors) was high from the first (proportion of performance variance explained = .66) to the last trial block (.69). The fact that the influence of heritability was high for the the initial 5 trial blocks (.66, .53, .52, .55, .52) was suggested by the authors to show that people rely on innate capacities when they attempt to perform a novel task. There was a clear MZA versus DZA distinction. Conclusions in favor of significant genetic effects for percent time on target, performance improvement rate over trial block, and improvement after a period of rest were based on "the simplest and most reasonable explanation for the greater MZA twin resemblance . . . that motor performance reflects genetic influence" (p. 357).

However, this conclusion is not so clear cut, because Fox and colleagues (1996) seemed to be confusing skill performance with skill acquisition. Although that study purported to investigate genetic constraints on skill acquisition, the groups were presented with only 75 practice trials, and it could be argued that performances of both groups were measured. Also, the potential confounding effects of unequal sample sizes in the study is nontrivial. In complete contrast to the data obtained by Fox and colleagues, other work examining differences on pursuit tracking performance between equal numbers ($n = 35$) of MZA and DZA twins proposed that the strength of the genetic constraints on performance systematically diminished throughout the course of practice, fitting a monotonic trend over trials (Marisi, 1977). More recent work has examined heritability in neuromuscular coordination (Missitzi, Geladas, & Klissouras, 2004). As with the study by Fox and colleagues, a twin model was used, this time to investigate monozygotic–dizygotic variations in accuracy and economy of effort, assessed by analyzing kinematic data and electromyographical records of muscle activity. The results showed that heredity accounted for the greatest proportion of MZ–DZ differences in movement accuracy and economy for fast elbow flexion movements, not slow-velocity movements.

Genetic Constraints on Physical Performance

The past few years have seen increasing work on the role genes play in defining individual athletic performance. Research has focused primarily on genetic and environmental contributions to physical endurance (e.g., Rankinen et al., 2000). The significant amount of interindividual variation observed in response to cardiovascular training has led many investigators to question the extent to which genetic diversity may be responsible for the data (e.g., Feitosa et al., 2002). Recently, the angiotensin-converting enzyme (ACE) gene has received considerable attention in the sports medicine literature. The ACE gene is one of a number of genes that researchers have associated with interindividual variability in physical endurance (e.g., Alvarez et al., 2000; Montgomery et al., 1999; Myerson et al., 1999; Nazarov et al., 2001; Taylor, Mamotte, Fallon, & van Bockxmeer, 1999; Williams, Alty, & Lees, 2000; Woods, Humphries, &

Montgomery, 2000; Woods et al., 2001; Woods et al., 2002). In muscle, the angiotensin I–converting enzyme degrades two vasodilators, bradykinin and tachykinin, and stimulates the production of the vasoconstrictor angiotensin II during physical performance (e.g., Sonna et al., 2001). Sequence variation in DNA creates two alleles of the ACE gene, I (i.e., insertion) and D (i.e., deletion), which combine to produce polymorphisms in genotype (II, ID, DD).

The D variant of the gene has been linked with relatively higher ACE activity. For example, early work with army recruits found that the II polymorphism of the gene has been associated with lower activity levels of ACE in muscle than the DD allele, as well as an increased response to physical training (Montgomery et al., 1998). In response to repetitive upper-arm exercises, recruits with ACE genotype II differed by as much as 1,100% compared with their DD genotype peers. Individuals with a heterogeneous genotype (DI) demonstrated levels of performance between both homozygous genotypes. In sport, a higher prevalence of the II genotype has been found in elite endurance athletes, including mountaineers who can climb up to 7,000 meters without the aid of oxygen, Olympic-standard endurance runners, and elite rowers (Gayagay et al., 1998; Montgomery et al., 1998; Myerson et al., 1999).

To summarize what is already known in this area of research, most geneticists working on physical performance understand that genes work in combination to influence biological function. This refutes the idea of successful athletes being differentiated on the presence of a single allele such as the ACE gene (for a similar argument in developmental theory, see Johnston & Edwards, 2002). The arguments against a biologically deterministic view of gene transmission are important to note because of the prevalence of the common philosophy among sport practitioners that there is a single gene that is a so-called magic bullet. Over the years, the view of DNA as information bearer has somehow been replaced with the mechanistic fallacy of DNA as blueprint, plan, or master molecule (Lewontin, 2000).

Fortunately, the traditional rationale of genes as blueprints is giving way to a better understanding of the mechanisms and processes of genetic transmission, including transcription and translation, revealing that expression levels of single genes or networks of genes are far more open to stochastic fluctuations in constant environments than previously thought (Kærn, Elston, Blake, & Collins, 2005). Scientists now understand that molecular interactions are inherently random, leading to stochasticity in the biochemical processes of transcription, protein synthesis, and the basis of gene transmission (Kærn et al., 2005). Therefore, presence of genetic material should not be viewed as a blueprint for success in sport. A review of the theoretical ideas and empirical research for learning and performance theories has revealed major implications for understanding how environmental and genetic constraints function. We can conclude that neither approach accounts for all the data on performance variability. There is now clear evidence rejecting the idea that there is a single gene predisposing an athlete to superior performance in a specific domain (Davids & Baker, in press).

These insights are examples of how advances in research are uncovering myths and biases in the scientific literature on individual differences. In the following sections, we examine how changes in research and statistical methodologies are providing insights into the functional structure of movement variability as performers seek individualized coordination solutions during performance.

Research Issues: Data Collection

Since the 1970s, there have been comprehensive changes in the way human movement patterns are collected, analyzed, and interpreted. These developments have been fueled by the introduction of cine filming, high-speed digital cameras, three-dimensional analysis, accelerometers, and computer modeling and simulations (Allard, Stokes, & Blanchi, 1995). This equipment has allowed researchers and practitioners to look at coordination patterns with greater depth and sensitivity (see Alderson, Sully, & Sully, 1974). Early researchers attempting to study coordination of multiarticular actions such as one-handed catching were limited by the technology available and tended to focus on performance outcome variables such as number of successful catches and number of catches dropped. In the 1970s, technology such as high-speed filming began to reveal insights into the timing and coordination of hand positioning and grasping of the ball with the fingers (Alderson, Sully, & Sully, 1974). Consequently, researchers began to study movement variables underpinning coordination in some depth.

The development of sophisticated measuring devices also has facilitated research that examines complex, multiarticular actions rather than the simplistic, laboratory-based tasks (e.g., linear positioning, reaction time, pursuit rotor) that characterized much of the earlier research (Williams, Davids, & Williams, 1999). Studying multiarticular actions can provide meaningful insights into adaptive behavior, which involves analyzing the interactions between complex organisms and their task constraints and environments. Increasingly, the experimental models that many psychologists and movement scientists use to study adaptive behavior of complex movement systems are being provided by a rich range of sport and physical activities (e.g., Davids et al., 2006). Complex movement models from sport are also gaining in popularity because of the powerful influence of a theoretical framework suggesting that movement coordination is best viewed as adaptive, emergent behavior that self-organizes under constraints, particularly informational and other task constraints.

Thus, technological and theoretical advances have gone hand in hand to promote a greater emphasis on idiographic analyses of how people solve

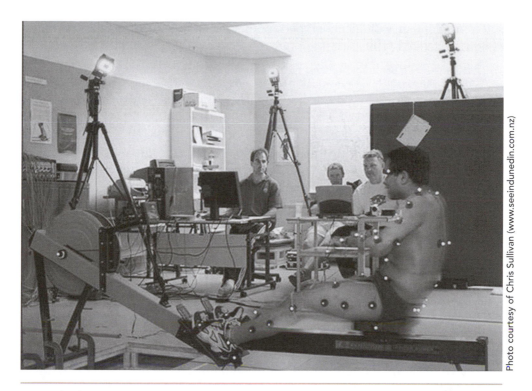

New technology such as this online motion analysis system (rower) has enabled researchers and practitioners to analyze coordination patterns with greater depth and sensitivity.

motor problems (that is, examining unique functional adaptations of people to the environment). In the human movement sciences, idiographic methods exemplify how participants solve movement problems, providing rich insights into individual variations in satisfying constraints. Refined methodologies for studying human movement can now be used to conduct in-depth analyses on unique movement solutions by each participant. The data that emerge from such in-depth analyses are better examined without the traditional techniques of grouping data from several individuals together. Grouping data can prevent the interpretation of subtle variations in coordination that emerge as people attempt to satisfy the unique constraints acting on them.

Research Issues: Statistical Analysis

Advances in data collection have resulted in alternative data analysis methods (see Spotlight on Research). For example, researchers traditionally have used pooled group data in their statistical analysis of outcome or error data from motor control research. Presumably, they used pooled group data in an effort to establish laws of action that apply to a wider population. Indeed, the type of analysis demanded by inferential statistics forms a cornerstone of traditional science. From an ecological perspective, pooled group data have limited value, prompting Kelso (1995) to point out the following:

> Because each person possesses his or her own 'signature', it makes little sense to average performance over individuals. One might as well average apples and oranges. This does not mean that putative laws and principles of learning cannot be generalized across individuals; laws wouldn't qualify as such if it were not possible to do so. It only means that the way the law is instantiated is specific to the individual. (p. 147)

The argument is that individual analyses (profiling) of kinematics are preferable to the traditional pooling of group data, especially if one is interested in unraveling the complex processes that govern motor control as each person attempts to satisfy constraints (Button et al., 2006).

In statistical terms, variability is the variance of data about the mean of a distribution of scores and is usually quantified by the magnitude of the standard deviation statistic (Riley & Turvey, 2002). The standard deviation is useful if one is interested in the level of performance variability on a specific task at any one point in time. However, it is of little use if one is interested in changes in variability of selected measures of movement coordination over time by participants in a group, such as during development or as a result of learning (Newell & Slifkin, 1998; Riley & Turvey, 2002). Statistics such as standard deviation, coefficient of variation, and range assume little association between discrete measurements taken at different points in the performance timeline. A good example of the emphasis on discrete measurements of kinematic variables is the report that elite javelin throwers achieve higher peak speeds of distal segments of the arm than novice throwers and that 50% of peak speed is generated in the last 50 milliseconds before release (for an overview of statistical procedures in biomechanics and motor control, see Mullineaux, Bartlett, & Bennett, 2001).

However, performance analysis of complex motor tasks as a continuous time series is predicated over selected portions of the movement, not isolated points (for example, during the final 50 milliseconds of the javelin throw). Time-series analysis allows us to plot key kinematic variables against each other as a movement pattern unfolds. We can compare values of a particular variable early in a movement to values of the same variable later in the movement. In this way, we can examine the structure of movement variability in a given performance rather than simply the magnitude of outcome variability. In a similar vein, using techniques like phase plots has allowed researchers to demonstrate how variability within movement patterns, such as gait and rehabilitation (Clark, 1995; Heiderscheit, Hamill, & van Emmerik, 1998), can be helpful in satisfying task constraints. Phase plots display the velocity characteristics of a moving body against its position as a function of time. By overlaying trials on top of each other, we can gain a clear picture of how these derivatives are related. The data displayed in figure 6.2 demonstrate how we can use phase plots to distinguish among different coordination tendencies in the basketball free throw, such as increased between-throw consistency for expert players.

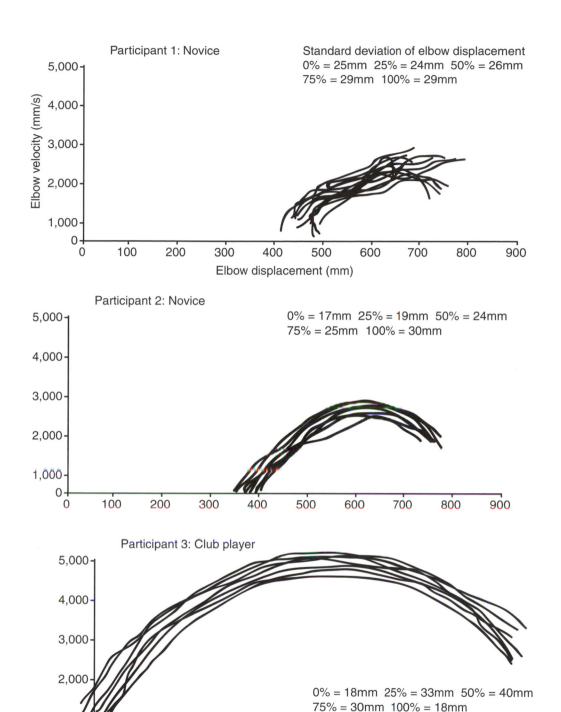

Figure 6.2 Phase plots of elbow displacement and velocity taken during the basketball free throw. Six players (from novice to international standard) throwing up to 30 attempts are depicted.

Reprinted with permission from *Research Quarterly for Exercise and Sport*, Vol. 74, No. 3, 257-269, Copyright 2003 by the American Alliance for Health, Physical Education, Recreation and Dance, 1900 Association Drive, Reston, VA 20191.

(CONTINUED)

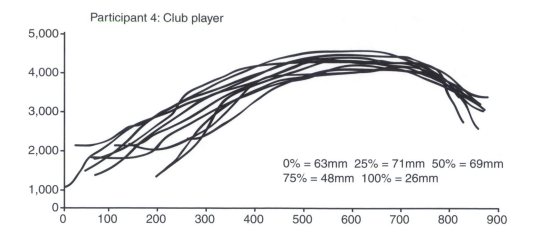

Participant 4: Club player

0% = 63mm 25% = 71mm 50% = 69mm
75% = 48mm 100% = 26mm

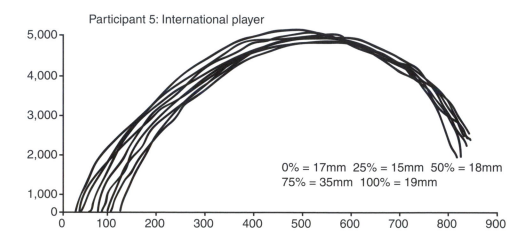

Participant 5: International player

0% = 17mm 25% = 15mm 50% = 18mm
75% = 35mm 100% = 19mm

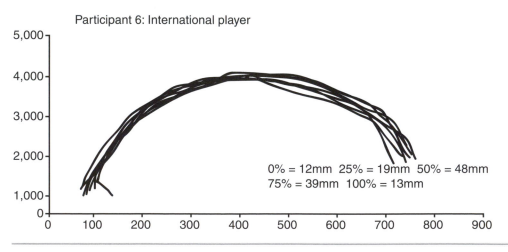

Participant 6: International player

0% = 12mm 25% = 19mm 50% = 48mm
75% = 39mm 100% = 13mm

Figure 6.2 *(continued)*

Individual Differences in Practical Settings

Many counselors, psychotherapists, physiotherapists, life coaches, personal trainers, and sport psychologists have been quick to realize that an individual approach is the only effective way to understand the complex problems that learners present them with, and consequently they spend very little time working with large groups. Despite the arguments for a focus on the individual learner in a nonlinear pedagogy, however, many practitioners have little choice but to work with large groups of learners on a daily basis. For example, it is not uncommon for teachers and coaches to assume sole responsibility for groups of 30 students during a practice session. Given the multiple demands these practitioners must manage, it is not surprising that many may question the feasibility of the hands-off approach that we advocate. However, there are several simple strategies that practitioners can use to shift the focus back to the individual without demotivating other learners in the group.

Demonstrations of Model Behavior

The evidence that there are important variations in the structure of coordination variability has many implications for practitioners, especially when we consider that an idealized expert image of an action is often advocated as a model in traditional learning methods. In nonlinear pedagogy, the structure of coordination variability offers a different view of learning from watching a model. **Modeling** or observational learning is the process whereby learners observe and then attempt to reproduce a desired behavior demonstrated by another person. Although demonstrations of a skill are a valuable tool in the practitioner's toolbox, individuals across a group may not benefit similarly from watching expert demonstrations and then reproducing the same movement themselves. As Hodges and Franks (2001) pointed out, "[Ability level] will affect what information an athlete is able to extract from a demonstration" (p. 808). As expertise develops, the nature of the perceptual variables or informational constraints that performers use to support movements will differ considerably (Beek, Jacobs, Daffertshofer, & Huys, 2003).

The ideas on individual differences presented in this chapter imply that we need a clear understanding of the processes of observational learning that are used in practice. An important theoretical framework for aiding our understanding is Scully and Newell's (1985) proposal of a visual perception perspective on observational learning. Central to this perspective is the idea that the main function of visual demonstrations is to transmit relative motion information essential to the task being learned or performed. The visual perception perspective on observational learning processes is based on Gibson's (1979) conceptualization of invariance in optic information (see chapter 3). It has been shown that the identification and classification of different types

The individual nature of the human gait has received considerable research attention recently. Future applications could include kinematic screening for the unique relative motion characteristics of known terrorists and criminals at airports.

of movement activities (e.g., walking, cycling, gymnastics) have occurred on the basis of invariance in the relative motion of topological characteristics (movement form) peculiar to each activity (Hoenkamp, 1978; Scully, 1988). The relative motion pattern underlying each movement event leads to unique spatiotemporal relationships between the person's torso and limbs, or among the limbs, as well as the organization of the body in relation to the surrounding environment. Recently, the individual nature of gait analysis has received considerable research attention (Schöllhorn, Nigg, Stefanyshyn, & Liu, 2002), and future applications of this work could include kinematic screening for the unique relative motion characteristics of known terrorists and criminals at airports.

Spotlight on Research

META-ANALYSIS

Meta-analysis is a rubric description for quantitative review methods that are used to combine results across studies. The process has been called "an analysis of the results of statistical analysis" (Hedges & Olkin, 1985, p. 13). Meta-analytic procedures offer protocols for synthesizing, interpreting, and summarizing research literature that uses quantitative statistical procedures. It can be particularly useful when there is some ambiguity in research literature. For example, although many studies have investigated the effects of observational modeling on motor behavior, until recently there has been a lack of consensus on whether it actually provides a significant learning advantage.

Attempting to resolve this ambiguity, Ashford, Bennett, and Davids (2006) used meta-analytic procedures to quantify the generalized effect of observational modeling. Effects were derived from 68 independent investigations reporting modeling results from motor learning studies on a variety of movement skills. A significant advantage of modeling over practice-only control conditions was reported for movement dynamics (i.e., the emphasis on approximating the coordination patterns of the model observed) and for movement outcome measures (i.e., the emphasis on approximating the achievement of a specific movement outcome regardless of the coordination pattern involved). In terms of effect magnitude, a stronger effect was noted for movement dynamics (δ_{Bi}^{u} = 0.77) compared with a more modest mean effect for movement outcomes (δ_{Bi}^{u} = 0.17). Further, the increased effect magnitude for movement dynamics compared with movement outcome was evident across different types of tasks. For example, for serial tasks involving performance of subtasks in particular sequence, there was a significant treatment effect of δ_{Bi}^{u} = 2.17 for movement dynamics and δ_{Bi}^{u} = 0.61 for movement outcome measures.

APPLICATION

As a learner, what do you do when you watch a coach or teacher perform an action during practice: copy the action exactly, or use the demonstration as a guide to facilitate your own learning?

The results of Ashford and colleagues (2006) support Scully and Newell's (1985) visual perception perspective, which proposes that observational modeling provides relative motion information conveying topographical characteristics associated with the modeled movement dynamics. More specifically, results were consistent with the view that perception of relative motion information enables people to reproduce an observed movement during the process of acquiring movement coordination. Findings were also consistent with the view that the influence of modeling on movement outcomes would be less effective early in learning because individuals would need to focus on acquiring an unfamiliar movement pattern. In other words, during early stages of learning, observational modeling is more likely to facilitate the assembly of movement coordination patterns that approximate the modeled behavior rather than the achievement of specific movement goals such as accurately shooting a ball at a target or jumping over an object.

Nonlinear pedagogy advocates that coaches and teachers identify the nature of information that learners acquire so that the content and the presentation of information during a visual demonstration can be enhanced to promote skill acquisition. Visual demonstrations facilitate the early stage of skill learning because they convey relative motion information that is essential for the assembly of an unfamiliar coordination pattern. Later in learning, when the goal of the task demands the refinement of an acquired coordination pattern, modeling may help learners develop control. In other words, perception of dynamic features can lead to optimal scaling of a movement pattern (e.g., producing a pattern that varies in force, timing, or duration). Interestingly,

Herbert and Landin (1994), among others, demonstrated that learners benefit more from watching other learners who are at similar developmental stages. Due to the specificity of the information (scaled to the intrinsic dynamics of a specific model) and learners' inexperience, observation may not facilitate learning unless verbal instructions or other optimization procedures are incorporated into the demonstration.

In summary, using live and videotaped demonstrations of model behavior can help learners find suitable coordination solutions more quickly and safely. The aim should not necessarily be to imitate the model; rather, it may be to demonstrate an approximate coordination solution that guides the learners' physical practice and problem-solving activities (search patterns). Theoretically, it would seem important for models to have similar scaling of limb segments when conveying relative motion information to learners (i.e., adult models for adult learners and child models for children), but this idea needs to be empirically verified. However, body scaling of equipment is an important aspect of nonlinear pedagogy, as we discuss next.

Manipulating Constraints: Body-Scaled Equipment

The idea that practice equipment needs to be body scaled if learners are to efficiently acquire information–movement couplings has some theoretical substance. As described in chapter 5, the practitioner can help direct the learner by altering relevant task constraints. One of the most important task constraints during practice is the size and mass of equipment (e.g., ball or racket) relative to relevant limb segments (e.g., leg or arm). This task constraint has implications for the implementation of coaching strategies during practice and training, particularly with children. Konczak (1990) proposed that children's skill acquisition would be enhanced if sport equipment were correctly scaled to their body dimensions, which change regularly during childhood.

Given children's relative lack of experience, one might question to what extent they are able to distinguish between body-scaled and conventional sport equipment. Beak, Davids, and Bennett (2000) used an innovative experimental design to examine the ability of novice tennis players (mean age = 10 years) to perceive the weight-distribution characteristics of tennis rackets when swung. They manipulated the moment of inertia of a tennis racket by placing a 50-gram weight at various points along its longitudinal axis. They then asked the players to wield the rackets and judge which racket would allow them to hit a ball to a maximum distance with a forehand drive. This is a typical judgment learners must make in tennis classes where a pool of rackets is made available to the group before practice.

To ascertain which sources of sensory feedback informed the children's decisions, Beak and colleagues (2000) implemented the experiment with and without racket visibility. In the latter condition, an opaque screen occluded sight of the racket, and the children showed great sensitivity to the haptic information of the racket. They tended to select rackets that were more suited to their age range—rackets at the lower end of the inertia scale where the weight was distributed toward the handle. When both vision and haptic information was available, intraindividual variability of racket selection increased even more.

Beak and colleagues suggested that the children were experiencing a conflict between intrinsic feedback sources that made them less certain about which racket to select. It seems that even young children use haptic information to provide sensory feedback about the characteristics of a manipulated object. The implication is that we typically rely too much on vision when learning and need to increase our sensitivity to other feedback sources. The authors also suggested that tennis rackets specifically designed for use by 10-year-old children are still too universal to be useful for all 10-year-old children. The marketing of a universal racket for 10-year-old children does not account for the huge variation in the moments of inertia in the upper limbs at that age (Beak, Davids, & Bennett, 2002).

Children's skill acquisition may be enhanced if sport equipment is correctly scaled to their body dimensions.

© Icon Sports Media

The implications of these data for practitioners are reinforced when one considers similar studies. With respect to upper- and lower-limb interceptive actions, motor development research has revealed decrements in skill acquisition when practice has occurred with balls that are too large or too heavy for children to grasp, throw, or kick (e.g., Herkowitz, 1984). The research literature has consistently recommended the use of appropriately scaled equipment for children, including smaller playing field dimensions, changed height and width of goals and baskets, and use of balls and implements scaled to key limb dimensions (e.g., see Pangrazi & Dauber, 1989; Siedentop, Herkowitz, & Pink, 1984; Wright, 1967). Children are able to perceive clear preferences based on small differences between identical items of sport equipment. In basketball, Regimbal, Deller, and Plimpton (1992) examined the ball size that 10-year-olds preferred in shooting. They found that 66% preferred the smaller ball over an adult-sized ball, with accuracy of motor responses correlating with the improvement of fit between ball and hand.

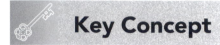

Key Concept

The reason why some learners produce successful movement patterns early in learning and others take a considerably longer time is linked to the fit between the intrinsic dynamics of the movement system and the task demands. Where there is a good fit between the two, positive transfer will occur. Where the task dynamics and the learner's intrinsic dynamics clash, negative transfer will result. Provision of appropriately scaled equipment for practice might enhance the fit between intrinsic and task dynamics and reduce any competitive tendencies of other nearby attractors. Additionally, providing models with similar body scaling of limb segments might convey more accurate relative motion information to learners attempting to reorganize motor system dfs during practice.

Reflective, Learner-Paced Practice Organization

Because people learn at different rates, practice organization should be flexible enough to cope with these variations. Practitioners are faced with the problem of how to deal with this demand when working with a group. However, the idea that task, environmental, and organismic constraints operate at different timescales has strong implications for coaches' judgments of learners' rates of progress. When learning a new coordination pattern, more permanent changes in behavior take longer to appear than immediate adaptations to task constraints during practice. Therefore, practitioners need to understand that some behaviors might represent transient attempts to adapt to immediate task constraints imposed during practice, which in turn interact with organismic constraints related to developmental status. Important constraints here include the effects of the specific equipment, location, and instructions that a learner experiences at a given state of development. Practitioners need to ensure that emergent behavior under constraints is not due to transient effects, but is a stable characteristic of each learner's current level of performance.

Using nonlinear pedagogy as a theoretical basis, practitioners can promote an individual focus and a more active learning style by delegating some of the responsibility for the practice organization to the learners themselves (see the TGfU approach in chapter 5 as an example). They can achieve this goal in several ways. For example, practitioners can encourage self-reflection during breaks in play, such as asking a group to discuss why they lost possession of a ball during subphase practice in a team sport. Another approach is to allow the timing and provision of augmented feedback to be student driven. Janelle and colleagues (1997) found that children who were allowed to choose when they received visual feedback about their technique retained the skill of a precision throwing task better than groups who had no choice in the feedback scheduling. Despite the fact that the children were comparative novices, they only asked for video feedback of themselves on about 11% of trials.

Practitioners also should consider whether practice organization actively engages the learners in problem solving and opportunities to search the perceptual-motor workspace. For example, a simple strategy like asking children to devise three different ways of throwing a ball toward a target encourages each child to deal with a common problem in unique ways. Splitting large groups of learners into smaller ability-based groups also can facilitate this sort of approach. Capel (2000) highlighted the benefits of children practicing in small groups by arguing that "small-sided games are more varied, and provide more opportunities to each pupil to be involved in the play, to try things out and to develop skills" (p. 83).

Therefore, practitioners who have to work with large groups should not be tempted to use only group-based teaching styles with the belief that there are no alternatives. Instead, teachers and coaches can apply several simple ideas that promote greater mental and physical engagement from learners during group practice sessions.

Developing Decision-Making Skills

A key factor that distinguishes performers is decision-making skills under pressure. Regardless of how many learners the practitioner must work with, teaching someone to make quick and appropriate decisions in practice environments is no easy task. From the perspective of ecological psychology, there is growing evidence that decision making is an emergent process rather than a completely predefined process based on knowledge stored in memory (Araújo, Davids, & Serpa, 2005). Research has shown that emergent decision making is apparent at different performance levels. Next, we discuss how people use information to make judgments for action before focusing on emergent processes in tactical decision making at the level of team performance.

Intrinsic Metrics

In chapter 3, we noted that information is a physical variable available in the environment to constrain action and support decision making (Turvey, 1992). To detect such information, performers need an intrinsic metric scaled to the dimensions of their perceptual-motor system. Athletes perceive environmental properties not in arbitrary extrinsic units (such as meters, inches, and so on), but in relation to their own body, action capabilities, and relative location to important objects and surfaces in the environment (Konczak, Meeuwsen, & Crees, 1992).

A landmark study addressing intrinsic metrics showed that young adults of a wide range of statures could, by visual inspection alone, decide which in a series of stairs of varied riser heights afforded bipedal climbing and which were most energy efficient (Warren, 1984). In the study, participants of different statures viewed slides of stairs that varied in riser height (13-102 centimeters) and attempted to judge whether the stairs were climbable. Despite absolute differences in leg length, the participants were able to perceive the maximum riser heights by using a constant proportion of leg length to riser height (0.88) in their decision making. In the words of Ulrich, Thelen, and Niles (1990), Warren's study showed that "individual choices varied but were body-scaled; participants' choices were the same mathematical function of the leg length, regardless of stature" (p. 2). Therefore, as van der Kamp, Savelsbergh, and Davis (1998) argued, "body-scaled ratios can be used as a critical determinant of action choice—a change beyond the critical ratio value demands a new class of action" (p. 352).

Other research has shown that despite differences in absolute leg length, individuals make similar judgments about limits to angle of incline and tread depth in negotiating stairs, with 60° being a general threshold below which stairs are judged as climbable (Maraj, 2003). Clearly, transitions between movement patterns emerge as a function of people perceiving possibilities for actions afforded by information from environmental surfaces, objects, and gaps. As we will discuss next, these ideas have implications for decision-making behavior in sport.

Emergent Decision Making in Team Sports

Recently sport performance has been considered as a dynamical system, and there have been some attempts to apply relevant concepts and tools from dynamical systems theory and ecological psychology to the study of emergent game structure and tactical patterns in team sports (McGarry, Anderson, Wallace, Hughes, & Franks, 2002; Lebed, 2007). Research concerning individual coordination in team sports is relevant to practitioners in relation to decision making. Subphase work (e.g., 1v1, 2v2, 3v3) is typical of the practice organization in many ball sports, including basketball, soccer, hockey, lacrosse, and rugby. The assumption is that changes in the stability of such subsystems are based on the dynamics among people involved in the subphase context (Schmidt, Carello, & Turvey, 1990).

For example, in the common 1v1 practice task, the dyad formed by an attacker and defender comprises a system. The aim of the attacker is to destroy the stability of this system. When the defender matches the movements of the opponent and remains in position between the attacker and the basket or goal, the symmetry of the system remains stable. When an attacking player dribbles past a defending opponent near the basket, the player creates a break in the symmetry of the system. Even though the defender may run to stay in front of the attacker, it will be after the attacker has moved the ball toward the basket. This constant adjustment of the opposing players' positioning is a characteristic of dribbling tasks in ball games that we can understand as a type of interpersonal coordination.

Recent research has examined the feasibility of this new theoretical explanation of dribbling in basketball (e.g., Davids, Button, Araújo, Renshaw, & Hristovski, 2006). Coaching literature suggests that an important order parameter to describe the coordination dynamics of attacker–defender dyadic systems is the distance between the median point of the dyad and the basket. They tested the following hypothesis in their study: As interpersonal distance decreases, the order parameter should radically change at some critical value of the interpersonal distance (the control parameter). The researchers predicted the order parameter would change dramatically as a consequence of the attacker successfully exploring the constraints that guide decision making about when to attack the basket.

Ten male players (regional level, 15-16 years old) participated in the experiment and formed five dyads of attackers and defenders. Each dyad started on the free-throw line, with the other members of both teams positioned on court based on the attack system 1:2:2 (see figure 6.3). Each member of the dyads performed each attacking and defending function for 15 trials. The task was selected on the advice of an expert panel of basketball coaches who unanimously agreed that it represented a real pattern in basketball games. Instructional constraints were for the attacker to score and the defender to prevent a score within the rules of basketball. The eight other players were passive, only participating in the play 5 seconds after the beginning of the task and keeping the positions shown in figure 6.3 (providing temporal and spatial task constraints for the dyad). Upon a signal from the experimenters, the action sequence began when the defender passed the ball to the attacker. Before initiating the task, 10 minutes of one-on-one practice took place in order to eliminate the warm-up effect (Adams, 1961). To permit examination of symmetry breaking, the trials chosen for analysis were those where the attacker did not shoot immediately after receiving the ball and instead tried to dribble past the defender.

Figure 6.4 shows the relative movements of both the attacker and defender in the practice task. Note that the attacker-defender-basket system exhibited initial symmetry, which was broken during

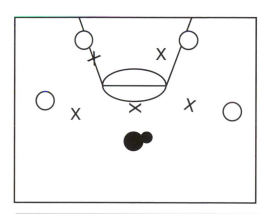

Figure 6.3 The positioning of attackers (circles) and defenders (Xs) on a basketball court forms dyads.

Reprinted, by permission, from D. Araújo et al., 2004, Emergence of sport skills under constraints. In *Skill acquisition in sport: Research, theory and practice*, edited by A. M. Williams and N. J. Hodges (London: Routledge, Taylor & Francis), 409-433.

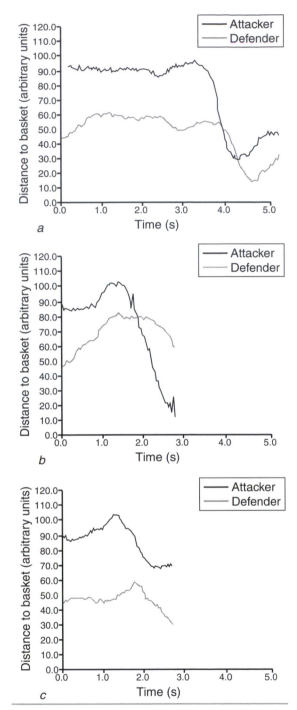

a

b

c

Figure 6.4 Relative movements of both the attacker and defender in the practice task. The movement trajectories of the players show system symmetry (a) being maintained, (b) broken in favor of the attacker, and (c) broken in favor of the defender.

Reprinted, by permission, from D. Araújo et al., 2004, Emergence of sport skills under constraints. In *Skill acquisition in sport: Research, theory and practice*, edited by A. M. Williams and N. J. Hodges (London: Routledge, Taylor & Francis), 409-433.

transition to a new state at a specific value of the control parameter. In other words, the attacker was trying to dribble past the defender while the defender was attempting to maintain the initial system state. The attacker increased the number of dribbling actions (fluctuations) in order to create information on the emergence of a system transition (i.e., a decision on when to go). Suddenly, the decision emerged in the intending-perceiving-acting cycle (Kugler, Shaw, Vincente, & Kinsella-Shaw, 1990). Importantly, the emergence of the decision was a result of the breaking of symmetry between the dyad. In figure 6.4, the movement trajectories of the players show system symmetry being maintained *(a)*, broken in favor of the attacker *(b)*, and broken in favor of the defender *(c)*.

Summary

In this chapter, we discussed how a constraints-based framework focuses attention on individual differences, viewing variability of behavior as attempts to satisfy unique constraints on performers within specific contexts. We also discussed the implications of this theoretical perspective for a nonlinear pedagogical approach to practice. Technological advances and new analytical methods have helped us to gain a more detailed appreciation of the structure of movement variability, which provides a relevant focus when one is concerned with how motor system dfs are reorganized during practice. Due to the potentially unique matching of an individual's intrinsic dynamics with a set of task dynamics, each person may exploit system variability in a slightly different way. When working with groups, practitioners must allow this fact to inform their instructional methods rather than neglecting individual problems and rates of learning. The emergence of behavior under interacting constraints is a key theoretical idea that promises to help us understand decision making at many different levels of analysis in sport and physical activities.

Due to the detailed individualized analyses used in many of the experiments described in this chapter, we have been able to uncover interesting differences across participants in a range of tasks. From fine, static motor tasks like free-throw shooting in basketball to more dynamic, explosive tasks like dribbling against an opponent, an enhanced emphasis on variability has highlighted some important implications for motor control and learning.

By adopting a nonlinear pedagogical view, coaches and teachers can enhance learning. Practitioners' traditional emphasis on reducing error during skill practice by encouraging consistency in motor patterns should be revised to acknowledge the valuable role of variability in moment-to-moment control as well as long-term learning. A struggling learner can be viewed as a system that is temporarily trapped in a stable attractor state that does not correspond well with a behavioral solution that would satisfy task demands. As Corbetta and Vereijken (1999) suggested, a strategy of perturbing the movement system may be necessary to help the learner let go of previous movement solutions. Techniques such as manipulating task constraints like rules, spaces, equipment, and number of opponents should be regarded as useful ways to induce functional movement variability and to encourage exploration for alternative solutions. These ideas question the traditional concepts of repetitious practice to memorize standardized motor patterns and breaking down skills during practice to minimize movement variability. Because performance can fluctuate as a consequence of motor system reorganization, practitioners should acknowledge that the learner may need additional encouragement and reassurance.

In this chapter, we have argued for and demonstrated the insightful strategy of employing individual analysis in movement research to gain a clearer picture of how different performers exploit variability. As more studies that employ methods such as coordination profiling and cluster analysis continue to emerge, researchers are becoming increasingly convinced that a linear, causal relationship between the commands of the CNS and motor output cannot exist. This idea is harmonious with the view in nonlinear pedagogy that the aim of learning is not to acquire an ideal motor pattern that is common to all learners. Latash (1996) suggested that the brain does not care exactly how motor system dfs interact to produce goal-directed activity. Instead, varied movement trajectories emerge as a result of the interplay between the specific task, environmental, and organismic constraints that each unique situation brings. This is particularly apparent in sport, where such factors change so frequently and unexpectedly. Expert performers are increasingly recognized as having the ability to continually adapt their technique as perceptual demands change. The mechanisms humans use to progress to this level of control as a function of learning will provide a productive focus for future research.

SELF-TEST QUESTIONS

1. How are learners able to perform novel movement patterns that they have never attempted before? Answer this question by distinguishing between traditional and constraints-led theoretical approaches to skill acquisition.

2. How might a physical education teacher encourage discovery learning while managing a group of 30 children who are learning basic gymnastic skills?

3. To what extent do genetic factors influence skill acquisition? Discuss this question in relation to common talent identification and development strategies.

4. Provide some examples of rate-limiting constraints on a chef rehabilitating from a repetitive strain injury of the wrist.

5. Explain some of the advantages of time-dependent measures of variability taken from javelin throws.

ADDITIONAL READING

1. Araújo, D., Davids, K., & Serpa, S. (2005). An ecological approach to expertise effects in decision-making in a simulated sailing regatta. *Psychology of Sport and Exercise, 6,* 671-692.

2. Button, C., Davids, K., & Schöllhorn, W.I. (2006). Co-ordination profiling of movement systems. In K. Davids, S. Bennett, & K.M. Newell (Eds.), *Variability in the movement system: A multi-disciplinary perspective* (pp. 133-152). Champaign, IL: Human Kinetics.

3. Ridley, M. (2004). *Nature via nurture: Genes, experience and what makes us human.* New York: Harper Collins.

4. Scully, D.M., & Newell, K.M. (1985). Observational learning and the acquisition of motor skills: Toward a visual perception perspective. *Journal of Human Movement Studies, 11,* 169-186.

CHAPTER 7

Organizing Practice to Optimize Learning

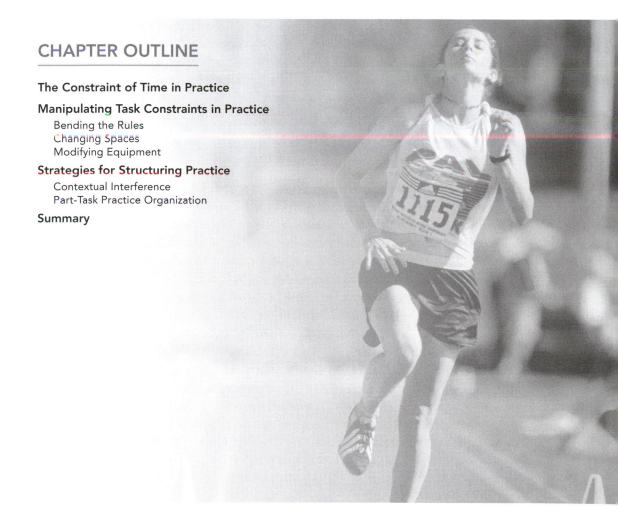

CHAPTER OUTLINE

As we noted in the previous chapter, some of the most important task constraints that practitioners can manipulate are practice variables. For example, a comprehensive review of practice research highlighted a range of variables that could constrain the process of skill acquisition (see Lee, Chamberlin, & Hodges, 2001). These variables included amount of practice, type of practice (e.g., directed versus discovery-based practice), nature of feedback, number of skills practiced in one session, and structure of practice sessions (see also chapter 1). Bernstein (1967) referred to the process of practice as "repetition without repetition," signifying less of an emphasis on the reproduction of an identical movement pattern over practice trials and more attention to the adaptation of movement patterns during practice to achieve consistent outcome goals. In this chapter, we will analyze the process of practice and construct an argument that views practice as a search activity rather than simple repetition or rehearsal of a movement form. The search process during practice involves the modification and perfection of movement solutions from trial to trial without relying on identical performance, a type of "repetition without repetition" as Bernstein (1967) noted. Viewing practice as an exploratory process is a consequence of the self-organization properties found at all levels of the human movement system and the emergent nature of adaptive behavior. Our aim is to flesh out the details of the practice process by examining the practitioner's role in manipulating constraints and organizing the structure of practice sessions.

The Constraint of Time in Practice

An important feature of the constraints-led approach concerns how change in movement behavior can be incurred as a function of learning and development. A major goal in traditional research on practice has been to provide general laws to describe the function of change and development (see chapter 1). The dominant theory of change with learning is the power law of practice, which has been called "the ubiquitous law of learning" (Newell & Rosenbloom, 1981, p. 2). Research examining the accumulated effects of prolonged practice and rates of learning suggested that the function that best describes this relationship is monotonic. A monotonic relationship between two variables (e.g., rates of learning and amount of practice) indicates that as one variable increases (i.e., amount of practice), the other variable (i.e., rate of learning) changes in the same direction. Therefore, the power law of practice states that learning occurs at a rapid rate after the onset of practice, but that the rate of learning negatively accelerates over time as practice continues. Taken together, these ideas suggest that the amount of learning people acquire is typically a function of the amount of practice they perform. Late in learning, however, there tends to be a leveling off in the amount of improvement gained from a given amount of practice trials.

Some analyses of reported and observed data on the amount of time musicians spend in deliberate practice have supported the **monotonic benefits assumption.** For example, as mentioned in chapter 1, Ericsson, Krampe, and Tesch-Römer (1993) highlighted the monotonic relationship between the number of hours musicians deliberately practiced and the performance level they achieved. Their research indicated that the difference between expert and nonexpert pianists and violinists was due to the amount of time the musicians spent in intense practice. The most competent musicians in their study had spent in excess of 10,000 hours practicing alone, whereas the less skilled musicians had spent no more than 7,000 hours practicing alone. During deliberate practice, the learner also typically receives instruction from a practitioner over prolonged periods. The concept of deliberate practice suggests that because expertise is domain specific, learners should expect little transfer of their capabilities to other fields. For example, highly skilled dancers with several years of experience might expect little transfer of their technical ability to gymnastics or ice-skating unless they undertook an extended period of deliberate practice in those activities.

Although these data are useful in helping us to understand the levels of practice that learners might typically require, they fail to capture the uniqueness of each learner's personal struggle, which is at the forefront of the constraints-led

© Jim Whitmer

A monotonic relationship exists between the number of hours musicians deliberately practice and the performance levels they achieve.

perspective. Research on deliberate practice exhibits the familiar weakness of grouping together data from different learners, failing to recognize the unique constraints that each person needs to satisfy, as described in chapters 4 and 5.

These findings also are challenged by the many examples of precocious athletes who rise to the top of their profession at a young age. For example, in 2003, basketball player LeBron James was offered a multimillion-dollar sponsorship deal with a large American sportswear manufacturer at age 18, the second biggest deal ever and more than twice the amount paid to the legendary Michael Jordan. In soccer, 11-year-old Freddy Kofi Adu was the subject of a million-dollar bid by the European team, Inter Milan. He was selected for the USA under-17 team at age 13 and was later approached to sign multimillion-dollar deals by English Premier League clubs in 2003 and trialed with Manchester

Soccer player Freddy Adu. The precocial nature of many performers' abilities challenge the idea that time spent in deliberate practice is the major constraint on skill acquisition and talent development.

United, one of the world's biggest clubs, in 2006. Countless examples of such prodigies exist in other performance domains such as music, art, and dance (van Lieshout & Heymans, 2000). The precocial nature of many performers' abilities challenges the idea that time spent in deliberate practice is the major constraint on skill acquisition and talent development.

Some theoreticians have suggested that the microstructure of activities (i.e., the specific routines and exercises) undertaken during deliberate practice is most important (Starkes, 2000), but existing empirical research in this field has several limitations (see Davids & Baker, in press; Davids, 2000). For example, deliberate practice activities are usually inferred from retrospective estimates over many years, and this is open to recording bias by participants. Further, the lack of control groups in research designs that aim to directly test the predictions of the theory is noticeable. The earlier point about problems in precisely recording the microstructure of practice rather than quantifying how much practice time has been accumulated is important because, in extreme situations, learners may suffer from overpracticing skills within a narrow range of task constraints, particularly if bad habits are inadvertently formed or if overtraining or repetitive strain injuries result. Merely knowing the number of hours that learners need to spend in deliberate practice is not enough. Movement practitioners need to manage changes in learning, and one crucial method is by manipulating the constraints on learners as they attempt to discover their own movement solutions.

Manipulating Task Constraints in Practice

In chapter 4, we acknowledged that retention and transfer are indicators of motor learning, and many of the strategies we will discuss in this chapter emphasize these concepts. Practitioners should be aware that the techniques we suggest may lead to slower rates of skill acquisition than traditional teaching strategies. However, just like a good wine, the process of skill acquisition should be given time to mature naturally for better results in the long term. Not all learners are as gifted as the extraordinary young stars mentioned earlier.

Bending the Rules

Each sport has its own rules that are designed to constrain participants' behavior to varying degrees and create a fair competitive context. For example, to avoid gaining an unfair advantage of their opponents, javelin throwers must not step across the throw line. In more general movement activities, rules may coexist with sociocultural conventions, such as following traffic signals when driving. Regardless of the activity, learners attempt to move within the constraints of the rules or risk failing to achieve the task goal. In many sports and activities, practitioners typically forgo teaching the rules until after learners have practiced some basic techniques in isolation (see chapter 5). Consequently, learners may have little opportunity to search and discover movements in gamelike situations.

The capacity of learners to adhere to rules and produce movement patterns accordingly can be harnessed as a powerful practice strategy. Rather than trying to receive and interpret specific verbal instructions on how to achieve the task goal, learners need to engage with and solve realistic problems for themselves. Practitioners can use small rule changes to influence players to modify their existing intrinsic dynamics in order to match the behavioral information introduced in a game-specific manner (Corbetta & Vereijken, 1999). The task for the practitioner is to manipulate constraints by providing realistic rule changes that permit learners to seek and translate appropriate movement solutions into actual performances (Handford, Davids, Bennett, & Button, 1997). Next we will consider two examples from team and individual sport to help us understand how this type of constraints manipulation might work.

Team Sport: Soccer A common technique in physical education and coaching has been to alter the rules of practice games to encourage acquisition of specific skills (Capel, 2000; Rink, 2001). This is sometimes referred to as *conditioning* a practice game. For example, a soccer coach can help learners to improve their ball control and passing skills in a modified (conditioned) practice game where individual players are permitted a limited number of ball touches. The two-touch rule requires that the player in possession must pass or shoot with only two touches of the ball; otherwise the player commits a foul and loses possession to the opposition.

How can a simple rule change like this affect skill acquisition? First, the two-touch rule demands a good first touch to control and place the ball for the important second contact. To gain a good first touch, the receiver must learn to perceive important information as the ball approaches in order to adopt an appropriate body position (Button, Smith, & Pepping, 2005). The optical image of the approaching ball on the retina will help to specify how an interceptive movement with the kicking leg should be guided (see chapter 3). The practitioner does not explicitly teach the learner to attend to such information sources or adopt better ball control; instead, learners are encouraged to discover these solutions for themselves. By following these rules, learners will seek movement solutions that allow them to quickly control and pass the ball to a teammate. Through extensive practice under these constraints, the movement system will evolve to pick up key perceptual invariants from the ball and movement of teammates. Gradually, relevant task-specific coordination patterns will emerge and these links will become stronger and actions will appear more fluid and automatic (Anderson & Sidaway, 1994; Broderick & Newell, 1999).

After learners have acquired a basic coordination pattern, the practitioner can introduce a rule-bending task constraint that approximates game situations in which the presence of opponents imposes time limits on actions. The following are some other artificial rules that are designed to stabilize certain coordination patterns within soccer practice. Consider the nature of the skills that coaches may wish to enhance by introducing these artificial rules into practices:

- Restrictions are placed on shooting from areas of the pitch or court very close to goal.
- Each member of the team must touch the ball before a shot can occur.
- Only goals scored from high passes (or crosses) count.
- Goals from headers or volleys count double.

Individual Sport: Squash An example from an individual sport is useful to develop the idea of constraints manipulation on learners by imposing certain rules or conditions. Squash coaches encourage their players to return to the T-position on the court between shots since this represents a central location from which it is easier to retrieve the ball from all areas of the court. Unfortunately for players, the movement toward the T-position after a shot is unfamiliar and often forgotten in the heat of a rally. How might a rule change help a player to develop this positioning skill? One approach might be to instruct each player to step on a small target area around the T-position between points or forfeit the point being played. This rule should encourage players to recognize this court position as an important spatial pivotal location around which conventional shots such as the backhand or drop shot might be played. Bending the rules in this way can constrain actions where adherence to verbal instructions from the coach might not.

In their study of coordination dynamics, Carson, Goodman, Kelso, and Elliott (1995) termed this phenomenon *inherent anchoring*. By implementing inherent anchoring, the performer develops stronger movement links to key environmental sources of information. As a training drill, this type of practice is also likely to improve cardiovascular fitness as each player is forced to move between shots to focus on optimal court positioning. By implementing this sort of task constraint relatively early in learning, static, predictable sequences of action can be made more dynamic. An added benefit of implementing task constraints as conditions during practice is that learners are encouraged at an early stage to take responsibility for their own actions and to practice decision-making activities that may be relevant during competition.

Changing Spaces

Because all physical activities occur within environments that are restricted by boundaries to some degree, the potential to either increase or reduce performance areas within practice is ubiquitous. Consider the benefits field hockey players might gain when practicing under task constraints in which one player must dribble past an opponent within a limited space. First, the task constraints direct the dribbler toward movement patterns that help keep close possession of the ball, such as maintaining control of the ball and stick, dribbling at pace, and changing directions. Second, defenders learn how to position themselves to prevent opponents dribbling around them and how to time an interception with their stick. As learners improve their dribbling skills, the practitioner may gradually change the task constraints by reducing the playing area further or by adding extra players to encourage passing and ball-control movements.

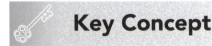

In badminton, manipulating task constraints by altering the spatial characteristics of the court can sometimes be advantageous to learners.

Manipulating task constraints by altering spatial characteristics of playing areas within racket sports, such as short tennis and badminton, also can be advantageous. During early learning stages when novice players are establishing new coordination patterns, it could be beneficial to play within a larger court or surface area so that fewer shots may leave the court and be considered as errors. As players establish basic coordination patterns, such as the forehand stroke, the court size can be reduced to force players to fine-tune movements of the racket arm to cope with the increased accuracy demands. For example, in tennis, moving the service line closer to the net on the opponent's court will demand a closed racket face at ball contact to impart an arched ball trajectory over the net. In addition, lowering or lifting the net during practice encourages tennis and badminton players to explore how and when different shot trajectories can be useful against opponents.

Key Concept

In many performance environments, players must learn to exploit space or exhibit skill within a confined area. Under restricted spatial task constraints, learners improve their transferability of skills because they have to adapt their coordination patterns to the new performance context. Again, it is clear that the most important benefit for learners is that they must create their own appropriate solution to the new task constraints. This situation represents a valuable learning opportunity in which the learner must reevaluate existing movement capabilities against realistic environmental demands. An additional benefit of changing the dimensions of the practice area is that learners remain interested and motivated since the task constraints can be continually adjusted to suit their level of expertise.

Modifying Equipment

The influence of sport science and technological improvements over the last 50 years has resulted in an increasing interest in the effectiveness of sport equipment. The substantial financial incentives associated with performance enhancement in modern-day sport have contributed to the many changes in equipment design, such as in speed skates (de Koning, de Groot, & van Ingen Schenau, 1992) and golf clubs (Iwatsubo, Kawamura, Miyamoto, & Yamaguchi, 2000). In this section, we will address how practitioners can use equipment and artificial aids during practice to constrain learners' movement patterns and promote skill acquisition. Modified equipment can restructure the practice environment and enable learners to cope with less stringent task constraints. Practitioners can use training aids to temporarily constrain the performer–environment system to encourage an appropriate focus on certain perceptual variables or the emergence of key information–movement couplings. Successful practitioners realize that the occasional use of modified equipment must be carefully integrated into an athlete's training program so that movement transfer into subsequent performance is optimal. Learners must not become dependent on the use of artificial devices.

Practicing With Blindfolds   Although using blindfolds or visual-occlusion goggles during volleyball, soccer, and basketball practice may seem unusual, several recent studies have supported the idea of occluding various information sources during learning to direct players to alternative perceptual information sources (see Spotlight on Research). Occlusion devices such as blindfolds, protruding bibs worn around the waist, and dribble aids worn under the eyes to occlude vision of limbs have been used in volleyball to direct blockers' search for acoustic information from setters' hand–ball contact, in basketball to prevent players from watching their hands as they bounce a ball, in soccer to direct players to raise their heads and search for visual information in the environment as they dribble the ball, and in golf to focus the player's attention on the proprioceptive feel of the golf swing. Alternatively, other movement practitioners, such as dance instructors, have advocated the use of mirrors or live video feedback to augment vision. The key point is that practitioners can remove or add information to help learners develop appropriate information–movement couplings.

Spotlight on Research

TEMPORAL AND INFORMATIONAL CONSTRAINTS ON ONE-HANDED CATCHING PERFORMANCE

In this one-handed catching experiment by Bennett, Button, Kingsbury, and Davids (1999), three groups of children were selected using a pretest of catching ability. Only those participants who caught less than 10% of trials were investigated. One group of children practiced the task with restricted vision (RV group), wearing a helmet with an opaque screen attached to it (see figure 7.1a). The helmet was designed to remove visual information of the catching limb. The researchers predicted that in the absence

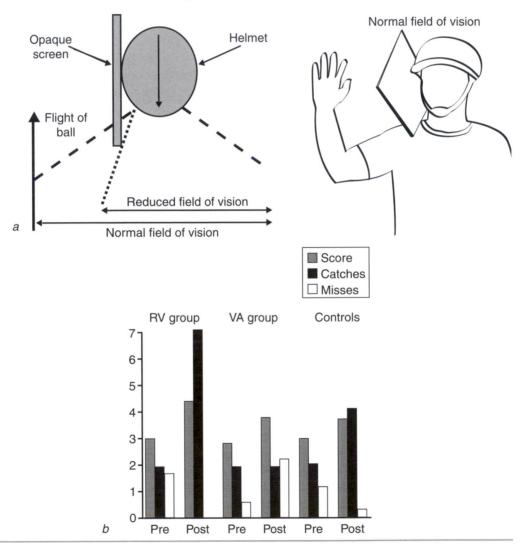

Figure 7.1 Manipulating access to information of the catching arm can benefit catching skill acquisition by directing learners' search for relevant information sources for catching a ball.

Reprinted with permission from *Research Quarterly for Exercise and Sport*, Vol. 70, 220-232, Copyright 1999 by the American Alliance for Health, Physical Education, Recreation and Dance, 1900 Association Drive, Reston, VA 20191.

of visual information, the children would be forced to search for alternative information sources such as proprioceptive information from the catching arm. The RV group transferred to a normal vision condition after 120 practice trials. A second group had vision available (VA group) during the practice trials but then transferred to the RV condition for 20 transfer trials. Finally, a control group trained for the same period of trials with normal vision throughout.

As shown in figure 7.1*b*, each group improved the number of catches made from pre- to posttest. Of particular interest was the significantly greater improvement of the RV group compared with the VA group. During transfer tests, the RV group showed no detrimental effects of catching in normal vision. However, the VA group performed poorly when vision of the catching arm was occluded. The sensitivity of the VA group to removal of visual information suggests that catchers in this group had relied heavily on vision and were somewhat less adaptable when this information was restricted. Another suggestion was that the RV group benefited from being directed toward information sources provided by vision of the ball early in flight, proprioception from the catching arm, and acoustic information from the ball machine.

APPLICATION

In summary, the data supported the use of equipment aids as a teaching strategy to manipulate informational constraints and direct novices toward appropriate information sources. Whether more experienced learners would show similar benefits in long-term performance in response to such manipulations during practice is an interesting question for future work. What are other types of movement activities where learners could benefit from practice with restricted vision? From the context of rehabilitation after injury, provide a similar example of how a practitioner might direct a patient toward critical information sources (e.g., acoustic, haptic, or visual) that support movements such as postural control, balance, or locomotion toward a target.

Futebol de Salão   Task constraints are often manipulated during ball sports in one way or another, but what benefits might be gained from changing the characteristics of the ball? Practitioners can use modified equipment to direct learners to alternative forms of sensory information in order to regulate motor behavior. For example, equipment that is heavier than normal might load the haptic sensory system with different moments of inertia, directing learners' attention to this important source of information (Beak, Davids, & Bennett, 2000).

Within the last decade, the futebol de salão (FDS), a South American football (soccer ball), has been introduced in England. The FDS ball is smaller and heavier than a regulation size-5 ball, which has a coefficient of restitution between 45% and 48% with a recommended pressure of 11.4 pounds per square inch (78.6 kilopascals). For FDS, the recommended rebound resilience ranges from 10% to 15% and the pressure is maintained at 8.5 pounds per square inch (58.6 kilopascals). The density of the FDS ball is manipulated by filling the bladder with a type of foam that reduces its bounce characteristics, thereby ensuring more playing time on the ground. It encourages the learner to use the sole of the foot to drag the ball away from defenders in close proximity. Similar training aids are now widely available for a variety of sports such as rugby and basketball. As with the FDS, the makers of such products claim these balls improve ball control during practice (for an example, see www.icfds.com).

However, the effects of ball design on ball control are unknown because there has been little scientific research on redesigned balls as a constraint on the emergence of ball skills. Button, Bennett, Davids, and Stephenson (1999) examined the training effect using a small football with a lower coefficient of restitution on the learning of two soccer-specific skills: dribbling and juggling. In this experiment, a group of novices who trained with the FDS ball were compared with a group who trained with a standard-sized football. In a juggling test conducted after 10 acquisition lessons, the experimental group showed significantly greater improvements in ball control than the control group (25% versus 9% improvements in juggling score from pretest to posttest).

Chapman, Bennett, and Davids (2001) extended the findings of Button, Bennett, Davids, and Stephenson (1999) by manipulating ball size and coefficient of restitution as a function of learners' skill level. In contrast to Button and colleagues, who studied children at the control stage of motor learning, Chapman and colleagues studied the ball control of children at the coordination stage of Newell's (1985) model of skill acquisition. A more precise definition of the learners in the Button et al. study may be beginners, whereas the children investigated by Chapman et al. have been aptly described as complete novices. Using the same tests as Button and colleagues, Chapman and colleagues found no effects on skill acquisition when ball characteristics were manipulated. The findings from both studies demonstrate how manipulating equipment design interacts with learners' skill level. In the case of the FDS, further research is needed to examine how equipment design influences children's skill acquisition at both the coordination and control stages. Refined analyses also should include study of coordination changes with learning.

Strategies for Structuring Practice

A considerable amount of research has been conducted on the variables that influence practice organization (Lee, Chamberlin, & Hodges, 2001). In this section we consider some of these concerns from the constraints-led approach, focusing particularly on the concepts of contextual interference and part-task practice.

Contextual Interference

Within a training session, randomly ordering the practice of different movement skills as opposed to practicing them in a blocked order has been shown to improve the retention and transfer of individual skills. As mentioned in chapter 1, this is called **contextual interference** (CI) (Magill, 2006; Newell

& McDonald, 1991; Schmidt & Lee, 2005). For example, a pilot practicing three different types of flying maneuvers (e.g., A, B, and C) in a simulator might experience short-term performance gains from practicing in a blocked format (e.g., AAABBBCCC), but long-term retention of the movements and a more adaptable technique should be encouraged within random training (e.g., CAABCABCB). The more diverse the scheduling of practice skills, the higher the level of CI present during practice.

The CI literature is dominated by cognitive explanations such as the elaboration hypothesis (Shea & Morgan, 1979) and more recently the reconstruction hypothesis (Immink & Wright, 2001). These hypotheses posit that the learning benefits of high CI can be attributed to learners engaging in demanding cognitive processing while practicing different variations of a skill. The constraints-led perspective takes a different stance, however, focusing on how learners must explore relevant constraints and solve task-related problems on a trial-by-trial basis (e.g., Newell & McDonald, 1991; Ollis, Button, & Fairweather, 2005).

Practice involving high levels of CI could be viewed as a frequent perturbation to the perceptual-motor landscape (as a function of altered task dynamics between trials). Practicing a set of skills (e.g., the dig, set, and smash in volleyball) randomly requires the movement system to engage in a high frequency of search and reorganization. This amount of exploration forces learners to adapt their movement patterns regularly but could delay the emergence of learning effects due to the amount of instability created in the perceptual-motor landscape during such an exhaustive search process. However, some long-term learning benefits arise from having searched such a large area of the perceptual-motor landscape. Provided that some motor characteristics of the skills set are common, the suggestion is that high CI creates a wider and more robust attractor basin that individuals can then apply when performing the skill within different effectors and transfer situations (Kelso & Zanone, 2002). This alternative interpretation has been supported by results with laboratory tasks involving fewer motor system dfs (i.e., aiming at targets with the hand). However, it still requires rigorous testing in practical situations in which the stability of acquired movement skills in high to low CI conditions should be probed.

Although several researchers have raised concerns about the consistency and durability of the CI effect (Brady, 1998; Newell and McDonald, 1991), it is likely that interactions of empirical factors have clouded the benefits somewhat. For example, Ollis and colleagues (2005) demonstrated that certain combinations of factors such as task difficulty, ability level, and transfer distality (relative change in performance conditions) can lead to smaller CI effects than may be expected based on previous work. In their study, experienced and inexperienced firefighters learned how to tie a combination of different knots in low, medium, or high CI conditions. High CI conditions were shown to be most beneficial when participants were asked to transfer the knot-tying skills into a different context such as tying while blindfolded. In the future, more holistic, real-world experiments should be conducted to establish a firm theoretical understanding of why and how the CI effect occurs.

Part-Task Practice Organization

Several relevant techniques for designing practice conditions based on task decomposition have been highlighted by Wickens (1997). These techniques include part-task training and adaptive instruction, which have both been used extensively as coaching strategies in sport and work-related training programs. As mentioned in chapter 1, **part-task training** involves practicing a subset of task components as a precursor to practice or performance of the whole task. For example, swimmers are encouraged to separately practice the leg kick for the front crawl by holding on to a floatation aid before the kicking and arm actions are integrated into the whole pattern.

In **adaptive training,** task difficulty is gradually increased as performance is mastered. For example, when coaching the skills of ball control and dribbling in basketball or hockey, opponents are only introduced once the players have mastered basic techniques. The dribbling task is broken down into its constituent parts such as ball or stick handling and feet movements. Learners are first taught to control the ball so that they can later concentrate on dribbling and running or skating with the ball. Coaches might consider using static obstacles, such as cones, passive players, or other markers, to outline a pathway for dribbling as a useful intermediate step before progressing to more realistic dynamic learning contexts with moving defenders. Similar progressions are evident in gait rehabilitation where patients may practice in an uncluttered laboratory environment before moving into more realistic, dynamic environments that might include surfaces, steps, and openings (e.g., doors). Therapists can increase the demands of such exercises by gradually introducing complexity into the environment such as moving on a motorized treadmill, walking around obstacles, or adding interceptive requirements. Eventually, the goal is to simulate the conditions of gait in natural environments.

Practitioners use this pedagogical strategy to teach many complex movement skills. Because practitioners have assumed that effective learning depends on people allocating finite resources to selectively attend to appropriate information sources, they have argued that part-task and adaptive training benefit beginners (e.g., see Magill, 2006; Schmidt, 1991; Wightman & Lintern, 1985). Attention overload could result in error-ridden performance and a loss of confidence and motivation to practice. Therefore, an interesting question for practitioners is how to decompose tasks for practice.

Traditionally, researchers have argued that the principle of component interdependence may be useful in helping practitioners decide how and when to break up complex tasks for practice (e.g., Naylor & Briggs, 1978).

They hypothesized that tasks high in organization (interdependence between components) and low in complexity do not readily lend themselves to decomposition and should be practiced as a whole. They considered that part practice might best be used in tasks low in organization and high in complexity. However, regardless of the amount of component interdependence perceived in task analysis, part practice leads to better learning than no practice, and the majority of motor actions can be acquired through task decomposition (Lee et al., 2001). The problem is that, as Lee and colleagues argued, "Component interdependence may not be telling the whole story" (p. 121). Clearly, complex motor actions need to be managed by practitioners during practice.

Preserving Information–Movement Couplings   The Gibsonian view of the relationship between information and movement discussed in chapter 3 supports the idea that effective practice organization should be based on the learner's functional integration of the perceptual and action subsystems. In ecological psychology, movement plays two important roles. First, movement orients performers to information sources in the environment and can create information for learning. Second, movement creates transformations in surrounding energy arrays, producing spatiotemporal changes to the environment (Bootsma, 1998; Gibson, 1979; Michaels & Carello, 1981). The implication of these ideas is that practice should occur in more or less dynamic circumstances with all key sources of information present (and flowing) for learners. People can learn to select key perceptual variables and calibrate movements to the information available in the practice environment.

This approach directly contradicts the traditional pedagogical doctrine of part practice in highly managed, static environments in order to reduce learners' information load. Instead, it suggests that practitioners should adopt simplification strategies. The challenge for practitioners is to design activities that help learners form information–movement couplings while managing the informational constraints on the learner. *Simplification* means that practice conditions should simulate natural performance conditions, but key performance variables such as velocities of objects and people, distances between surfaces and objects, and forces of moving people and objects should be reduced to simplify the task. It does not refer to practicing the components of complex tasks separately before reassembling them. This latter strategy risks decoupling perception and action systems. During practice, it is critical to keep important sources of perceptual information together with functional movements in simplified versions of the target task.

Examples of simplification strategies include the following:

- In rehabilitation, patients with postural control problems could practice standing in a quiet (static) stance before attempting a dynamic stance after stepping or landing.

- Long jumpers might reduce the run-up distance to the takeoff board so that they can practice the running and jumping components of the task together (Scott, 2002). They can begin a few steps from the takeoff board and gradually move the starting position back as learning occurs.

- In cricket, the velocity and distance of the cricket bowler in running up to deliver a ball could be reduced (Renshaw & Davids, 2004). Similar simplification strategies could be applied to learning a gymnastic vault or throwing a javelin.

- For the beginner catcher or batter, the velocity of approaching balls could be reduced, perhaps starting with intercepting rolling balls on the floor. To learn how to perceive transformations to surrounding energy arrays, novices should practice the interception of slow-moving balls in dynamic tasks, not static projectiles. Hitting static balls does not enable learners to form important information–movement couplings during practice.

- Novice servers in volleyball, table tennis, tennis, and badminton might reduce the distance to the target as well as gradually raise the net during practice so that they can practice the ball toss and strike together.

- Driving a car or riding a bike at slow speeds encourages learners to form crucial information–movement couplings as they acquire key information sources while navigating typical environments.

Oversimplification of Practice in Table Tennis   How can we be sure there are benefits of practicing sport tasks under dynamic conditions? Bootsma, Houbiers, Whiting, and van Wieringen (1991) examined this question in their analysis of practicing the forehand drive in table tennis. Bootsma and colleagues divided a sample of table tennis novices into two training groups that practiced over 4 days. One group practiced under dynamic task (DT) constraints with the ball rolling down a half-open tube before bouncing once to land at the leading edge of the table. During the entire approach, the ball remained clearly visible to the player. In a second condition, a static task (ST) constraints group practiced hitting a ball suspended 0.4 meters above the leading edge in the laminar airstream of an inverted vacuum cleaner. The practice conditions differed in the availability of time-to-contact information provided by the approaching ball in the dynamic conditions only. The researchers believed this information would support the formation of an information–movement coupling for the forehand drive (Bootsma & van Wieringen, 1990).

The researchers observed no statistical differences between the groups' levels of performance accuracy in hitting a 0.5- × 0.5-meter target on the table. However, an interesting finding was the significant negative correlations between the time to ball contact (tau margin) at stroke initiation and the mean acceleration of the bat found for both the DT and ST groups in the pretest. That is, as the tau margin value decreased, the mean acceleration of the bat increased. It seems that novices were quickly attempting to establish an information–movement coupling, possibly based on previous experiences in related interceptive actions or evolutionary sensitivity under dynamic task constraints. However, after a week of training under dynamic task conditions for this specific action, the negative relationship between the tau value at movement initiation and the mean acceleration of the bat actually decreased in strength for the DT group ($r = -0.33$ on the posttest compared with $r = -0.60$ on the pretest). This effect did not occur after training for the ST group ($r = -0.73$ on the posttest compared with $r = -0.70$ on the pretest).

These findings suggested that the ST group stabilized their performance after practicing under the same task constraints for 4 days, while the performance of the DT group might have deteriorated (indicated by the decrease in the value of the negative correlation) because the task was too complex for them at that stage of learning. In the context of the current analysis of practice structure, the findings imply how task simplification might be beneficial in sensitizing the learners to intermediate ball velocities between the static and highly dynamic task constraints. Rather than employing a dynamic and static condition, better management of the task constraints—perhaps by using lower ball velocities to reduce the dynamic nature of the task—might have resulted in learners stabilizing a stronger information–movement coupling. The implication for practice organization, which needs to be tested in further research, is that the ST group could experience some transfer difficulties if they were to encounter more dynamic constraints (as might be expected in a game). In addition, the DT group might have benefited from having the task simplified a little more. For example, a range of lower ball velocities during the practice of the DT group may have reduced the severity of the task constraints. Such innovative research highlights the importance of identifying and preserving relevant information–movement couplings in practice.

Summary

Constraints manipulation is an important strategy in a nonlinear pedagogy. Many of these practical ideas have been around for a long time, but the theoretical rationale for their value has not been clear. Indeed, many practitioners will be able to identify how their favorite strategies are actually simple manipulations of task constraints. Our goal in this chapter has been to develop a theoretical and scientific framework for understanding why manipulating constraints can benefit learning. Once the theoretical rationale for manipulating task constraints is understood, practitioners will become more precise in the ways they adapt learning environments. Clearly, task constraints play an influential role in motor learning and must be given careful consideration by practitioners. Practitioners must ensure that the movement patterns created within the new constraints are transferable to actual performance settings. In addition, the manipulation of constraints needs to be temporary and should occur with a specific performance-enhancement goal in mind, encouraging a particular adaptation in learners' behavior (Handford et al., 1997). From this viewpoint, skill acquisition is a process of gradually changing the existing coordination dynamics of each person to satisfy a set of novel task constraints. As such, the manipulation of task constraints can be beneficial, particularly early in the learning process.

The concept of information–movement coupling is significant in practicing many motor skills. The research discussed in this chapter demonstrated the significance of information that constrains movements by specifying or regulating ongoing movement behavior in sport. These findings support the role of task simplification as an important strategy in providing learners with opportunities to establish key information–movement couplings. Neuroscientific evidence also suggests that successfully performing interceptive movements in sport requires the establishment of strong cortical connections between the visual cortex and motor areas of the brain through extensive task-specific experience. For example, the ball toss in softball pitching provides perceptual information that learners can use to constrain the strike phase. A decoupling of the demands on the perceptual and motor subsystems during practice would not be commensurate with the establishment of cortical networks for perceiving information for movement (Davids, Kingsbury, Bennett, & Handford, 2001).

From a pedagogical standpoint, the empirical data from research programs of work on information–movement coupling are beginning to reveal some important avenues for research on teaching strategies employed during practice (see Handford et al., 1997; Renshaw & Davids, 2006; Savelsbergh & van der Kamp, 2000; Williams, Davids, & Williams, 1999). The major goals for researchers appear to be (a) gaining a better understanding of the information–movement relationship that constrains movement system components, (b) focusing on the implications of manipulating various constraints in the learning environment, (c) understanding how to organize practice regimes and break down sport tasks for the purposes of practice, and (d) understanding the role of task simplification in a range of physical activities and sports.

SELF-TEST QUESTIONS

1. Why have some theorists described the theory of deliberate practice as "very environmentalist"? (Tip: See Starkes [2000] in Additional Reading.)

2. Identify examples of teaching techniques from either a physical education or rehabilitation setting where the performer is placed under high and low levels of constraint.

3. List some task constraints that could be altered during skill learning. Which do you feel would have the most beneficial effect and why?

4. How might manipulating the size of the practice area encourage a defender in soccer to improve positional awareness in a match?

5. Discuss the value for a swimming student of practicing the front crawl in segments (i.e., the arm stroke separately from the leg kick).

6. Why would repetition without repetition (Bernstein, 1967) during practice be beneficial for the learner?

ADDITIONAL READING

1. Bootsma, R.J., & Van Wieringen, P.C.W. (1990). Timing an attacking forehand drive in table tennis. *Journal of Experimental Psychology: Human Perception and Performance, 16*(1): 21-29.

2. Davids, K., Kingsbury, D., Bennett, S., & Handford, C. (2001). Information–movement coupling: Implications for the organization of research and practice during acquisition of self-paced extrinsic timing skills. *Journal of Sports Sciences, 19,* 117-127.

3. Lee, T.D., Chamberlin, C.J., & Hodges, N.J. (2001). Practice. In B. Singer, H. Hausenblas, & C. Jannelle (Eds.), *Handbook of Sport Psychology* (2nd ed., pp. 115-143). New York: Wiley.

4. Starkes, J. (2000). The road to expertise: Is practice the only determinant? *International Journal of Sport Psychology, 31,* 431-451.

CHAPTER 8

Using Verbal Guidance as an Informational Constraint on Learners

CHAPTER OUTLINE

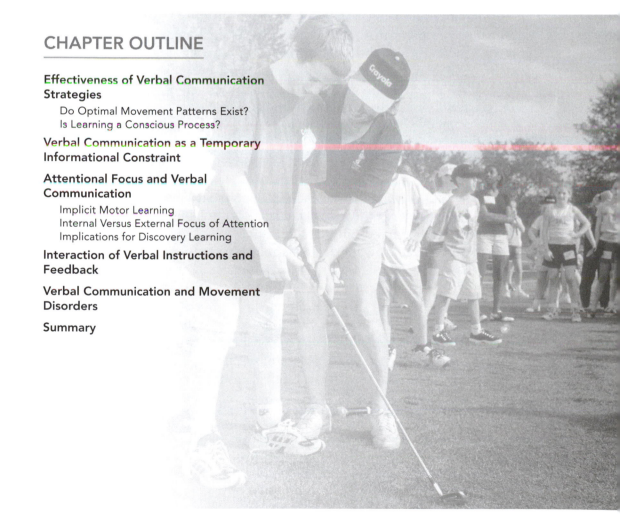

Traditionally, practitioners have used instructions to promote an optimal technique or movement pattern that may not necessarily be commensurate with each learner's intrinsic dynamics. In this chapter, you will learn that there are many situations in which verbal instructions and movement-related feedback can actually hinder learners. To what extent are verbal instructions compatible with the principle of information–movement coupling discussed in chapters 6 and 7? For example, while practicing a golf swing, does it help to verbally instruct learners to focus on the movement of their limbs, the club, or perhaps the intended trajectory of the ball? In this chapter, we consider how practitioners can use verbal instructions, feedback, and other attention-focusing strategies to help learners acquire skills.

Effectiveness of Verbal Communication Strategies

Practitioners often use verbal communication to direct learners toward an optimal way of performing a skill or to provide encouragement during practice. When we recall a former sport coach or teacher, it is often a common catchphrase or an inspirational pep talk that we remember. Traditional views of motor learning tend to emphasize the transmission of verbal information from the practitioner to the learner for purposes of retention (see chapter 1). This focus may explain why pedagogical strategies such as providing verbal instructions, feedback, and demonstrations are so popular among many practitioners. How do practitioners effectively use most verbal communications? For example, are certain kinds of instructions more or less beneficial for different types of learners? How much feedback should a practitioner provide at any one instance? What theoretical guidance is available to help practitioners plan how and when to best deliver feedback?

The key point is that, within the constraints-led approach, there is a greater emphasis on how learners who are harnessing self-organization processes in the motor system discover and acquire relevant coordination modes for complex actions. Given this nontraditional perspective, it is apparent that practitioners need to rethink how verbal guidance strategies can help facilitate this process. We begin our discussion by considering two theoretical questions relevant to our understanding of skill acquisition processes: Do optimal movement patterns exist, and to what extent is learning a conscious process?

Do Optimal Movement Patterns Exist?

Verbal communication enables practitioners to quickly communicate to learners a mental image of how they should perform the desired movement during practice. However, as we noted in chapter 4, an important preliminary task for the practitioner is to ascertain the coordination tendencies that already exist within each person. The relationship between the task constraints and the learner's intrinsic dynamics is critical. If the task dynamics match a learner's intrinsic dynamics, learning is likely to occur rapidly. If there is some discrepancy between the learner's task dynamics and intrinsic dynamics, the rate of learning may be slower and more demanding of the practitioner's resources. Recall that negative transfer can occur when the learner's intrinsic dynamics compete with the task dynamics. The implication is that practitioners should discard the strategy of verbally instructing learners to reproduce an idealized technique in favor of understanding how learners can best discover a specific movement solution that harnesses their unique intrinsic dynamics. With the practitioner's help, individuals can discover a biomechanically optimal pattern that is suitable for them.

From this perspective, the term *optimal* should be reinterpreted since it is not common (i.e., universal) among all learners, and it does not refer to a universal movement pattern toward which all learners should aspire. Rather, an optimal movement pattern for each learner is one that cooperates with the intrinsic dynamics of that person's specific movement system and that allows the achievement of the task goal in an accurate, timely, and energy-efficient manner. In short, an optimal movement pattern is one that satisfies the constraints on individual learners as they successfully achieve a specific, intended performance outcome (Button, Davids, & Schöllhorn, 2006; Davids, Glazier, Araújo, & Bartlett, 2003).

Is Learning a Conscious Process?

Traditional skill acquisition theories also suggest that learning results from the acquisition and storage of more appropriate representations of the movement skill (Schmidt, 1975). Conversely, the constraints-led approach does not place as great an emphasis on the construction of cognitive structures for supporting memory recall. Instead, coordinated movement is viewed as an emergent property of the key variables (including some verbal guidance from a practitioner) that help learners harness movement system dfs in deriving coordination solutions (Hodges & Franks, 2002). Regardless of the theoretical interpretation one favors, it is worthwhile to consider whether the learner needs to be aware of skill acquisition occurring. In other words, to what extent is learning a conscious process?

Bernstein (1967) provided insight into this issue by positing the view of the learner as an integrated movement system with at least four levels of organizational control (see figure 8.1). According to Bernstein, the four levels of control used for assembling movements are the level of tone, the level of synergies, the level of space, and the level of action. The four levels of control are differentiated hierarchically within the CNS, with leading levels of control being located at cortical levels of the CNS (for a detailed overview, see Beek, 2000). The level of tone provides the lowest level of control

Bernstein's levels of movement control

4. Action   **Conscious**
- Movements requiring action
sequences
- Adaptive changes
- Examples include changing gears
in a car, doing sets of gymnastic exercises

3. Space
- Movement in space adjacent to body
- Requires perception of workspace
- Examples include interceptive
actions, locomotion

2. Synergies
- Coordinated movement
- Linking multiple muscle groups
- Stable and reproducible
- Examples include controlling balance
and posture while reaching forward to pick
up a book from a shelf

1. Tone
- Involved in all movement
- Tonic or background muscular force
- Examples include adjusting forces in
postural muscles when walking on an
uneven surface.   **Subconscious**

Figure 8.1   Bernstein (1967) posited a view of the learner as an integrated movement system with at least four levels of organizational complexity.

Adapted from N.A. Bernstein, 1967, *The control and regulation of movements* (London: Pergamon Press).

associated with basic tonic and background muscle force associated with movement. The level of synergies is engaged in integrating muscle groups into coordinated action. The level of space focuses on the coordination of movements with respect to environmental objects, surfaces, and individuals. Finally, the highest level of control, the level of action, is used for planning and creating movement sequences and adapting movements in dynamic environments.

Bernstein's (1967) description of the different levels of organization in the CNS suggests that, typically, leading levels of the CNS are not involved in the process of basic perceptual-motor skill acquisition. Only the leading level of control, the level of action, features in the use of verbal information and explicit instructions during learning. According to Bernstein, the CNS is actually specialized for acquiring perceptual-motor skills in an implicit (subconscious) manner. This specialization helps explain how young infants can rapidly acquire basic motor patterns for controlling posture, picking up toys, and feeding without parental instruction or verbal feedback. The concept of discovery learning also fits with Bernstein's suggestion that more effective motor learning occurs through gaining a better understanding of the relationships between muscle force outputs and effects on important environmental properties. As we all know, the natural process of skill acquisition in infancy occurs when infants seek and discover appropriate task solutions through problem-solving movement behaviors (Thelen & Smith, 1994).

Theorists have tended to downplay these natural learning processes over the years, even though these processes are at the forefront of a constraints-led theory of motor learning. Some of the research that we discuss next suggests that these same implicit processes may be involved in the practice process. As learners become more skilled at a movement task through practice, responsibility for coordination control is delegated to subordinate levels of the CNS, which allows learners to explore self-organizing movement system dynamics. Asking a learner to understand complex verbal instructions about skill performance or referring in too much detail to body-part movements in space is likely to engage cortical levels of the learner's CNS during practice. This, in turn, disrupts the typical process of implicit motor learning that exploits the propensity for self-organization at lower levels of the CNS. An exception to this process occurs when performers acquire skills that are imbued with cultural or symbolic interpretation, such as learning stylized movements in dance, gymnastics, martial arts, and ice-skating (Beek, 2000). In these circumstances, the very basis of expertise involves the highly explicit processes of intentionality and interpretation in performing carefully considered motor patterns.

Verbal Communication as a Temporary Informational Constraint

Of course, verbal communication doesn't always have negative implications for learners. Recall from chapter 3 that changes to the energy in perceptual arrays can provide information that humans directly perceive to regulate action (Gibson, 1979). That is, learners couple movements, not words, to environmental information sources. Although learners may struggle initially to detect the key information sources that can effectively guide their behavior, one way in which practitioners can help them is by providing additional information to facilitate the search for the information they need to regulate movements. We can view verbal instructions and feedback as specific informational constraints that learners use to discover key perceptual invariants available for pickup in the environment. For example, in the absence of sufficient information, practitioners can use instructions to clarify the task goals, providing learners with a shortcut to begin exploring specific (rather than global) areas of the perceptual-motor landscape.

Verbal communication can thus be a powerful method of directing the learner's attentional focus to facilitate self-organization processes (Wulf, McNevin, & Shea, 2001). However, an important consideration for the practitioner is the extent to which performers learn to rely on verbal communication during practice to reproduce a given action. Recall that from a constraints-led perspective, the learner's goal is not to reproduce an idealized motor pattern, but to independently discover a relevant movement solution. It is also unlikely that verbal feedback will be readily available in all performance contexts and hence practitioners should use verbal communication sparingly to prevent this dependence from developing (Hodges & Franks, 2002). According to interpretations of Bernstein's (1967) insights, the learning process occurs most naturally in an implicit way, so it makes little sense for learners to be made overaware of their actions by practitioners, as we shall discover next.

Attentional Focus and Verbal Communication

Transmitting augmented information in the form of verbal instructions or visual demonstrations has been a primary concern of motor learning theorists for many years (Newell, Morris, & Scully, 1985). So far, we have argued that an emerging view in the constraints-led approach is to minimize prescriptive, verbal communication during practice while emphasizing its role in directing learners to explore key areas of task dynamics (Davids, Araújo, & Shuttleworth, 2005; Davids et al., 2003; Handford, Davids, Bennett, & Button, 1997). Indeed, we can use this viewpoint to reinterpret many conventional ideas about motor learning.

Results from a series of studies comparing the nature and role of implicit and explicit learning have questioned the traditional emphasis on numerous verbal instructions by practitioners, as well as the strategy of verbalization of motor control by learners (that is, asking learners to explain how they are attempting to regulate their actions). For example, Masters, Law, and Maxwell (2002) made the case for implicit learning of actions by drawing attention to recent literature supporting the significance of an external focus of attention in the provision of instructions and feedback to learners in sport. According to Masters and colleagues, it is inappropriate for learners to develop an overawareness of movement during practice. They referred to recent feedback studies by Wulf and colleagues demonstrating that a qualitative focus on feedback emphasizing awareness of specific body parts may be detrimental to learning (e.g., Wulf, McNevin, Fuchs, Ritter, & Toole, 2000). Before discussing this body of work, we need to begin with an analysis of the distinction between implicit and explicit learning and the implications for exploratory practice.

Implicit Motor Learning

According to Masters and colleagues (e.g., Abernethy et al. 2007; Masters et al., 2002; Maxwell, Masters, Kerr, & Weedon, 2001), if learners acquire movement skill explicitly—by learning a large pool of verbal rules and knowledge about how to execute such movements—they default to a conscious type of control in which movements are deliberately and cognitively controlled and learners verbally articulate their control strategies. Research has shown that this type of perceptual-motor control can be more easily perturbed by intervening factors such as anxiety, cognitions, and emotions (e.g., Masters, 1992). A better approach for practitioners is to avoid the acquisition of verbal information during practice by emphasizing implicit motor learning techniques.

Implicit motor learning occurs when individuals are not formally exposed to verbal instructions to perform a movement in a specific manner (Shea, Wulf, Whitacre, & Park, 2001). Masters and colleagues (2002) proposed that overloading learners with verbal instructions leads them to invest too much effort in acquiring verbal knowledge that might interfere with the sequencing of motor commands for controlling movements. Instead, they emphasized the use of nonverbal strategies for imparting information to learners, such as by using analogies for movement patterns (see Spotlight on Research).

Spotlight on Research

USING ANALOGIES TO PROMOTE IMPLICIT MOTOR LEARNING

Liao & Masters (2001) demonstrated the effectiveness of using analogies to promote implicit motor learning among learners practicing a table tennis stroke. They instructed an analogy group to imagine a right-angled triangle and to swing a table tennis racket up along the hypotenuse while hitting the ball, thus producing an appropriate movement pattern. The task required participants to strike a machine-fed ball to a target on a table tennis table. The group performed 300 practice trials. The analogy group's accuracy was compared with that of an implicit group, which practiced while repeating number sequences, and an explicit group, which was given 12 instructions for performing the stroke properly.

The results in figure 8.2 indicate that the analogy group did at least as well as the implicit learning group and outperformed the explicit learning group. When asked to reproduce the movement under stress (being evaluated by others) in a follow-up experiment, the analogy group still performed well.

APPLICATION

Analogy learning is popular within a variety of sports and among different types of learners as a method for reducing the amount of time spent verbally describing a movement pattern. For this reason, analogy learning might require learners to form shapes with limb movements to mimic the spatial orientation of specific movement patterns. In swimming, for instance, rather than describe a movement pattern in detail, many practitioners use analogies to help conceptualize the movement patterns required for learning a new stroke. For example, the breaststroke arm action is analogous to using the hands to make a keyhole shape in the water. Likewise, the breaststroke leg action resembles two semicircles. For the front crawl, many practitioners describe an S-shaped pattern during the catch, pull, and push phases of the arm stroke, and a shark fin conceptualizes the high elbow during the recovery phase. In summary, analogy learning reduces the technical information that the practitioner has to verbally communicate to each learner. It also creates an external focus for instructions and feedback.

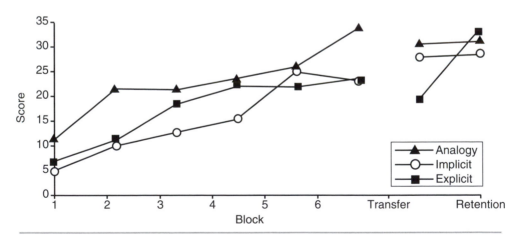

Figure 8.2 Data from Liao and Masters (2001) show the benefits of using analogies in learning a table tennis stroke.

Reprinted from C. Liao and R.S.W. Masters, 2001, "Analogy learning: A means to implicit motor learning," *Journal of Sports Sciences* 19: 307-319, by permission of Taylor & Francis Ltd. http://www.informaworld.com

Internal Versus External Focus of Attention

Abernethy and colleagues (2007) noted that research on implicit and discovery learning concurs with criticisms of an internal focus of attention in the instruction and feedback literature (e.g., Wulf et al., 2000; Wulf et al., 2001). In a series of studies, Wulf and colleagues (e.g., Shea & Wulf, 1999; Wulf et al., 2001; Wulf, Hoess, & Prinz, 1998; Wulf, Lauterbach, & Toole, 1999) provided strong support for the detrimental effects of directing learners' attention to the movements of their limbs. They observed that directing attention to the effects of learners' movements on the environment (e.g., ball trajectory after a striking action, the cutting action of a skate on the ice) can be more effective than directing their attention to their limb movements (see table 8.1 for some more examples).

Wulf et al. (1998) asked participants to learn to balance on a stabilometer. The internal-focus group focused on the movements of their feet and the external-focus group focused on the movement of the platform beneath their feet. Markers on the platform provided the external focus of attention on movement effects. This small change in focus of attention resulted in the external-focus group demonstrating superior balance learning relative to the internal-focus group. The viability of internal and external focus on learning a golf chip shot also led to similar conclusions (Shea & Wulf, 1999; Wulf et al., 1999). The internal-focus group was instructed to attend to limb movements

TABLE 8.1 Summary of Results From Focus of Attention Studies

Task	Location of attentional focus	Benefit of external focus	Study
Ski-simulator action	Feet (internal) Wheels of platform (external)	Enhanced performance (↑movement amplitude) Improved retention of skill	Wulf et al. (1998)
Golf pitch shot	Arms and legs (internal) Clubhead (external)	Improved accuracy of shot in both practice and retention	Wulf et al. (1999)
Balance on stabilometer	Feet (internal) Markers placed in front of feet (external)	Improved balance and better retention of balance Majority of performers preferred external focus	Wulf et. al. (2001)
Daily life tasks with cerebro-vascular accident patients	Limb to be used in task (internal) Object to be manipulated (external)	Movement times shorter Decreased peak velocity	Fasoli et al. (2002)
Basketball free throw	Wrist motion (internal) Basket (external)	Performance improvement Better economy of movement	Zachry et al. (2005)

and the external-focus group focused on the movement effects (the trajectory of the clubhead).

Implications for Discovery Learning

Although the benefits of an external focus of attention on learning have been demonstrated clearly in the literature, there have been few attempts to interpret the results from the constraints-led approach. By encompassing the findings within the benefits of a discovery learning strategy, dynamical systems theory provides a fruitful framework for understanding the effects of implicit learning and the role of an external focus of attention. The benefits include a deemphasis on the role of prescription through verbal communication, especially as it relates to specific body parts, and the provision of time to search for the essential relationships among performer, environmental, and task constraints in discovering a movement pattern to achieve an intended performance outcome.

Taken together, those findings support the relative efficacy of discovery learning compared with prescriptive approaches in which coaches instruct learners in step-by-step procedures. A constraints-led viewpoint suggests how learners can exploit self-organization processes in the movement system when attempting to assemble a coordination solution for a given task goal. It is interesting to note how the findings of Masters and colleagues (2002) on implicit learning coincide with the experimental outcomes on the role of self-organization processes during discovery-based practice on a ski simulator in the literature on dynamical systems (e.g., Vereijken, van Emmerik, Whiting, & Newell, 1992). It seems that an explicit emphasis on learning movement skills through verbal information provides too narrow a focus for individual learners. It does not permit them the time they need to search for their own task solutions, whereas adopting an implicit focus does provide such opportunities.

The literature on the relevance of an external focus of attention in feedback provision agrees with data from a study by Vereijken and Whiting (1990). They showed that discovery learners were free to attend to feedback information on movement effects on the environment because they were not overburdened with task instructions. Discovery strategies enabled participants to learn more effectively than prescriptive instructions on how to perform the slalom-like movements. This interpretation supporting the role of discovery learning resonates with data from two studies by Wulf and colleagues (2000) that extended understanding of the contrasting effects of an internal and external focus of attention. In these studies, Wulf and coworkers showed that an external focus of attention does not work simply because it distracts learners from thinking about their own body movements; instead, the reasons for its efficacy are far more complex.

The original question examined by Wulf and colleagues (2000) concerned whether a psychological approach of implementing a nonawareness strategy would account for the benefits of using an external focus of attention (see Singer 1985, 1988). Observing students of the tennis forehand, they first investigated the advantages of an external focus on movement effects relative to an external focus that was not related to movement effects. They instructed one group to attend to the anticipated arc of the ball leaving the racket after the forehand drive (effect group), while another group was required to focus on the trajectory of the approaching ball (antecedent information group). In both cases, the focus of attention was external and on the flight of the ball, although only one group focused on movement effects. The data in figure 8.3 demonstrate that an external focus can be more beneficial if it is directed toward the effects of learners' movements rather than toward other external information sources that distract attention away from their movements (as previously proposed by Singer, 1985, 1988).

Wulf and colleagues (2000) examined learning in two external, effect-related, attentional focus conditions in a golf-chipping task experiment. In one external-focus condition, the movement technique (arc of the clubhead) was emphasized, and in the other, the external focus of attention was the ball trajectory and target. Wulf and colleagues hypothesized that if focusing on the

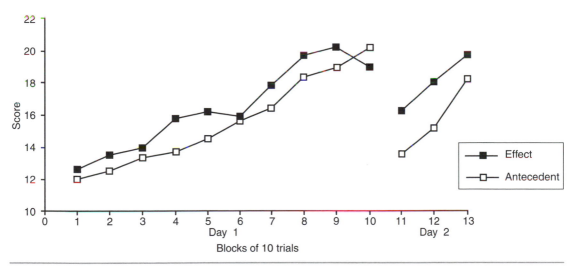

Figure 8.3 These data demonstrate that an external focus can be more beneficial if it is directed toward the effects of learners' movements rather than toward other external information sources.

Reprinted with permission from *Research Quarterly for Exercise and Sport*, Vol. 71, No. 3, 229-239, Copyright 2000 by the American Alliance for Health, Physical Education, Recreation and Dance, 1900 Association Drive, Reston, VA 20191.

action of the implement is more important than focusing on movement form, then the group that focused on the motion of the club should be more effective. Although both groups demonstrated improved efficiency with practice, the results showed yet again that instructions directing the learners' attention to an effect of the implement enhanced their learning of the task. Additionally, the benefits of focusing on movement effects related to technique were observed early in practice.

Most research has examined the distinction between internal and external focus of attention using performance outcome measures (e.g., movement accuracy or error scores) as the main dependent variable. Zachry, Wulf, Mercer, and Bezodis (2005) extended these findings to an electromyographical (EMG) analysis of movement. In this study, players shot basketball free throws while the researchers monitored electrical activity in the muscles of the players' shooting arm. Data showed that players were more accurate in shooting when using an external focus of attention. In addition, the EMG activity was lower in the biceps and triceps of the shooting arm with an external focus compared with an internal focus. Zachry and colleagues argued that the lower EMG activity signaled greater movement economy and noise reduction.

In summary, it seems that an external focus on instructions and feedback allows self-organization processes to support more effective learning and performance.

Interaction of Verbal Instructions and Feedback

Experimental research and practical examples support the benefits of an implicit learning approach that emphasizes infrequent provision of verbal communications with an external focus. However, in this chapter we have often referred to instructions and feedback interchangeably. It is possible that each type of verbal communication has different and interacting effects on behavior. Let us consider in more detail how the nature of the information that practitioners provide can influence learning.

During a bimanual coordination task, Lee, Blandin, and Proteau (1996) demonstrated the positive side of instructional constraints on coordination dynamics. As bimanual movement frequency was increased, one group of participants was instructed to maintain an antiphase pattern. Another group was told not to intervene if they felt the antiphase pattern changing to the in-phase pattern. This group's instructions matched those offered by Kelso (1981, 1984) in his original work in bimanual coordination (see Spotlight on Research, chapter 2). The nonintervention group provided support for Kelso's findings with spontaneous transitions to the in-phase mode as frequency increased.

However, the group instructed to maintain the antiphase mode were able to stick to the 180° pattern for a longer period of time. Therefore, instructions administered before practice can be an effective means of overriding the inherent dynamical tendencies of the motor system to adapt movement patterns to task requirements.

However, Hodges and Franks (2001) have questioned the wisdom of providing certain kinds of verbal instructions to learners. They were interested in whether instruction and different types of feedback interact during practice. In their experiment, participants in four groups were required to move two joysticks to create a circular pattern on a computer screen. One group received verbal instructions about how to create the circle and specific feedback about the shape they were creating (related to the task goal). Another group received verbal instructions and general feedback related to the concurrent movement of their limbs. The other two groups received no instructions and either specific or general feedback.

The results indicated that feedback related to the task goal was more beneficial than concurrent information concerning limb movement. In addition, compared with an equivalent noninstructed group, the group instructed on creating the circle showed a disadvantage in acquisition rate. It seems the instructions interfered with the learners' ability to use concurrent feedback to create the required shape. These studies indicate that when learning complex coordination patterns, detailed instructions and feedback are not always necessary and may waste valuable practice time. Interestingly, the noninstructed group showed more variability, indicating that this group initially was more actively involved in breaking from established patterns and searching for new functional behaviors.

These findings support the outcomes of an earlier study by Green and Flowers (1991), which indicated that verbal instructions can interfere with movement production. Learners were asked to catch an object on a computer screen using a cursor linked to a joystick. A group that received instructions before practice was less accurate (and less variable) than a group that learned without instructions. According to the authors, the implication is that verbal instructions simply add to the learner's attentional load in certain tasks, thereby interrupting the learner's ability to concentrate on satisfying task constraints.

These findings suggest that learners do not need overspecific instructions on movement patterns. Rather, the success of the task goal–oriented and noninstructed groups in finding appropriate movement behaviors signals that learners need time to search for their own solutions. Instructions and feedback in tandem may not be necessary provided that learners have a clear movement goal. In a more applied study, Magill and Schoenfelder-Zohdi (1996) manipulated both instructions and knowledge of performance feedback for learners of gymnastics skills. As in the Hodges and Franks (2001) experiment, instructions were beneficial only if they directed learners to information that they could use to achieve the task more successfully.

Due to observed temporary performance benefits, it is possible that practitioners are fooled into believing that augmented feedback is effective. For example, Mononen, Vitasalo, Kontinnen, and Era (2003) showed that rifle shooters who received kinematic feedback on 100% of acquisition trials outperformed a 50% group and a control group following a 2-day retention period. However, this enhanced performance effect did not last when the group's shooting performances were compared 10 days after acquisition. After 10 days without feedback, their accuracy had fallen to a similar level as the other groups in the study.

In summary, it seems that providing additional instructions on how to perform motor skills is often not helpful when task goal–related feedback is naturally available to constrain the learner's search activities (Hodges & Franks, 2001). Further, providing learners with detailed pretask instructions and concurrent movement-related feedback often can prove to be too much information, particularly in complex tasks where spatiotemporal demands are high. Moreover, the effects of providing verbal instructions on every trial are not long lasting, and less frequent use of performance-related feedback will suffice.

Verbal Communication and Movement Disorders

An interesting consideration concerning the relative value of verbal instructions involves learners who exhibit impairment in the development of motor coordination. For example, Wallen and Walker (1995) noted that practitioners who treat children with DCD use several different approaches due to the wide range of symptoms each child may present. Despite this suggestion, Niemeijer and colleagues (2003) found that pediatric therapists more frequently gave command- or feedback-style comments (mean of 60 times) as opposed to adopting a questioning style, sharing knowledge with comments in an attempt to elicit understanding in DCD children (mean of 21) affected by problems with motor coordination. Although conditions such as DCD are not associated with any form of clinical or neurological disorder, much research has focused solely on deficits in cognitive processing and movement planning (Henderson, 1992). Therefore, it is tempting to assume that simple verbal explanations and lots of feedback from the therapist may enable learners to better understand what is required of them.

However, it seems increasingly likely that the complex interaction of factors that contribute to movement disorders such as visual deficits cannot be easily remedied through the verbal commands of practitioners alone (Johnston et al., 2002; Mon-Williams, Tresilian, & Wann, 1999; Sigmundsson, Hansen, & Talcott, 2003). Given that the foundation of the constraints-led approach is the consideration of the human movement system as a complex, dynamical system, the application of this philosophy for DCD sufferers seems apt. We would argue that the same principles of directed search and guided discovery described throughout this book are applicable to all learners, and we believe that current and future research in this area will support our arguments (for a review of evidence-based practice for DCD, see Ayyash & Preece, 2003).

Summary

A practitioner's verbal communications seem to be the most powerful and direct form of informational constraint used to alter movement patterns. However, research suggests that verbal instructions can have both positive and negative effects on skill acquisition. Attentional focus and the availability of outcome-related feedback have been shown to be important factors in mediating the benefits that learners stand to gain from directed search. In addition, the nature of the task to be performed is important since the presentation of different information streams can interfere with the performance of complex coordination patterns.

The synthesis of theory and empirical findings provides a solid platform for understanding why discovery learning should form the foundation of practice. Practitioners should use verbal guidance, instructions, and feedback sparingly and only when the learner cannot gain information about the task goal in another way. Hodges and Franks (2002) suggest that "tasks which place more emphasis on the perceptual-motor demands and have complex response requirements will benefit less from explicit instruction about the details of the movement, at least early in learning" (p. 801). Optimal practice methods involve plenty of opportunities for learners to discover how to harness motor system dfs in coordination solutions with little emphasis on verbal instructions by practitioners. Such an approach signals a different role for the practitioner, as we suggested in chapter 4.

In chapter 9, we discuss the pedagogical challenge of decreasing learners' reliance on verbal instructions and feedback, particularly as they relate to body-part movements in space. The question for practitioners is, how do we facilitate search activities without overreliance on verbal instructions? One answer may lie in using video demonstrations and other common visual modeling techniques to direct the learner's search for suitable coordination solutions.

SELF-TEST QUESTIONS

1. Advise motor skills practitioners on how and when they should provide task instructions to learners.

2. For optimal skill acquisition to occur, do performers need to be aware that they are learning motor skills? Refer to the organizational complexity of the CNS in your answer.

3. Select a sport or physical activity and identify an important skill for learners to practice. Next, create a list of coaching instructions for learners using a traditional internal focus of attention. Finally, create a list of similar instructions using an external focus of attention.

4. Discuss how focus of attention mediates the benefit a learner gains from verbal instructions and feedback. (Tip: Consider the learner's experience, the nature of the task constraints, the availability of feedback, and so on.)

5. Using a skill of your choice, identify effective movement analogies that would encourage learners to search and explore different areas of the perceptual-motor landscape.

6. Why is a performer who learns by practicing a skill repeatedly without making any errors more likely to learn the skill implicitly?

ADDITIONAL READING

1. Abernethy, B., Maxwell, J.P., Masters, R.W.S., van der kamp, J., & Jackson, R. C. (2007). Attentional processes in skill learning and expert performance. In G. Tenenbaum & R. Eklund (Eds.), *Handbook of Sport Psychology* (3rd ed., pp. 245-265). New York: John Wiley & Sons.

2. Beek, P.J. (2000). Toward a theory of implicit learning in the perceptual-motor domain. *International Journal of Sport Psychology, 31*, 547-554.

3. Hodges, N.J., & Franks, I.M. (2002). Modelling coaching practice: the role of instruction and demonstration. *Journal of Sports Sciences, 20*, 793-811.

4. Wulf, G., Shea, C., & Park, J-H. (2001). Attention and motor performance: Preferences for and advantages of an external focus. *Research Quarterly for Exercise and Sport, 72*(4), 335-344.

CHAPTER 9

Observational Learning as Directed Search

CHAPTER OUTLINE

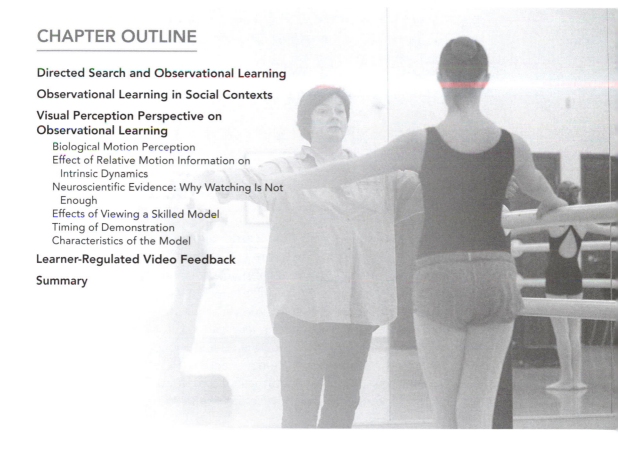

In chapter 8, we suggested that traditional theories of motor learning and teaching practices tend to overemphasize verbal information such as instructions and prescriptive feedback. Throughout this book we have acknowledged that search and discovery are important learning processes. In practical terms, however, it is often unwise to pursue a totally discovery-based pedagogical approach. This is one reason why we have proposed the strategy of directing learners' search for functional coordination solutions (see also Pettifor, 1999). In order to structure a safe and productive practice environment, a physical education teacher or coach would need to understand what we mean by the term *discovery learning* in this context. An unstructured practice environment would be inefficient in terms of the time it may take to learn a skill (Daly, Bass, & Finch, 2001), and it also might be physically and mentally harmful to the learner.

In this chapter, we will examine how practitioners can use visual images and skill demonstrations to direct and constrain the learner's search activities during practice. We will discuss how sensitivity to biological motion features in humans can be exploited when learning occurs by observation and modeling. It will emerge that, from a constraints-led perspective, the aim of observational learning is not to imitate a technique, but to use the demonstration to direct the search for a functional coordination solution for a particular movement problem. It is also important to note the similarities with the conceived role of verbal instructions in guiding search behavior during motor learning discussed in the previous chapter. Regardless of whether information is presented visually or verbally, the aim is not to prescribe a specific course of action during practice for each learner; rather, it will become apparent that augmented information (whether presented in visual or verbal mode) constrains exploratory search for movement solutions (Araújo et al., 2004).

Directed Search and Observational Learning

The nature of the constraints placed on learners limits their search for more functional movement patterns. The more constraints that learners need to satisfy, the less opportunity exists for experimentation and exploration through self-directed or discovery learning. In this respect, a visual demonstration of a skill should be conceptualized as an instructional constraint (part of the subset of task constraints) that guides learners' exploratory activity. For example, taekwondo students who practice a kick previously demonstrated by a teacher can be constrained by the model's action. However, if the learners are not given a demonstration but simply asked to defend themselves against an opponent, this type of exploratory practice would represent a lower level

A student practicing a kick previously demonstrated by a teacher can be constrained by the model's action.

of constraint because the learners' search activities have not been directed by the model's demonstration.

Imitating a model such as a parent, skilled performer, or coach demonstrating a motor pattern is a common activity in daily life and is intended to facilitate motor skill acquisition (De Maeght & Prinz, 2004). Also known as observational modeling, **observational learning** is the process whereby a person assimilates and sometimes adopts or replicates the behavioral patterns and actions of others as a direct consequence of observing those behaviors (Ashford, Bennett, & Davids, 2006). Observational learning initially became a focus of study in social psychological research on imitation (e.g., Bandura, 1962, 1969) and has experienced a recent resurgence in popularity in areas such as neurobiology, robotics, and artificial intelligence (e.g., Schaal, 1999; Schaal, Ijspeert, & Billard, 2003). Observers can include spectators, learners, students, teammates, and opposing athletes. The observed individuals could include demonstrators, performers, or models. A number of practitioners, including physical therapists, sports medicine specialists, physical trainers, physical education instructors, teachers, and coaches have increasingly used observational learning methods, suggesting that its role is recognized and well understood.

Observational Learning in Social Contexts

Observational learning can occur in formal teaching, coaching, and rehabilitation and training contexts such as when an image, mirrored view, or demonstration is provided to help people learn a particular task, skill, or behavior. Alternatively, incidental observational learning can occur whenever and wherever a person is exposed to the behavior of others (e.g., watching a sport event on television). People sometimes pick up subtle information regarding appropriate social behaviors in new or unfamiliar settings (Jarvis, Holford, & Griffin, 2003). People can also acquire a strong familiarity or awareness of many skills by simply observing others performing such tasks, even though their observations may not be associated with any conscious desire or intention to reproduce such behaviors or actions. In this respect, observational learning can act as a social affordance in gaining information on what actions are performed by a significant other (e.g., a parent, teacher, or another performer) prior to learning (for a discussion of social affordances, see Fajen et al., in press).

Although it has been argued that some motor learning can occur without movement (e.g., McCullagh & Weiss, 2001), when observational modeling is used as an instructional protocol to facilitate acquisition of new movement behaviors, it is rarely used in isolation. Instead, it is typically used in conjunction with other learning strategies, including verbal instructions, visual imagery, and physical practice, to establish information–movement couplings. An important aim in future research is to understand how these modes of transmitting information to learners interact to constrain search activities (see Spotlight on Research). From a constraints-led standpoint, a relevant theoretical framework for aiding understanding of the relation between modeling effects and practice as a search process is Scully and Newell's (1985) visual perception perspective on observational learning, which we discuss next.

 ## Spotlight on Research

HOW TO COMBINE WORDS AND IMAGES FOR EFFECTIVE MOTOR LEARNING

An interesting question concerns the ideal combination of verbal and visual information that practitioners can employ while learners observe a skilled model. Janelle, Champenoy, Coombes, and Mousseau (2003) predicted that a combination of verbal and visual cues would be most beneficial to a group of learners practicing a precision kicking task. They suggested that both information modalities would interact to constrain selective

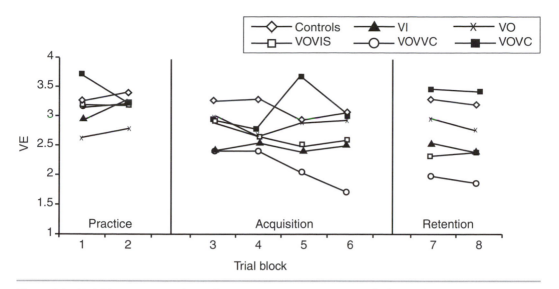

Figure 9.1 Variable error scores for each group in practicing a precision kicking task.

Reprinted from C.M. Janelle et al., 2003, "Mechanics of attentional cueing during observational learning to facilitate motor skill acquisition," *Journal of Sports Sciences* 21: 825-838, by permission of Taylor & Francis Ltd. http://www.informaworld.com

attention by accentuating important task components. Sixty novice adult players (18-27 years) participated in the study and were randomly allocated to the following groups: discovery (control); verbal instructions (VI); video only (VO); video and verbal cues (VOVC); video and visual cues (VOVIS); and video, verbal, and visual cues (VOVVC). A technique analysis of form and outcome accuracy scores were monitored over 80 trials of practice. The variable error scores for each group are presented in figure 9.1.

The VOVVC group receiving a combination of attention-focusing cues outperformed the other groups in acquisition and retention. Further, the accuracy scores were reflected by more appropriate movement form in this group compared with the other treatment groups, as revealed by the technique analysis.

APPLICATION

It seems clear that for a closed skill under stable environmental conditions, such as the precision kicking task, learners benefit from the practitioner giving detailed direction about the desired movement pattern and performance outcome. What remains unclear from this research is whether the treatments that each group received were actually powerful enough to redirect attentional strategies as suggested by the results. A combination of eye-movement registration techniques and self-report interviews may help to yield this information. In addition, the limited number of trials employed in the study and short retention period (24 hours) say little about the permanence of these effects. Future research is necessary to consider the generality of Janelle and colleagues' (2003) findings to other types of task constraints and cueing strategies.

Identify a sport or physical activity with task constraints that differ from precision kicking and outline how verbal and visual information can be provided to focus learners' attention on key variables that specify successful performance outcomes.

Visual Perception Perspective on Observational Learning

Although a variety of theoretical explanations have been proposed over the years for interpreting observational learning effects, the visual perception perspective advocated by Scully and Newell (Scully, 1986, 1987, 1988; Scully & Newell, 1985) provides a powerful, theoretically based account of the visual processes underlying this learning phenomenon. Specifically, it emphasizes the nature of the perceptual information that observers pick up to constrain movement production. According to this view, changes in motor behavior following observational learning depend on the perception of relative motion information from a model, which observers use to assemble stable coordination patterns during a particular movement activity. The term **relative motion** refers to the specific spatiotemporal relationships among and within limbs, as well as the organization of the performer's limbs relative to the surrounding environment. The literature on biological motion (e.g., Johansson, 1973, 1975) demonstrates that relative motion is the principal source of visual information that observers use to identify and classify different types of human movement activities, such as walking, cycling, and gymnastic moves.

Biological Motion Perception

The emphasis of the visual perception perspective on biological motion as the key information that learners perceive from demonstrations (for a review, see Johansson, von Hofsten, & Jansson, 1980) has been productively linked with Newell's (1985) framework of motor learning stages (see chapter 4). During skill acquisition, early learning requires the search for and assembly of a functional coordination pattern. The later stages, on the other hand, involve experimentation with the key parameters of the coordination pattern in optimizing performance (Newell, 1985). The visual perception perspective (Scully & Newell, 1985) advocates that the human visual system is able to minimize and directly perceive information about the topological characteristics of the relative motion of a demonstrated action (Cutting & Proffitt, 1982). Humans are surprisingly good at selecting and using information from biological motion to identify actions, and the information on the relative motions between the body's limbs and joints can aid motor learning.

Once a learner perceives relative motion (i.e., the movements of body segments relative to one another), it acts as an informational constraint on the emergence of a coordination pattern that is essential to a task being learned. Recall from chapter 3 that informational constraints guide the learner's search for the optimal task solutions within the perceptual-motor landscape (Warren, 1988, 1990). Some evidence exists for the idea that observation of relative motion information is enough to guide the search for appropriate coordination solutions during motor learning.

For example, Ward, Williams, and Bennett (2002) examined the relationships among visual-search strategy, anticipation, and biological motion perception in tennis. Tennis players were required to perform motor responses to forehand and backhand drive shots presented in video film format and as point-light images. The point-light images were created by attaching reflective markers to the players' major anatomical sites before filming the players performing various shots against a black background. In this scenario, the point-light display presentations contained the same relative motion pattern as conveyed in the film but with the background and structural information removed. When viewing point-light sequences, participants employed fewer fixations (5.8 versus 7.2) of longer duration (597 versus 457 milliseconds) to a smaller number of fixation locations (3.8 versus 4.6) compared with the normal film display. Despite these differences in fixation usage, participants under the point-light constraints were able to perceive as much relevant relative motion information to support movement approximation as when viewing films.

Effect of Relative Motion Information on Intrinsic Dynamics

Horn, Williams, and Scott (2002) also reported changes in search behavior when female soccer players viewed demonstrations of a chipped soccer pass presented in point-light compared with video format. Compared with controls, no learning differences were reported for the point-light display and video-presentation groups. Interestingly, the point-light display group showed a more selective visual-search strategy than the video-presentation group. The differences in search strategy resulted from the removal of key environmental information related to the mainly irrelevant background structure within the display. These variations in search strategy illustrate how performers might acquire information to guide skill acquisition.

Studies by Ward and colleagues (2002) and Horn and colleagues (2002) showed how the presentation of key informational constraints in relative motion of models can direct learners' search for coordination solutions and constrain visual-search activities. It follows that coaches and teachers need to identify the nature of information that learners acquire so that the content and presentation of information during a visual demonstration can be enhanced to promote skill acquisition. Linking these findings to Newell's (1985) model of motor learning, it seems that visual demonstrations should facilitate the early stage of skill learning by conveying relative motion information essential for the assembly of a novel coordination pattern (Scully & Newell, 1985). Later in learning, when the goal of the task demands the refinement of an already established coordination pattern, observational modeling should help the perception of dynamic features for optimal scaling of a movement pattern (e.g., producing a pattern that varies in force, timing, or duration).

Ashford and coworkers (2006) have conducted an extensive meta-analysis on the published and unpublished observational modeling literature to quantify the relative strength of the effects of observational learning on movement performance or movement dynamics being learned. The overall mean observational modeling treatment effects were $\delta_{Bi}^u = 0.77$ for movement dynamics and $\delta_{Bi}^u = 0.17$ for movement outcome measures. For both measures, the literature showed a significant advantage of observational modeling over practice-only control conditions. The magnitude of effects obtained for observational learning was far stronger for movement dynamics compared with movement outcome measures, confirming the advantage of observational modeling during motor learning. Observational learning was particularly beneficial for skill acquisition in serial tasks ($\delta_{Bi}^u = MD = 1.62$ and $MO = 0.61$). There were slightly reduced effects for continuous tasks ($\delta_{Bi}^u = MD = 1.01$ and $MO = 0.51$), and smaller to medium effects for discrete tasks ($\delta_{Bi}^u = MD = 0.56$ and $MO = 0.10$). These findings are consistent with the predictions of the visual perception perspective on observational learning and confirm that demonstrations primarily convey relative motions required to approximate modeled movement behaviors.

However, due to the specificity of the information scaled to a specific model's intrinsic dynamics, such as anatomical and physical characteristics and coordination tendencies, observation may not facilitate learning unless verbal instructions or other optimization procedures are incorporated into the demonstration. For example, as noted earlier, Janelle and colleagues (2003) have demonstrated that learners who received a combination of verbal and visual information while learning a soccer-kicking task reproduced a model's kicking technique better than learners who received either informational source separately.

Neuroscientific Evidence: Why Watching Is Not Enough

It has been argued that human brains have evolved to mentally simulate actions by using **mirror neurons** (e.g., Calvo-Merino, Glaser, Grèzes, Passingham, & Haggard, 2005). These neurons are activated when a learner performs an action or watches another person perform an action, and neuroscientific research is starting to pinpoint which areas in the brain are active while observers watch biological motion (e.g., Michels et al., 2005; Pelphrey et al., 2003). For example, researchers have used functional magnetic resonance imaging (fMRI) to show that perception of biological motion versus arbitrary point-light displays is differentiated by the level of activation in the brain's superior temporal sulcus region (Pelphrey et al., 2003).

But it seems that watching movement performance is not enough. For example, when expert and nonexpert dancers watched video images of classical ballet and capoeira performances, fMRI of the expert dancers' cortical interconnections revealed greater bilateral activation of visual and motor sections mediated by mirror neurons (Calvo-Merino et al., 2005). These findings suggest that observation enhances learning when a motor pattern is already an established part of a performer's intrinsic dynamics. It seems likely that mirror neurons play a crucial role in constraining motor learning through both learning and doing. They also may enable humans to perceive and approximate relative motion information from images.

Empirical work on the visual perception approach to observational learning (Scully & Newell, 1985) is beginning to reveal its validity, and there has been a tendency to examine coordination changes associated with observational learning. A few early studies investigating the effects of modeling on movement coordination with kinematic measures gave it some credibility (e.g., Magill & Schoenfelder-Zohdi, 1996; Southard & Higgins, 1987; Whiting, Bijlard, & den Brinker, 1987). In later studies, comparisons have actually been made between participants' specific movement coordination patterns in control or modeling groups compared with the pattern demonstrated by a model (e.g., Al-Abood, Davids, & Bennett, 2001; Al-Abood, Davids, Bennett, Ashford, & Marin, 2001). This comparison procedure is essential to determine whether modeling or control groups have approximated the model's relative motion pattern underlying movement coordination. The model's pattern is considered to be a potentially optimal solution to the coordination problem, and so approximating it supports the benefits of observational learning. This is a considerable advance in the literature from the visual perception perspective; early studies tended to examine whether modeling participants developed coordination patterns different from those of the control participants.

Effects of Viewing a Skilled Model

What is the evidence that visual demonstration of a skilled model can actually direct learners' search for functional coordination patterns? In one study, Schoenfelder-Zohdi (1992) examined some of Scully and Newell's (1985) main predictions. Novices learned the ski-simulator task (Vereijken, van Emmerik, Whiting, & Newell, 1992) over 5 days of practice after being assigned to one of three groups. Participants in the discovery learning group received written instructions about the experimental procedures and the task goal and did not observe any visual demonstrations. Participants in the modeling-1 group observed a skilled model before the first practice trial and during the intertrial intervals only on the first day of practice. Participants in the modeling-5 group followed the same procedures but continued to observe the model throughout 4 ensuing practice days. Schoenfelder-Zohdi recorded movement outcome (amplitude and frequency of the platform derived from displacement data) and coordination data (displacement and velocity of the platform and angular displacement of the body's joints relative to one another, that is, ipsilateral and contralateral relationships).

If observational learning effects were due to visual demonstrations directing the learner's search for a movement solution, then the modeling-5 group,
which received the greatest amount of guidance during their physical practice,
would have shown the best results. By the end of the first day of practice, the
modeling participants exhibited coordination patterns similar to the model's,
while the discovery learners showed coordination patterns different from the
model's. By the end of day 5, however, the discovery group's patterns approximated the model's pattern, with movement coordination becoming similar to
that of the modeling participants. For movement outcomes, modeling groups
performed significantly better than the discovery group.

We can conclude that the model conveyed relative motion information
to observers who spent less time (1 day) assembling a solution that was
approximate to the model's coordination pattern. Although it is interesting
to note how powerful discovery learning seems as a practice strategy, in this
study it did lead to a longer search time (5 days). Therefore, it appears that
modeling reduced the practice time required to assemble the appropriate
coordination pattern by directing novice observers' search of the perceptual-
motor workspace.

Timing of Demonstration

Schoenfelder-Zohdi's (1992) findings were extended in studies by Al-Abood
and colleagues (Al-Abood, Davids, & Bennett, 2001; Al-Abood, Davids, Bennett,
Ashford, et al., 2001) of a dart-throwing task. Al-Abood and colleagues
attempted to build upon Schoenfelder-Zohdi's findings by analyzing learning
with a continuous, high-constraint task. Their objective was to examine the
generality of the findings using a low-constraint, discrete throwing action.
Due to the need to examine the effects of visual demonstrations on learners' capacities to find appropriate coordination solutions, an investigation of
changes in coordination was necessary.

Because observational modeling conveys relative motion information
essential for finding appropriate movement coordination patterns, one of the
questions Al-Abood and colleagues examined concerned whether the observation of visual demonstrations, particularly early in learning, facilitates skill
acquisition (Scully & Newell, 1985). In one study, Al-Abood, Davids, and Bennett (2001) investigated whether observational modeling to direct a search
toward the model's coordination was required throughout the learning phase,
or whether early presentation of the model could be complemented by physical practice to enhance search activity during practice. They expected that
the participants in modeling groups would approximate the model's relative
motion more quickly and accurately than participants who practiced without demonstrations, as found by Schoenfelder-Zohdi (1992). An additional
question concerned whether adequate relative motion information could be
acquired from the model to constrain observers' search activities early in learn-

ing, or whether continuous exposure to the model was necessary to direct search throughout practice. They anticipated that discovery learners would not necessarily assemble coordination solutions similar to the model's pattern because their search was not being directed to an appropriate attractor as a stable task solution.

In the study, the task was to learn an underarm, intralimb coordination pattern so that the participants could throw a modified dart (larger than a typical dart, with greater mass at the throwing end that affected its flight path) to a modified dartboard (22.5-centimeter radius) located 3 meters away in the horizontal plane (Al-Abood, Davids, & Bennett, 2001; Al-Abood, Davids, Bennett, Ashford, et al., 2001). The task goal was to score a high number of points by throwing the dart as close as possible to the central concentric ring on the board. The score of each trial ranged from 10 to 0 points, with 10 points being allocated for darts landing in the central ring and 0 points for the outer ring.

Three experimental groups (discovery learning, early modeling, and continuous modeling) performed 100-KR acquisition trials (trials with knowledge of results provided) on day 1 and 20-KR retention trials on day 2. The groups varied in their amount of exposure to visual demonstrations to direct their search during task practice. The early-modeling group observed six videotaped visual demonstrations performed by a skilled model just before the beginning of the acquisition phase and were instructed to use the demonstration information to help them learn the task. The continuous-modeling group observed the visual demonstration tape throughout the practice period after every block of 20 trials. The discovery group was left to assemble a task solution without any visual demonstrations. To quantify coordination, a ratio of upper-arm angle to lower-arm angle was calculated for each data point in a time series of a trial that each participant performed and was compared with the mean normalized ratio of the model's trials.

An analysis of coordination measures revealed that both modeling groups' coordination patterns approximated the model's relative motion early in learning and in retention more closely than the discovery learners' (see figure 9.2). There was also a difference between the early-modeling and continuous-modeling groups early in practice, although the beneficial effects of physical practice could be clearly seen in the lack of differences between both groups during the retention phase.

The data confirmed that observational learning could facilitate skill acquisition by directing learners' search toward appropriate coordination patterns. It seems that video presentation of a movement skill can act as an important instructional constraint on the learner's exploratory search activities. Discovery of appropriate coordination solutions by the early-modeling group occurred as a result of early guided physical practice. This conclusion can be drawn from the continuous-modeling group's faster time to approximate the coordination shown by the skilled model during the acquisition phase and the lack

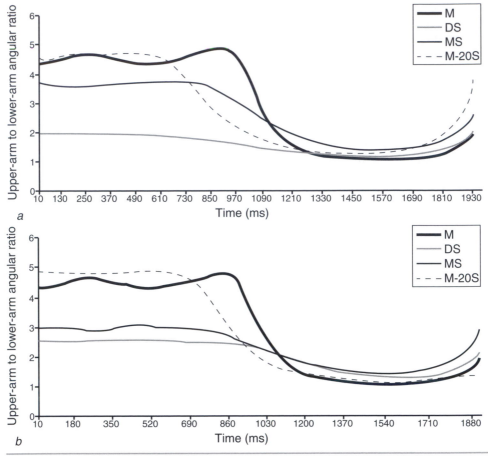

Figure 9.2 Data from Al-Abood, Davids, and Bennett (2001) show how modeling influences discovery learning. Note how exposure to the expert model in both modeling groups (early and continuous) helped them to approximate the expert's coordination pattern more effectively than the discovery group, who were not exposed to modeling effects. M = expert model's coordination pattern; DS = discovery learning group; MS = early modeling group; M-20S = continuous modeling group

Adapted, by permission, from S.A. Al-Abood et al., 1999, Visual modeling and discovery learning as constraints on the acquisition of coordination. In *Psychology of sport and exercise: Enhancing the quality of life*, edited by V. Hosek, P. Tilinger and L. Bilek (Prague: FEPSAC), 56-58.

of differences between the early- and continuous-modeling groups in retention. Finally, it seems that continuous direction of search is not necessary if opportunities for physical practice are provided.

Characteristics of the Model

If the logic of a constraints-led perspective is valid, then we would expect the characteristics of a model to have an important bearing on learners' practice activity. Because modeling constrains search during motor learning, it follows that model characteristics have to be carefully selected to facilitate search. For example, children learning to ski may benefit from watching a child rather than an adult because of the closer fit between learner and model psychophysical constraints. Differences in limb lengths, strength, and hand sizes between an adult model and child learner might result in some demonstrated movement solutions being less useful for the learner.

Some existing evidence has shown that using peer-group models is beneficial in motor learning, particularly when there is a skill differential between learners and models. D'Arripe-Longueville, Gernigon, Huet, Cadopi, and Winnykamen (2002) found that in a swimming task for children, peer models who were more skilled elicited more effective learning, primarily by constraining the children's desire to emulate the models through hard work in practice. Novice models did not influence the self-efficacy of learners as much as the skilled peer-group models. Other work by d'Arripe-Longueville, Gernigon, Huet, Winnykamen, and Cadopi (2002) found that gender differences in peer-group modeling led to a greater amount of modeling in asymmetrical (different-sex) dyads, particularly affecting the number of practice trials undertaken by male children.

Another explanation of such findings is that when watching a novice model, learners are more actively involved in problem solving and goal attainment than when observing a skilled model (Hodges & Franks, 2002). In addition, learners are benefiting from receiving variable information during practice and discovering what works as well as what does not work. These factors may also contribute to the apparent benefits of learners observing models and not simply copying an idealized technique.

Learners watch as a child demonstrates a skill.

Clearly, further work is needed on the psychophysical constraints of models on learners, particularly concerning child–adult variations and gender differences between model and learner. Another interesting issue is whether models for disabled athletes need to have the same physical characteristics as the learners. For example, would a disabled model or a model without disabilities best facilitate practice of disabled or injured learners? If modeling directs learners' search, then it follows that congruence between model and learner constraints should be relatively high to optimally constrain exploratory activities.

This is an important area for future research on observational learning. It reflects ideas from ecological psychology research on affordances for action, which suggests that variations in learners' body dimensions and action capabilities can occur over different timescales (e.g., instantaneous changes can occur due to fatigue, injury, and use of implements, whereas long-term changes occur due to growth, development, and training). According to Fajen and colleagues (in press), a period of perceptual-motor calibration is needed to habituate to such short- and long-term changes so that affordances for action can be detected by learners. Similarly, it appears that model characteristics need to be calibrated with those of learners to enhance learning from visual demonstrations.

Learner-Regulated Video Feedback

Video feedback is becoming increasingly popular as a practical tool for movement practitioners. Janelle, Barba, Frehlich, Tennant, and Cauraugh (1997) considered two questions of particular interest. First, is video feedback better than other types of feedback? Second, to what extent do learners benefit from choosing when and how much feedback they receive? Janelle and colleagues used a precision ball-throwing task with the nondominant limb to address these questions. To ascertain whether movement-related feedback (KP) was of greater benefit than outcome-related feedback (KR), three groups of learners received KP via video feedback while another group received KR.

Another concern of Janelle and colleagues (1997) was whether learners should receive KP in summary format. For this reason, one of the KP groups received KP after every 5 trials (summary format). They also suggested that learners would benefit most from choosing the schedule of KP provision. Therefore, the final two groups consisted of a group that decided when KP was given (self) and a group that had no choice but did have a feedback schedule matching that of the self group (yoked). All participants were filmed performing the acquisition trials and had access to KR as they observed where the ball landed on the target.

The form scores from Janelle and colleagues' (1997) study clearly supported the use of video feedback (see figure 9.3). The KR group consistently

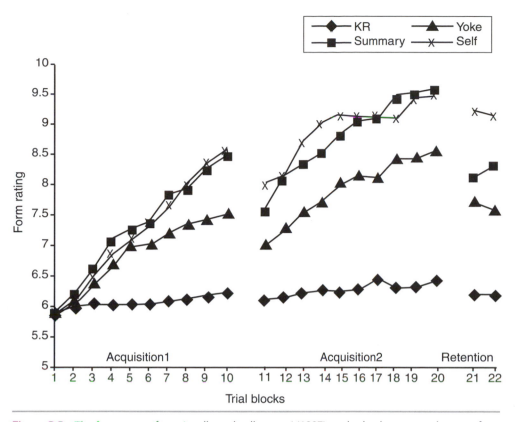

Figure 9.3 The form scores from Janelle and colleagues' (1997) study clearly support the use of video feedback.

Reprinted with permission from *Research Quarterly for Exercise and Sport*, Vol. 68, No. 4, 269-279, Copyright 1997 by the American Alliance for Health, Physical Education, Recreation and Dance, 1900 Association Drive, Reston, VA 20191.

showed poorer throwing form than the KP groups. Accuracy scores were also lowest in the KR group. During acquisition trials, the summary and self groups performed equally well. However, in no-feedback retention trials, the better movement form came from the self group. Finally, the yoked group appeared to have suffered from not being able to choose when KP was administered. Despite receiving the same amount of KP at the same time as the self group (on 11% of trials), the retention of the yoked group was not as high.

The findings of Janelle and colleagues' (1997) study raised several questions for practitioners and performers alike. First, the similarity in movement form and outcome scores indicates that when learners focus on achieving good form, they tend to successfully achieve outcomes as a by-product. Second, it seems important to allow the learner some control in determining when movement-related feedback is supplied. It is likely that self-regulation of feedback enhances motivation and also leads to more effective learning strategies. Also, this research has clearly demonstrated that in multiple-df tasks, KR alone is insufficient to optimize learning. The learner benefits most from a modest provision of movement-related feedback in order to develop the most salient aspects of the skill. Finally, as Newell (1996) pointed out, demonstrations only provide the learner with kinematic information about motion. Tasks like precision throwing that are primarily regulated by kinetic feedback may also benefit from other forms of feedback delivery.

Summary

Practice may be best described as a search process in which learners find appropriate coordination solutions for movement problems under varying task constraints. The role of observational learning methods is to direct learners' search activities. The literature reviewed in this chapter and chapter 8 suggests that, in order to facilitate the learner's search activities, practitioners need to avoid providing too many verbal instructions or feedback during practice. Establishing a visual demonstration or image of a skill gives learners the time to exploit strategies of discovery learning and to harness self-organization processes in finding suitable coordination patterns for carrying out specific tasks. As with verbal instructions that focus too much on the movements of specific body parts during skill acquisition, the use of visual demonstrations to focus on specific joints or limb segments should be avoided. Instead, visual demonstrations should emphasize the effects of the movements on environmental properties such as flight trajectory after a ball has been hit or thrown.

Videotaped demonstrations or images of model behavior can help learners find suitable coordination solutions more quickly and safely, although the aim should not be to imitate a model. Rather, the model demonstrates a possible coordination solution that may guide learners' physical practice activities (search patterns). The role of the demonstration is to get learners in the ballpark, so to speak, for relevant coordination solutions. To this extent, learners may benefit from choosing when they view demonstrations or augmented feedback, therefore taking greater responsibility for their own learning (Janelle et al., 1997). Research suggests a new role for pedagogists based on a strategy of directing learners' search for relevant coordination patterns through the use of limited verbal instructions and visual demonstrations.

Although various tasks have been used across many different investigations since early research contributions in the 1960s and 1970s, limited effort has been directed toward methodically building on the early exploration of the effects of task constraints. Further, equivocality in the literature on observational learning seems to be due to a number of key weaknesses, including limited disclosure of the verbal instructions accompanying investigations, inconsistency in implementing control conditions, and the tendency to confuse motor performance and motor learning in experimental designs.

Many of these methodological concerns have since been addressed by researchers (e.g., Al-Abood, Bennett, Moreno Hernandez, Ashford, & Davids, 2002; Horn et al., 2002). Investigators now are more likely to use a wide range of methodologies to explore observational modeling processes, including various neuropsychological brain-scanning techniques (e.g., Decety et al., 1997; Decety & Grèzes, 1999), visual eye-tracking procedures (e.g., Horn et al., 2002), and qualitative or quantitative movement analysis (e.g., typically approximated to the modeled action) allied with traditional performance outcome measures. The former measures represent recent innovations in the literature and a small percentage of data, whereas the latter measures have produced a considerable quantity of data, particularly for performance outcomes. There remains an ongoing need for the extensive use of statistical techniques like meta-analysis to verify specific trends and examine contentious issues in the huge amount of published and unpublished data in the literature on observational learning (see Ashford et al., 2007). Such techniques would permit more reliable generalization of the principal effects associated with observational learning.

SELF-TEST QUESTIONS

1. List the advantages and disadvantages of a learner engaging in discovery learning without any intervention from a practitioner.

2. Choose a motor skill from a sport with which you are familiar and identify relative motion characteristics from a demonstration that an observer should be guided toward.

3. What research evidence exists for the visual perception perspective proposed by Scully and Newell (1985)?

4. What factors should a practitioner consider when planning a practice session with respect to demonstrations?

5. How can learner-regulated feedback be an effective strategy for practitioners?

6. What is perceptual-motor calibration, and how might it enhance a learner's capacity to perceive affordances for action from observing visual demonstrations? Outline your answer with reference to different groups of learners, including disabled athletes, children, and older adults.

ADDITIONAL READING

1. Ashford, D., Bennett, S., & Davids, K. (2006). Observational modelling effects for movement dynamics and movement outcome measures across differing task constraints: A meta-analysis. *Journal of Motor Behavior, 38,* 185-205.

2. Calvo-Merino, B., Glaser, D.E., Grèzes, J., Passingham, R.E., & Haggard, P. (2005). Action observation and acquired motor skills: An fMRI study with expert dancers. *Cerebral Cortex, 15,* 1243-1249.

3. D'Arripe-Longueville, F., Gernigon, C., Huet, M.L., Cadopi, M., & Winnyka-men, F. (2002). Peer tutoring in a physical education setting: Influence of tutor skill level on novice learners' motivation and performance. *Journal of Teaching in Physical Education, 22,* 105-123.

4. Janelle, C. M., Champenoy, J. D., Coombes, S. A., & Mousseau, M. B. (2003). Mechanics of attentional cueing during observational learning to facilitate motor skill acquisition. *Journal of Sports Sciences, 21,* 825-838.

5. Scully, D.M., & Newell, K.M. (1985). Observational learning and the acqui-sition of motor skills: Toward a visual perception perspective. *Journal of Human Movement Studies, 11,* 169-186.

CHAPTER 10

Implementing the Constraints-Led Approach
Case Studies

CHAPTER OUTLINE

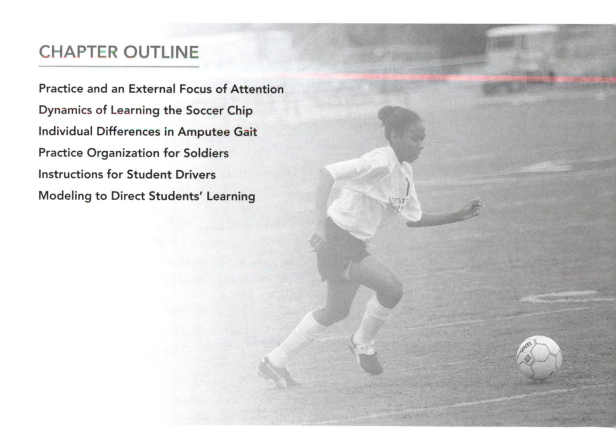

In this final chapter, we provide some ideas on how you might approach a particular movement problem through a case study. For each problem we have provided additional questions and application exercises. We also have included relevant chapter readings and research if you are interested in learning more. Keep in mind that the suggested solutions are not necessarily the only correct answers. Instead, each case study is based on the theoretical insights provided in the previous chapters and contains one of many possible answers. This final chapter is merely intended to help you gauge your level of understanding and to supplement your learning.

Practice and an External Focus of Attention

IDENTIFY THE PROBLEM

How to provide feedback and instructions to learners and advanced performers during practice

SETTING

Practice in the lead-up to an international rugby competition

PRIMARY CONSTRAINTS

Organismic (integrating feedback into practice of a well-established movement pattern), task (kicking a ball to satisfy height, distance, and accuracy constraints)

Some athletes use external-focus strategies intuitively, such as Jonny Wilkinson, who kicked the winning points in the last seconds of the 2003 Rugby World Cup. Jonny Wilkinson revealed the secret to his goal-kicking prowess: an imaginary woman named Doris. Five years earlier, when Wilkinson was preparing for his first test against the Australian national team in Brisbane, he was having serious problems with his kicking technique. Despite hours of training with England's kicking coach Dave Alred, Wilkinson was still spraying balls all over the place as time ticked down to kickoff. Alred eventually told Wilkinson to forget about technique and the goalposts. His advice to Wilkinson was to imagine a lady sitting in the crowd behind the posts and try to hit her. "She became known as Doris; we picked out a seat for her and tried to hit her," Wilkinson confided ahead of his team's World Cup pool C match against Samoa in Melbourne. "And then we imagined her reading a newspaper and we tried to kick that out of her hands. When things were going a little better, we imagined her with a can of cola and we tried to hit that."

The results were not immediate. England was thrashed by Australia by a record score of 76-0. However, the unusual visualization technique subsequently paid dividends. "The idea was instead of aiming at the posts you were aiming at something specific 30 yards [27 meters] back, and that way we changed the emphasis of where I was aiming. It made me really kick through the ball and it worked."

Whenever kicking practice is a challenge for Johnny Wilkinson, it helps him to think about hitting Doris!

Wilkinson likened a practice session to a jigsaw puzzle. "Every night you go to sleep you may have something on your mind that you have to deal with. That shakes the box up and when you kick the next day you're not the finished product anymore. The aim of every kicking session, the reason I practice the way I do, is to find those pieces and, by the end of the session, to have packed them back in." When Wilkinson fears he is in a flat patch, he will change focus by "doing a few Dorises" or some lazy sevens—a lobbed 7-iron golf shot where he tries to land the ball on the crossbar. "That blots out the panic of trying to get it over or on line—all you think about is the weight; you take the line for granted."

NZPA Staff Correspondent, Sydney, Australia. Copied with permission of *Otago Daily Times*, 27-October 2003 http://www.odt.co.nz

ANALYSIS QUESTIONS

1. What does the experience of this successful international athlete tell you about the stability of acquired movement patterns?

2. What are the implications of this real-life scenario for the way that instructions and feedback should be communicated to athletes?

3. Would you take the same approach with a complete beginner in rugby kicking?

APPLICATION EXERCISE

Select a sport or physical activity of your choice and identify the key skills involved. Under the task constraints of that sport or physical activity, consider how a coach could encourage an external focus of attention during practice of key skills.

READING

Chapters 8 and 9; Wulf and Shea (2002)

Dynamics of Learning the Soccer Chip

IDENTIFY THE PROBLEM

Scanning initial coordination patterns and monitoring the progress of a learner performing a pass in soccer

SETTING

Recreational women's soccer club

PRIMARY CONSTRAINTS

Organismic (lack of experience), task (goals—lift the ball over an opponent to a teammate)

Kirsten was beginning to wonder what she'd gotten herself into. Her roommates had encouraged her to try out for the local soccer club because she was physically fit and they were short on numbers. However, she had never even kicked a soccer ball before. "Initially we're going to focus on the basics—passing, shooting, and tackling—before we start to work on some specific skills," the coach had told the squad of 15 players. The first few training sessions went reasonably well for Kirsten. She had no problems in keeping up with the others during the training runs and shuttle races, and she'd even managed to score a goal in one practice game. But the skills practices were proving a little more difficult.

"I'm sorry, Coach, the ball doesn't seem to go where I want it to," Kirsten said after slicing an intended pass and smashing the window of the adjacent changing rooms. The coach quickly realized that Kirsten needed some help—before she broke anything else!

The coach closely examined Kirsten's kicking technique. She suspected that Kirsten's early coordination patterns for kicking were beginning to limit her ability to pass accurately. When Kirsten was asked to pass a stationary ball to a teammate, some key concerns immediately became apparent. For one thing, she tended to plant her nonkicking foot quite far from where she made contact with the ball. In addition, her upper body seemed to be leaning backward on most practice attempts. And sometimes she tended to punt right through the midline of the ball indiscriminately, leading to the large window-replacement bill.

Manipulating task constraints can encourage exploration of preliminary coordination patterns in learners.

The coach decided to manipulate task constraints to ascertain how adaptable Kirsten's technique was. In the first instance, she placed a 1-meter-high barrier 2 meters away from Kirsten and asked her to alternate passing the ball under and over the barrier. This modified skill forced Kirsten to regularly search for appropriate body positions and foot placements to achieve the desired pass. After a few minutes of practice, the coach asked Kirsten's teammate to stand behind the barrier and act as a target receiver for a pass. Finally, in a more advanced version of the practice, she asked Kirsten's teammate to roll the ball under the barrier toward Kirsten and then move either to the left or right to receive the pass. As Kirsten started showing improvement in these modified games, the coach continued to modify some key constraints. For example, on certain occasions she increased the barrier height to encourage Kirsten to lift the ball higher. She also regularly encouraged Kirsten to swap positions and practice roles with her teammate and watch her attempt the skill.

Kirsten began to notice her improvement. "It took me quite awhile to get the ball over the barrier, but after I managed that a few times, it all seemed to come together," she commented. The coach was also pleased with her improvement. "That's good, Kirsten. But now I want to see you using these skills in a game—you're starting in midfield for Saturday's match!" Kirsten gave a nervous groan and asked, "Are there any windows near the playing pitch?"

ANALYSIS QUESTIONS

1. If you were Kirsten's coach, how would you go about assessing her kicking technique?

2. What other practices could you devise to assess Kirsten's progress in this soccer chipping skill? What other key constraints could you manipulate to direct her search?

3. Why not just tell Kirsten what the problems are with her technique and provide a demonstration to show her how she should accomplish the task?

APPLICATION EXERCISE

Develop a 6-week practice program for Kirsten's soccer squad that is primarily focused on improving passing accuracy. Consider the following factors in your plan:

- There are 15 players and 1 coach. Access to training facilities and equipment is available (you can also borrow a video recorder).
- You have 90 minutes per session, and 2 training sessions per week.
- Two players are recovering from leg injuries and can only do light jogging exercises for the first 3 weeks.
- What modified games could you devise that emphasize passing skills?
- What verbal instructions and feedback should you provide and when?

READING

Chapters 4 and 5; Chow et al. (2006)

Individual Differences in Amputee Gait

IDENTIFY THE PROBLEM

Recommending rehabilitation exercises for transtibial amputee patients with different gait patterns

SETTING

Therapist providing clinical rehabilitation following major trauma

PRIMARY CONSTRAINTS

Organismic (loss of foot and ankle on one side), task (goals—walk in a functional, efficient way), environmental (social stigma of disability)

In the past year, A.J. and T.T. were involved in traumatic accidents that resulted in transtibial amputations of the left foot and ankle. Both patients had stated that they would like to start walking again as soon as possible so they could

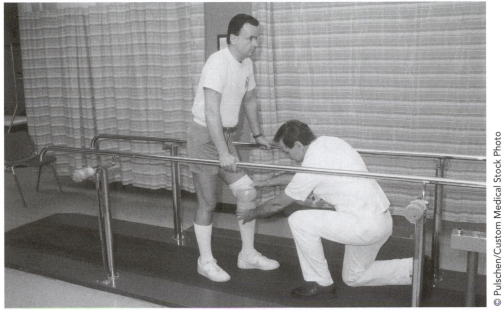

Learning to reacquire movement patterns after trauma requires variability in practice contexts just as much as when acquiring a skill for the first time. For example, lower limb amputees can benefit from walking in cluttered environments rather than solely on treadmills.

return to a normal life. "My short-term goal is to walk without assistance and then eventually get back to work," said A.J. However, T.T.'s primary motivation was different. He said, "I'm conscious that people keep looking at me because of my limp. I just wish it weren't so obvious." The hospital provided both patients with below-knee prostheses. Having recovered from the accidents, A.J. and T.T. worked with Charlie, a movement therapist, on their rehabilitation programs.

Charlie met A.J. and T.T. for the first time within a few days of each other. During his initial diagnosis, Charlie noticed a number of similarities between them. They were both male, and nearly the same age, height, and weight. However, as Charlie soon discovered, although each adapted to his prosthesis over the first few weeks, that is where the similarities ended.

For instance, A.J. seemed to be adapting to his new prosthesis better than T.T., whose walking technique was markedly slower and asymmetrical. Charlie also noticed that A.J. was better able to adapt to subtle changes in speed when walking on a motorized treadmill. Conversely, T.T.'s stride length, particularly on his amputated side, was less variable when Charlie modified the treadmill speed, which created an awkward-looking asymmetry between T.T.'s strides. Charlie believed that A.J.'s quicker habituation was due to the fact that he was fitter and had better leg strength. A.J. had worked as a mail carrier for over 8 years, although he was currently limited to helping out in the mail-sorting department. However, T.T.'s job as an office worker rarely offered him opportunities to be physically active.

Some more interesting differences between the patients emerged when Charlie observed them walking around the clinic. To add complexity to the walking task, Charlie placed a number of objects on the floor to act as obstacles. In this situation, A.J. completed the set route quicker than T.T. but tended to make more mistakes. For example, he often accidentally brushed his prosthesis against an obstacle, causing him to stumble. Although T.T. took longer to walk across the clinic floor, he preferred to use longer strides on his healthy leg to walk over the obstacles.

Considering all this information, Charlie made some different suggestions to his patients as part of their rehabilitation. For A.J., Charlie recommended balance and walking tasks with considerable accuracy demands. For example, he gave A.J. a rope ladder to place on the ground and practice walking through the gaps. He recognized that T.T. needed to improve his general fitness and leg strength and to develop his confidence so that he used his amputated leg more often. Charlie recommended a local gym for T.T. to attend and a number of specific conditioning exercises. He warned both A.J. and T.T. not to expect dramatic improvements, saying, "These things can take time, but try to practice using your prosthesis in a range of different situations—don't be afraid to make mistakes. Sometimes you have to take two steps backward to go one step forward!"

ANALYSIS QUESTIONS

1. If you were in Charlie's position, how would you deal with differences between patients such as A.J. and T.T.?

2. What other exercises can you think of to help A.J. and T.T.? Consider the key constraints at this early stage and the emerging constraints later in their rehabilitation.

3. Amputee patients typically change their prosthesis a number of times in the first few months to account for changes in leg strength, stump size, and so on. How would these changes in organismic constraints influence the practice programs that Charlie organized?

4. Can you think of any benefits in getting A.J. and T.T. together for rehabilitation sessions?

APPLICATION EXERCISE

Using a movement-related illness or injury of your choice, devise a rehabilitation program that is underpinned by nonlinear pedagogy. Consider the following factors:

- Key emerging and decaying constraints on the patient
- Short- and long-term recommendations
- Suggested rehabilitation equipment
- Patient goals

READING

Chapter 5; Schöllhorn, Nigg, Stefanyshyn, and Liu (2002)

IDENTIFY THE PROBLEM

Training a unit of newly recruited soldiers to defend a specified location from enemy attack

SETTING

Army training environment

PRIMARY CONSTRAINTS

Task (goal—defend base location), environment (unpredictable attack scenarios, group dynamics)

"Be on your guard, Blue Unit, the enemy could arrive at any time." A special unit trainer in the army for several years, Sergeant Bella Thornton was accustomed to issuing such warnings to trainee soldiers. However, she had rarely seen a more disorganized rabble of trainees than these 20 soldiers as they dispersed frantically, attempting to cover all access points to the mock base building. "This could be a long year," Bella mused to herself as she realized that not one soldier had remained to guard the front door. Over the next 9 months, Bella's job would be to train the Blue Unit to work as a unit and to protect strategic locations from potential enemy assaults.

Even teams and groups can benefit from identifying key task constraints for training perceptual-motor skills in coordinated activity.

Returning to the barracks later that afternoon, Bella began to plan some of the skills and practice activities that she would use to train the Blue Unit recruits. The first skill the soldiers needed to learn was how to identify key sources of strategic information such as optimal locations for potential intruders and all the potential entrances to the base building. To achieve this goal, Bella decided to take the unit to different buildings and locations over the first month of training. Upon arrival at the practice destinations, the Blue Unit would be given 5 minutes to scope the area and building and report back to the unit leader with details about the layout of the base building and surrounding area. As the unit improved its production of surveillance reports, Bella would reduce the time available and ask for more detailed information, such as asking whether anyone had checked access points on the roof.

The second important skill Bella wanted to work on was the unit's ability to work as a team. This skill would involve the unit clarifying each trainee's role (e.g., early warning guards) as well as each trainee's ability to cooperate and execute effective decisions quickly. To improve teamwork and role identification, Bella encouraged the Blue Unit to work together to plan for mock strategic scenarios such as sabotaging a guarded bridge, rescuing a captive, and transporting a prisoner to a secure location. For each scenario, she devised a number of rules or conditions that would require the unit to cooperate or risk failure.

Finally, Bella wanted the unit to be able to adapt its surveillance strategies to unpredictable attack scenarios, such as a night raid or a chemical weapons attack. To achieve this goal, she planned to return the Blue Unit to the mock scenario she had created earlier that day and gradually add in unforeseen events. For example, some of the key factors that she could change included the number of assailants, the weapons and resources available to the unit, the time that the siege occurred, and even the weather conditions in which the attack occurred. "One thing's for sure," thought Bella as she saved her training plan on her computer and watched the Blue Unit trudge in dejectedly from a 10-mile (16-kilometer) training run, "they won't leave the front door unguarded again!"

ANALYSIS QUESTIONS

1. Assume some of the Blue Unit trainees start to blame each other and argue over failed scenarios. How could you encourage the unit to become a more coordinated team?

2. What other training exercises would you suggest that Bella use to develop key military skills, such as precision rifle shooting and vigilance?

3. Would a complex motor skill such as checking a building for intruders benefit from practice in parts? What do you think the implications for performance acquisition, retention, and transfer might be?

APPLICATION EXERCISE

Create a mock scenario for the Blue Unit to help develop their teamwork skills. Consider the following factors:

- What is the task goal for the unit?
- What are the rules for the scenario (what behaviors do you wish to encourage)?
- How can contextual interference be introduced into the soldiers' training?
- How many possible solutions exist for your scenario? How do the task constraints affect the number of potential solutions?

READING

Chapters 6 and 7; Ollis, Button, and Fairweather (2005)

Instructions for Student Drivers

IDENTIFY THE PROBLEM

How driving instructors should use verbal communication to improve students' driving skills

SETTING

Dual-control student's car on a public highway

PRIMARY CONSTRAINTS

Task (goal—drive the car safely, presence of other traffic, junctions, and so on), organismic (lack of driving experience, anxiety)

Norman was a nervous and shy man at the best of times. His driving instructor, Janice, had caused him to blush deeply during his first lesson when he had tried to pull away without releasing the emergency brake. "Aren't you forgetting something, Norman?" she said as the engine had reached a deafening level.

"I . . . oh . . . I'm sorry, it's just that there's so much to think about, isn't there?" he stammered. Janice recognized immediately that she'd have to be careful not to confuse Norman during his lessons. This was not a problem for Janice; she actually felt that most instructors talked too much and tended to confuse drivers with overly complex information. Her aim was to try to make the driver feel at ease and to make the process of learning a pleasant experience, even for drivers like Norman.

Janice had driven Norman to a quiet industrial estate for his first lesson. She decided to focus on his general driving skills before progressing to more complex maneuvers. One of her first instructions concerned changing gears. "When changing gears," she told him, "the gas and clutch pedals are like a set of scales. As you ease off the gas, you push on the clutch." This analogy soon enabled Norman to coordinate these two pedals effectively. Later, when working on turning, Janice said, "Norman, a good driver is aware of others and lets other drivers know what he's about to do. Whenever you're about to turn at a junction, remember three simple words: mirror, signal, and maneuver." And when Norman attempted a hill start, Janice said, "The key here is to listen to the engine. Adjust the pedals until you hear the biting point, then release the emergency brake." In each case, Janice was careful to keep her instructions short, simple, and focused on achieving the task goal.

To help Norman with his lack of confidence, Janice was mindful of encouraging him and giving critical feedback only when it was necessary. On one occasion as he drove up onto the sidewalk while reversing around a bend, Janice said, "Your speed control was excellent there. Unfortunately, you just turned the wheel a little too early, so let's go back and try again." As Norman improved over the next few lessons and started to develop some confidence, Janice provided some feedback. After a more successful trial, she said, "That was a much better attempt, Norman. You're keeping the car nicely under control and close to the curb—but remember to keep checking your mirrors for other traffic." Janice knew that statements like this helped Norman to maintain an external focus of attention while learning this tricky maneuver.

Ten weeks later, Norman was a different driver as he pulled the car up outside the driving school. He told Janice, "I can't believe how quickly I've picked up some of these skills. At first it seemed like there was too much going on at the same time, but you've taught me to focus on all the right things." Janice was confident that with more practice and careful prompting, it wouldn't be long before Norman could take his proficiency test, and she said as much when he was getting out of the car. "You've done really well, Norman. Your awareness and patience with other traffic and pedestrians is particularly good. See you next week!"

ANALYSIS QUESTIONS

1. What verbal communication strategies would you employ as you instructed Norman how to approach and drive through a roundabout?

2. What other verbal instructions might Janice use in busy traffic situations where Norman is likely to become anxious again with less time to make decisions?

3. Imagine that you had to teach someone who tended to talk too much at the expense of concentrating on driving. How would you instruct that person?

APPLICATION EXERCISE

Develop a lesson plan for an intensive residential driving school that teaches novices to drive in 6 days. Consider the following factors:

- You have 6 days, with 4 hours of practice and 2 hours of theory per day.
- What are the learning objectives of each session?
- How will you prevent learners from acquiring bad habits?
- How can you ensure that your program has been successful (i.e., how will you know the drivers are proficient)?

READING

Chapters 8 and 9; Wulf and Shea (2002)

Modeling to Direct Students' Learning

IDENTIFY THE PROBLEM

Providing demonstrations for a class of 30 schoolchildren who are learning to serve a tennis ball

SETTING

School tennis courts (4) and a long wall

PRIMARY CONSTRAINTS

Task (goal—hit the ball over the net from the service line to land in the opposite serving court area; equipment—1 tennis ball for every 2 children)

Physical education teacher Anthony Emersons took a good look at the 30 students in his class as they each picked up their rackets from the equipment cupboard. "You do know you're holding the racket at the wrong end, Simon," Anthony said as one of the least coordinated students walked onto the court. "Yes, Mr. Emersons, but the other end's a lot better for poking people with!" Simon chirped cheekily back. "Try to act like a 10-year-old Simon, not a 3-year-old," he answered. "Okay everyone, find a partner and line up about 5 meters from the wall on the far side for some warm-up drills."

After 10 minutes of warm-up drills, Anthony could see that, as usual, there was a fair range of ability levels in the class. "Today we're going to focus on the tennis serve. Who can tell me the basic rules about serving?" he asked. Having ascertained that the aim was to hit the ball from behind the service line into the opposing service area, Anthony then asked for a volunteer to demonstrate. Two students' hands shot up in the air. The first was Jenny, who

Traditional coaching methods emphasize the decomposition of a task into separate components during practice, such as practicing the ball toss independently of the hitting action in the tennis serve.

seemed to excel at most sports, and the second was Simon. "Simon, if you can serve toward the wall so that the ball rebounds to Jenny, then she can serve back to you," he instructed. "The rest of you line up on either side of these two and watch carefully."

Simon milked the sudden attention by asking for new tennis balls and then bouncing his ball at least eight times. Standing and facing the wall, he launched the ball in the air at least three times his own height in preparation for the serve. Eventually the ball started to drop back down and in a blur of arms, racket, and a huge grunt, the ball bounced off Simon's head and bobbled over to Jenny's feet. Jenny's attempt was considerably more successful. She carefully threw the ball in the air, brought her racket behind her head, and swiveled fluidly to smash the ball just above the line marking the net's height on the wall.

"Everyone, what have you learned from observing both of those demonstrations?" Anthony asked, trying to avoid further embarrassment for Simon.

"That an accurate ball toss is important," shouted one student.

"Good. Anything else?"

"You need to stand side-on to the net to generate power." Anthony was impressed by the students' comments and it was clear that the class had picked up a considerable amount from watching his two volunteers.

"Now I want you to serve to each other. Remember what you've just seen and help each other if you can." While the class practiced their serves, Anthony took his video camera and recorded each pupil at least once. Using the slow-motion playback function, it was relatively easy to recognize timing and positional errors. Finally, he divided the class into fours and had them play serving games where the aim was to serve consistently over the net toward a target. Having explained this to the group, Anthony added, "Once the game is underway, if anyone wants to come and look at the video, just let me know."

Perhaps not surprisingly, Simon was one of the first to review his video replay. "Jenny learned everything she knows from watching me," he said sarcastically as he watched his much improved serve. "Yes, Simon, it's clear that everyone here has learned a lot from you today!" Anthony said, smiling knowingly.

ANALYSIS QUESTIONS

1. How could you use visual feedback to encourage a group of children to experiment with different serving techniques, such as might be used for first and second serve attempts?
2. Can you think of other ways to provide feedback for this task?
3. What if no one in the group could demonstrate the serve effectively? Is the only solution for Anthony to demonstrate?
4. What information sources on the video would you highlight for each learner to observe?

APPLICATION EXERCISE

Develop a lesson plan to teach the children how to play the forehand drive. Consider the following factors:

- Space limitations (there are only four courts)
- Time (90 minutes, including warm-up time)
- Different ability levels (at least four pupils are fairly advanced players)
- Games that would teach the children the tactics of when to play attacking and defensive shots

READING

Chapter 9; Ashford et al. (2006)

GLOSSARY

adaptive training—A technique in which task difficulty is gradually increased as performance is mastered.

affordances—The perception of information by what it offers, invites, or demands of an organism in terms of action.

associative stage—The second stage of Fitts' model. Connections are made between specific intended outcomes and particular movement patterns, and these associations become more refined as the learner becomes more consistent.

attractor—Stable and functional pattern of organization.

autonomous stage—The third stage of Fitts' model. The learner can perform a skill with minimal mental effort and few errors, and the movement pattern requires less cortical association involvement that has been interpreted as leading to greater control from lower brain centers.

closed-loop control—A form of movement control based on ongoing regulation by sensory feedback.

cognitive stage—The first stage of Fitts' model. The learner uses simple rules and verbal instructions to gain basic understanding of the movement and to assemble a basic solution to a motor problem.

complex systems—Highly integrated systems that are made up of many interacting parts or subsystems, each of which is capable of affecting other subsystems.

constraints—The numerous variables that influence the region of phase space that a dynamical system visits. Constraints both limit and enable the different behavioral trajectories that a neurobiological system, for example, can adopt. Constraints can be personal, task related, or environmental.

contextual interference (CI)—The learning effectiveness of practicing several motor tasks randomly as opposed to practicing the same tasks in a blocked order.

contextual interference effect—Practice organization that is blocked appears to lead to better performance during acquisition of the skill. Conversely, random practice organization benefits the learning of a skill.

control-based theory (COBALT)—A neurocomputational perspective proposing that the brain creates different types of representations so important information can be symbolically represented and stored. Learners can thus create mental models of the world and include categories based on features of the environment, intentions, and spatial or temporal patterns of muscle activation.

coordinative structures—The coordination or temporary order that emerges, in the form of a synergy, among system components during goal-directed behavior. Coordinative structures are designed for a specific purpose or activity, such as when groups of muscles are temporarily assembled into coherent units to achieve specific task goals.

degeneracy—Refers to the idea that different parts of neurobiological systems (e.g., muscles, joints, limbs) can achieve same or different movement outcomes leading to different patterns of movement coordination.

degrees of freedom (dfs)—The independent components of a system that can fit together in many different ways.

dynamical systems theory—A theoretical approach that views the learner as a complex, neurobiological system composed of independent but interacting dfs or subsystems.

environmental constraints—Constraints that are global, physical variables in nature, such as ambient light, temperature, or altitude. Some environmental constraints are social rather than physical.

experiential coaching—Coaching method that draws upon the wealth of knowledge and experience that many coaches have developed during their participation in a specific sport or physical activity.

facilitation approach—Based on traditional ideas of stimulus–response associations, this approach emphasizes the replication of specific movement patterns.

forward modeling—The mapping of motor commands to a movement's related sensory consequences. Located within the brain, this representation is used to predict the sensory consequences of planned movements.

habituation—The need for a warm-up period after people have been away from practice or training for some time. Habituation alleviates poor movement timing and coordination and reduces the number of errors made during performance.

homunculus—A central controlling mechanism in the brain believed to be responsible for the creation, selection, and timing of generalized motor programs.

implicit motor learning—Learning that occurs when people are not formally exposed to verbal instructions to perform a movement in a specific manner.

intrinsic dynamics—The set of movement capabilities that people bring with them when learning a new skill.

invariant—When an underlying essential structure remains constant despite changes in the superficial structure.

inverse modeling—A model of how the CNS controls an action by predicting the sensory consequences of a movement and determining the motor commands needed to achieve it.

metastability—A dynamic form of stability in biological systems in which system parts adhere together to achieve functional movement goals while maintaining their own separate identities and flexibility of operation.

method coaching—Coaching method whereby practitioners break down and teach specific movement skills in a mechanistic manner in order to piece together the correct or textbook technique.

mirror neurons—Neurons in the brain that are activated when a learner performs an action or watches another person perform an action.

modeling—The process whereby learners observe and then attempt to reproduce a desired behavior demonstrated by another person.

moment of inertia—A product of the mass of an implement and the radius of rotation (i.e., $I = mr^2$).

monotonic benefits assumption—The amount of time a person engages in deliberate practice is monotonically related to that person's acquired performance.

motor development—Behavioral changes that are typically attributed to growth and maturation.

motor learning—Behavioral changes that are typically attributed to practice or experience.

motor program—An abstract concept describing a set of movement commands that are stored within the CNS.

nonlinear pedagogy—A theoretical foundation that views learning systems as nonlinear dynamical systems. It advocates that the observed properties of dynamical human movement systems form the basis of a principled pedagogical framework. In particular, nonlinear pedagogy advocates the manipulation of key constraints on learners during practice.

numerical phase space—All the hypothetical states of organization into which a dynamical system can evolve.

observational learning—A process whereby a person assimilates and sometimes adopts or replicates the behavioral patterns or actions of others as a direct consequence of observing these behaviors.

open-loop control—A mode of movement regulation responsible for the control of quick, ballistic movements in which a set of preplanned instructions for action can be executed without feedback modification.

organismic constraints—Constraints that refer to the personal characteristics of the learner, such as genes, height, weight, muscle–fat ratio, connective strength of synapses in the brain, cognitions, motivations, and emotions.

part-task training—Practicing a subset of task components as a precursor to practice or performance of the whole task.

perceptual-motor landscape—The range of attractors that performers need to coordinate their actions with their environment in order to perform skills effectively.

phase transitions—Movements of a system's microcomponents into a different state of organization. Phase transitions form the basis of self-organization in complex systems.

power law of practice—A law that simply states that practice improves performance, although there is an upper limit to the gains that can be made as a function of increasing practice.

relative motion—The specific spatiotemporal relationships between and within limbs, as well as the organization of the performer's limbs relative to the surrounding environment.

retention—Given the right practice conditions, humans can usually retain some essence of a movement pattern regardless of the type of task they perform.

scanning procedure—An empirical technique that requires the participant to intentionally vary an order parameter in steps. As the behavior of the order parameter is monitored, the observer is effectively scanning the perceptual-motor landscape for stable and unstable regions.

schema—Rules concerning the execution of a movement response that is linked to feedback received during and after performance.

schema theory—An information-processing theory stating that a generalized motor program is an abstract representation containing the general characteristics for a given class of actions.

self-organization—A system's capacity to use environmental energy to spontaneously achieve stable states of functional organization. Self-organizing systems have a propensity for pattern formation under constraints.

skill acquisition—The internal processes that bring about relatively permanent changes in a learner's movement capabilities. Skill acquisition requires learners to produce consistent outcomes by interacting effectively with their environment, detecting important information, and timing their responses appropriately.

task constraints—Constraints that are usually more specific to particular performance contexts and include task goals, rules associated with a specific activity, activity-related implements or tools, surfaces, performance areas, and boundary markings.

tau—Optical information specified on the retina about the remaining time to contact (Tc) between the point of observation and an approaching object.

Teaching Games for Understanding (TGfU)—The most prominent model of pedagogical practice in the teaching of team games. TGfU enables learners to learn the tactical and movement skill aspects of games through playing modified versions of target games. A major focus of TGfU is developing an understanding of tactics before the development of component motor skills.

transfer—The influence of previous practice or performance of a skill on the acquisition of new skill.

variant—An energy flow is considered variant when some element of the superficial structure in the informational array changes as the performer moves relative to surfaces, objects, or events.

REFERENCES

Abernethy, B. (2001). Acquisition of skill. In F.S. Pyke (Ed.), *Better coaching: Advanced coach's manual* (2nd ed., pp. 161-170). Lower Mitcham, Australia: Human Kinetics.

Abernethy, B., Maxwell, J.P., Masters, R.S.W., van der Kamp, J., & Jackson, R.C. (2007). Attentional processes in skill learning and expert performance. In G. Tenenbaum & R. Eklund (Eds.), *Handbook of Sport Psychology* (3rd ed., pp. 245-265). New York: Wiley.

Abraham, A.K., & Collins, D. (1998). Examining and extending research in coach development. *Quest, 50,* 59-79.

Adams, J.A. (1961). The second facet of forgetting: A review of warm-up decrement. *Psychological Bulletin, 58,* 256-268.

Adams, J.A. (1971). A closed-loop theory of motor learning. *Journal of Motor Behavior, 3,* 111-150.

Aglioti, S., DeSouza, J.F.X., & Goodale, M.A. (1995). Size-contrast illusions deceive the eye but not the hand. *Current Biology, 5,* 679-685.

Al-Abood, S.A., Bennett, S.J., Moreno Hernandez, F., Ashford, D.G., & Davids, K. (2002). Effect of verbal instructions and image size on visual search strategies in basketball free throw shooting. *Journal of Sport Sciences, 20,* 271-278.

Al-Abood, S.A., Davids, K., & Bennett, S.J. (2001). Specificity of task constraints and the effect of visual demonstrations and verbal instructions on skill acquisition. *Journal of Motor Behavior, 33,* 295-305.

Al-Abood, S.A., Davids, K., Bennett, S.J., Ashford, D., & Marin, M.M. (2001). Manipulating relative and absolute motion information during observational learning of an aiming task: Effects of slow-motion and real-time video analysis. *Journal of Sports Sciences, 19,* 507-520.

Alderson, G.J.K., Sully, D.J., & Sully, H.G. (1974). An operational analysis of a one-handed catching task using high speed photography. *Journal of Motor Behavior, 6,* 217-226.

Allard, P., Stokes, I.A.F., & Blanchi, J.-P. (1995). *Three-dimensional analysis of human movement.* Champaign, IL: Human Kinetics.

Alvarez, R., Terrados, N., Ortolano, R., Iglesias-Cubero, G., Reguero, J.R., Batalla, A., et al. (2000). Genetic variation in the renin-angiotensin system and athletic performance. *European Journal of Applied Physiology, 82,* 117-120.

Anderson, D.I., & Sidaway, B. (1994). Coordination changes associated with practice of a soccer kick. *Research Quarterly for Exercise and Sport, 65,* 93-99.

Anderson, J.R. (1982). Acquisition of cognitive skill. *Psychological Review, 89,* 369-406.

Anson, G., Elliott, D., & Davids, K. (2005). Information processing and constraints-based views of skill acquisition: Divergent or complementary? *Motor Control, 9,* 217-241.

Araújo, D., Davids, K., Bennett, S.J., Button, C., & Chapman, G. (2004). Emergence of sport skills under constraint. In A.M. Williams & N.J. Hodges (Eds.), *Skill Acquisition in Sport: Research, Theory and Practice* (pp. 409-433). London: Routledge, Taylor & Francis.

Araújo, D., Davids, K., & Serpa, S. (2005). An ecological approach to expertise effects in decision-making in a simulated sailing regatta. *Psychology of Sport and Exercise, 6,* 671-692.

Arbib, M.A., Érdi, P., & Szentágothai, J. (1998). *Neural organization: Structure, function and dynamics.* Cambridge, MA: MIT Press.

Arutyunyan, G.H., Gurfinkel, V.S., & Mirskii, M.L. (1968). Investigation of aiming at a target. *Biophysics, 14,* 1162-1167.

Ashford, D., Bennett, S., & Davids, K. (2006) Observational modelling effects for movement dynamics and movement outcome measures across differing task constraints: A meta-analysis. *Journal of Motor Behavior, 38,* 185-205.

Ashford, D.G., Davids, K., & Bennett, S.J. (2007). Developmental effects influencing observational modelling: A meta-analysis. *Journal of Sports Sciences, 25,* 547-558.

Ayyash, H.F., & Preece, P.M. (2003). Evidence-based treatment of motor co-ordination disorder. *Current Paediatrics, 13*(5), 360-364.

Baker, J., & Davids, K. (2006). Genetic and environmental constraints on variability in sports performance. In K. Davids, S.J. Bennett, & K.M. Newell (Eds.), *Variability in the movement system: A multi-disciplinary perspective* (pp.109-129). Champaign, IL: Human Kinetics.

Ball, K.A., Best, R.J., & Wrigley, T.V. (2003). Body sway, aim point fluctuation and performance in rifle shooters: inter- and intra-individual analysis. *Journal of Sports Sciences, 21,* 559-566.

Bandura, A. (1962). Social learning through imitation. In M.R. Jones (Ed.), *Nebraska symposium on motivation* (pp. 211-269). Lincoln, NE: University of Nebraska Press.

Bandura, A. (1969). *Principles of behaviour modification.* New York: Rinehart-Winston.

Bandura, A. (1977). Self-efficacy: Toward a unifying theory of behavioral change. *Psychological Review, 84*(2), 191-215.

Beak, S., Davids, K., & Bennett, S.J. (2000). One size fits all? Sensitivity to moment of inertia information from tennis rackets in children and adults. In S.J. Haake & A. Coe (Eds.), *Tennis science and technology* (pp. 109-118). London: Blackwell.

Beak, S., Davids, K., & Bennett, S.J. (2002). Child's play: Children's sensitivity to haptic information in perceiving affordances of rackets for striking a ball. In J.E. Clark & J. Humphreys (Eds.), *Motor development: research and reviews* (Vol. 2, pp. 120-141). Reston, VA: NASPE.

Beek, P.J. (2000). Toward a theory of implicit learning in the perceptual-motor domain. *International Journal of Sport Psychology, 31,* 547-554.

Beek, P., Jacobs, D., Daffertshofer, A., & Huys, R. (2003). Expert performance in sport: views from the joint perspectives of ecological psychology and dynamical systems theory. In J. Starkes & K.A. Ericsson (Eds.), *Expert performance in sports: Advances in research on sport expertise* (pp. 321-344). Champaign, IL: Human Kinetics.

Bennett, S., Davids, K., & Craig, T. (1999). The effect of temporal and informational constraints on one-handed catching performance. *Research Quarterly for Exercise and Sport, 70*(2), 206-211.

Bernstein, N.A. (1967). *The control and regulation of movements.* London: Pergamon Press.

Berthouze, L., & Lungarella, M. (2004). Motor skill acquisition under environmental perturbations: on the necessity of alternate freezing and freeing degrees of freedom. *Adaptive Behavior, 12,* 47-64.

Bingham, G. (1988). Task-specific devices and the perceptual bottleneck. *Human Movement Science, 7,* 225-264.

Bootsma, R.J. (1998). *Ecological movement principles and how much information matters.* Paper presented at the Second Symposium of the Institute for Fundamental and Clinical Human Movement Sciences, Amsterdam.

Bootsma, R.J., Bakker, F.C., van Snippenberg, F.J., & Tdlohreg, C.W. (1992). The effects of anxiety on perceiving the reachability of passing objects. *Ecological Psychology, 4,* 1-16.

Bootsma, R.J., Fayt, V., Zaal, F.T.J.M., & Laurent, M. (1997). On the information-based regulation of movement: What Wann (1996) may want to consider. *Journal of Experimental Psychology: Human Perception and Performance, 23,* 1282-1289.

Bootsma, R.J., Houbiers, M., Whiting, H.T.A., & van Wieringen, P.C.W. (1991). Acquiring an attacking forehand drive: The effects of static and dynamic environemtal conditions. *Research Quarterly for Exercise and Sport, 62,* 276-284.

Bootsma, R.J., & van Wieringen, P.C.W. (1990). Timing an attacking forehand drive in table tennis. *Journal of Experimental Psychology: Human Perception and Performance, 16,* 21-29.

Brady, F. (1998). A theoretical and empirical review of the contextual interference effect and the learning of motor skills. *Quest, 50,* 266-293.

Brisson, T.A., & Alain, C. (1996). Should common optimal movement patterns be identified as the criterion to be achieved? *Journal of Motor Behavior, 28,* 211-223.

British Government (1999). *Saving Lives: Our Healthier Nation.* London: The Stationery Office.

Broderick, M.P., & Newell, K.M. (1999). Coordination patterns in ball bouncing as a function of skill. *Journal of Motor Behavior, 31,* 165-188.

Bryan, W.L., & Harter, N. (1897). Studies in the physiology and psychology of the telegraphic language. *Psychological Review, 4,* 27-53.

Bullock, D., & Grossberg, S. (1989). VITE and FLETE: Neural modules for trajectory formation and tension control. In W. Hershberger (Ed.), *Volitional action* (pp. 253-297). Amsterdam: North Holland.

Bunker, D., & Thorpe, R. (1982). A model for the teaching of games in the secondary school. *Bulletin of Physical Education, 10,* 9-16.

Bunker, D., & Thorpe, R. (1986). Is there a need to reflect on our games teaching? In R. Thorpe, D. Bunker, & L. Almond (Eds.), *Rethinking games teaching* (pp. 25-33). Loughborough, England: Loughborough University of Technology.

Button, C. (2002). Auditory information and the co-ordination of one-handed catching. In K. Davids, G. Savelsbergh, S. Bennett, & J. van der Kamp (Eds.), *Interception actions in sport: Information and Movement* (pp. 184-194). London: Taylor & Francis.

Button, C., Bennett, S. J., & Davids, K. (2001). Grasping a better understanding of the intrinsic dynamics of rhythmical and discrete prehension. *Journal of Motor Behavior, 33*(1), 27-36.

Button, C., Bennett, S.J., Davids, K., & Stephenson, J.M. (1999, 9 September). *The effects of practicing with a small, heavy soccer ball on the development of soccer related skills.* Paper presented at the British Association of Sports and Exercise Sciences Annual Conference, Leeds, UK.

Button, C., & Davids, K. (2004). Acoustic information for timing. In H. Hecht & G.J.P. Savelsbergh (Eds.), *Time-to-contact: Advances in psychology* (pp. 355-370). North-Holland: Elsevier.

Button, C., Davids, K., Bennett, S.J., & Tayler, M. (2000). Mechanical perturbation of the wrist during one-handed catching. *Acta Psychologica, 105,* 1, 9-30.

Button, C., Davids, K., & Schöllhorn, W. (2006). Co-ordination profiling of movement systems. In K. Davids, S. Bennett, & K.M. Newell (Eds.), *Variability in the movement system: A multi-disciplinary perspective* (pp. 133-152). Champaign, IL: Human Kinetics.

Button, C., Macleod, M., Sanders, R., & Coleman, S. (2003). Examining movement variability in the throwing action at different skill levels. *Research Quarterly for Exercise and Sport, 74*(3), 257-269.

Button, C., & Pepping, G-J. (2002). Enhancing skill acquisition in golf: Some key principles. Retrieved May 14, 2002, from www.coachesinfo.com.

Button, C., Smith, J., & Pepping, G.-J. (Eds.). (2005). *The influential role of task constraints in acquiring football skills.* London, UK: Routledge, Taylor & Francis.

Calvo-Merino, B., Glaser, D.E., Grèzes, J., Passingham, R.E., & Haggard, P. (2005). Action observation and acquired motor skills: An fMRI study with expert dancers. *Cerebral Cortex, 15*(8), 1243-1249.

Capel, S. (2000). Approaches to teaching games. In S. Capel & S. Piotrowski (Eds.), *Issues in Physical Education* (pp. 81-98). Cornwall, UK: TJ International.

Carello, C., Thuot, S., & Turvey, M.T. (2000). Aging and the perception of a racket's sweet spot. *Human Movement Science, 19,* 1-20.

Carr, G. (1997). *Mechanics of sport: A practitioner's guide.* Champaign, IL: Human Kinetics.

Carr, J.H., & Shepherd, R.B. (1998). *Neurological rehabilitation: Optimizing motor performance* (2nd ed.). Amsterdam: Elsevier Health Sciences.

Carson, R.G., Goodman, D., Kelso, J.A S., & Elliott, D. (1995). Intentional switching between patterns of interlimb coordination. *Journal of Human Movement Studies, 27,* 201-218.

Chapman, G., Bennett, S.J., & Davids, K. (2001). The effects of equipment constraints on the acquisition of juggling and dribbling in soccer. Communication to 6th Annual Congress of European College of Sports Science (Perspectives and Profiles), Cologne, Germany.

Chase, W.G., & Simon, H.A. (1973). Perception in chess. *Cognitive Psychology, 4,* 55-81.

Chen, H.H., Liu, Y.T., Mayer-Kress, G., & Newell, K.M. (2005). Learning the pedalo locomotion task. *Journal of Motor Behavior, 37,* 247-256.

Chow, J.-Y., Davids, K., Button, C., & Koh, M. (2006). Organisation of motor system degrees of freedom during the soccer chip: An analysis of skilled performance. *International Journal of Sport Psychology, 37,* 207-229.

Chow, J.-Y., Davids, K., Button, C., & Koh, M. (in press). Variation in coordination of a discrete multi-articular action as a function of skill level. *Journal of Motor Behavior.*

Chow, J-Y., Davids, K., Button, C., Shuttleworth, R., Renshaw, I., & Araújo, D. (2006). Nonlinear pedagogy: A constraints-led framework to understanding emergence of game play and skills. *Nonlinear Dynamics, Psychology and Life Sciences, 10,* 71-103.

Christina, R.W., & Corcos, D.M. (1998). *Coaches guide to teaching sport skills.* Champaign, IL: Human Kinetics.

Clark, J.E. (1995). On becoming skillful: Patterns and constraints. *Research Quarterly for Exercise and Sport, 66,* 173-183.

Clarke, D., & Crossland, J. (1985). *Action systems: An introduction to the analysis of complex behaviour.* London: Methuen.

Cobner, D., & Cardiff, M.A. (1980). *Auditory perception: A study of its contribution to motor learning and performance.* Paper presented at the British Association of Sport Psychology V.9, Bedford, UK.

Coleman, S. (1999). Biomechanics and its application for coaching. In N. Cross & J. Lyle (Eds.), *The coaching process* (pp. 130-151). Oxford: Butterworth-Heinemann.

Corbetta, D., & Vereijken, B. (1999). Understanding development and learning of motor coordination in sport: The contribution of dynamic systems theory. *International Journal of Sport Psychology, 30*(44), 507-530.

Court, M.L., Bennett, S.J., Williams, A.M., & Davids, K. (2002). Local stability in coordinated rhythmic movements: Fluctuations and relaxation times. *Human Movement Science, 21,* 39-60.

Court, M.J.L., Bennett, S.J., Williams, A.M., & Davids, K. (2005). Effects of attentional strategies and anxiety constraints on perceptual-motor organisation of rhythmical arm movements. *Neuroscience Letters, 384,* 17-22.

Crossman, E.R.F.W. (1959). A theory of the acquisition of speed-skill. *Ergonomics, 2,* 153-166.

Curtner-Smith, M.D., Todorov, J.R., McCaughtry, N.A., & Lacon, S.A. (2001). Urban teachers' use of productive and reproductive teaching styles within the confines of the national curriculum for physical education. *European Physical Education Review, 7*(2), 177-190.

Cutting, J.E., & Proffitt, D.R. (1982). The minimum principle and the perception of absolute, common, and relative motions. *Cognitive Psychology, 14,* 211-246.

Daly, R.M., Bass, S.L., & Finch, C.F. (2001). Balancing the risk of injury to gymnasts: How effective are the countermeasures? *British Journal of Sports Medicine, 35*(1), 8-18.

D'Arripe-Longueville, F., Gernigon, C., Huet, M.L., Cadopi, M., & Winnykamen, F. (2002). Peer tutoring in a physical education setting: Influence of tutor skill level on novice learners' motivation and performance. *Journal of Teaching in Physical Education, 22,* 105-123.

D'Arripe-Longueville, F., Gernigon, C., Huet, M.L., Winnykamen, F., & Cadopi, M. (2002). Peer-assisted learning in the physical activity domain: Dyad type and gender differences. *Journal of Sport and Exercise Psychology, 24,* 219-238.

Davids, K. (2000). Skill acquisition and the theory of deliberate practice: It ain't what you do, it's the way that you do it! Commentary on Starkes, J., "The road to expertise: Is practice the only determinant?" *International Journal of Sport Psychology, 31,* 461-465.

Davids, K., Araújo, D., Button, C., & Renshaw, I. (2007). Degenerate brains, indeterminate behavior and representative tasks: Implications for experimental design in sport psychology research. In G. Tenenbaum & R. Eklund (Eds.), *Handbook of Sport Psychology* (3rd ed., pp. 224-244). New York: John Wiley & Sons.

Davids, K., Araújo, D., & Shuttleworth, R. (2005). Applications of dynamical systems theory to football. In T. Reilly, J. Cabri & D. Araújo (Eds.), *Science and football V* (pp. 537-550). London: Routledge, Taylor & Francis.

Davids, K. & Baker, J. (in press). Genes, environment and sport performance: Why the Nature-Nurture dualism is no longer relevant. *Sports Medicine.*

Davids, K., Bennett, S., & Newell, K.M. (Eds.). (2006). *Movement system variability.* Champaign, IL: Human Kinetics.

Davids, K., Button, C., Araújo, D., Renshaw, I., & Hristovski, R. (2006). Movement models from sports provide representative task constraints for studying adaptive behavior in human movement systems. *Adaptive Behavior, 14,* 73-94.

Davids, K., Glazier, P., Araújo, D., & Bartlett, R. M. (2003). Movement systems as dynamical systems: The role of functional variability and its implications for sports medicine. *Sports Medicine, 33,* 245-260.

Davids, K. & Handford, C.H. (1994). Perception and action in sport: The practice behind the theories. *Coaching Focus, 26,* 3-5.

Davids, K., Handford, C.H., & Williams, A.M. (1994). The natural physical alternative to cognitive theories of motor behaviour: An invitation for interdisciplinary research in sports science? *Journal of Sports Sciences, 12,* 495-528.

Davids, K., Kingsbury, D., Bennett, S.J., & Handford, C. (2001). Information–movement coupling: Implications for the organisation of research and practice during acquisition of self-paced extrinsic timing skills. *Journal of Sports Sciences, 19,* 117-127.

Davids, K., Savelsbergh, G.J.P., Bennett, S. J., & van der Kamp, J. (2002). *Interceptive actions in sport: Information and movement.* London: Routledge, Taylor & Francis.

Davidson, D.L.W., & Wolpert, D.M. (2003). Motor learning and prediction in a variable environment. *Current Opinion in Neurobiology, 13*(2), 232-237.

Decety, J., & Grèzes, J. (1999). Neural mechanisms subserving the perception of human actions. *Trends in Cognitive Sciences, 3,* 172-178.

Decety, J., Grèzes, J., Costes, N., Perani, D., Jeannerod, M., Procyk, E., et al. (1997). Brain activity during observation of actions: Influence of action content and subject's strategy. *Brain, 120,* 1763-1777.

De Koning, J.J., de Groot, G., & van Ingen Schenau, G.J. (1992). Ice friction during speed skating. *Journal of Biomechanics, 25*(6), 565-571.

De Maeght, S., & Prinz, W. (2004). Action induction through action observation. *Psychological Research, 68*(2-3), 97-114.

den Duyn, N. (1996). Why it makes sense to play games! *Sports Coach,* Spring issue, 7- 9.

DiPaolo, E. (2002). Spike-timing dependent plasticity for evolved robots. *Adaptive Behavior, 10,* 243-263.

Duchon, A.P. & Warren, W.H. (2002). A visual equalization strategy for locomotor control: Of honeybees, robots and humans. *Psychological Science, 13,* 272-278.

Ebbinghaus, H. (1964). *Memory: A contribution to experimental psychology.* New York Dover.

Edelman, G.M., & Gally, J.A. (2001). Degeneracy and complexity in biological systems. *Proceedings of the National Academy of Science, 98,* 13763-13768.

Ehrlich, P.R. (2000). *Human natures: Genes, cultures, and the human prospect.* Washington, DC: Island Press.

Ericsson, K.A., Krampe, R.T., & Tesch-Römer, C. (1993). The role of deliberate practice in the acquisition of expert performance. *Psychological Review, 100*(3), 363-406.

Fairweather, M. (1999). Skill learning principles: Implications for coaching practice. In N. Cross & J. Lyle (Eds.), *The coaching process* (pp. 113-129). Oxford: Butterworth-Heinemann.

Fairweather, M., Button, C., & Rae, I. (2002). A critical examination of motor control and transfer issues in putting. In A. Cochran, M. Farrally, & E. Thain (Eds.), *Science and golf IV* (pp. 100-112). London: Routledge.

Fajen, B., Turvey, M.T. & Riley, M. (in press). Information, affordances, and the control of action in sport. *International Journal of Sport Psychology.*

Fajen, B.R, Warren, W.H., Temizer, S. & Kaelbling, L.P. (2003). A dynamical model of visually-guided steering, obstacle avoidance and route selection. *International Journal of Computer Vision, 54,* 13-34.

Feitosa, M.F., Gaskill, S.E., Rice, T., Rankinen, T., Bouchard, C., Rao, D.C., et al. (2002). Major gene effects on exercise ventilatory threshold: the HERITAGE Family Study. *Journal of Applied Physiology, 93,* 1000-1006.

Fitch, H.L., Tuller, B., & Turvey, M.T. (1982). The Bernstein perspective: III. Tuning of coordinative structures with respect to perception. In J.A.S. Kelso (Ed.), *Human motor behavior: An introduction* (pp. 271-282). Hillsdale, NY: LEA.

Fitch, H., & Turvey, M.T. (1978). On the control of activity: Some remarks from an ecological point of view. In D.H. Landers & R.W. Christina (Eds.), *Psychology of motor behavior and sport* (pp. 3-35). Champaign, IL: Human Kinetics.

Fitts, P.M. (1964). Perceptual-motor skills learning. In A.W. Melton (Ed.), *Categories of human learning.* New York: Academic Press.

Fitts, P.M., & Posner, M.I. (1967). *Human performance.* Belmont, CA: Brooks/Cale.

Flash, T., & Sejnowski, T.J. (2001). Computational approaches to motor control. *Current Opinion in Neurobiology, 11*(6), 655-662.

Fox, P.W., Hershberger, S.L., & Bouchard, T.J. (1996). Genetic and environmental contributions to the acquisition of a motor skill. *Nature, 384,* 356-358.

Gauthier, G.M., Martin, B.J., & Stark, L.W. (1986). Adapted head-and-eye-movement responses to added-head inertia. *Aviation, Space & Environmental Medicine, 57*(4), 336-342.

Gayagay, G., Yu, B., Hambly, B., Boston, T., Hahn, A., Celermajer, D.S., et al. (1998). Elite endurance athletes and the ACE I allele—the role of genes in athletic performance. *Human Genetics, 103,* 48-50.

Gentilucci, M., Chieffi, S., Daprati, E., Saetti, C.M., & Toni, I. (1996). Visual illusion and action. *Neuropsychologia, 34,* 369-376.

Gesell, A. (1928). *Infancy and human growth.* New York: Macmillan.

Gibson, J.J. (1979). *The ecological approach to visual perception.* Hillsdale, NJ: Erlbaum.

Gleick, J. (1987). *Chaos.* London: William Heinemann.

Goldfield, E.C. (2000). Development of infant action systems and exploratory activity: A tribute to Edward S. Reed. *Ecological Psychology, 12*(4), 303-318.

Goodale, M.A., Milner, A.D., Jackobson, L.S., & Carey, D.P. (1991). A neurological dissociation between perceiving objects and grasping them. *Nature, 349,* 154-156.

Gordon, D. (2007). Control without hierarchy. *Nature, 446,* 143.

Green, T.D., & Flowers, J.H. (1991). Implicit versus explicit learning processes in a probabilistic, continuous fine-motor catching task. *Journal of Motor Behavior, 24*(3), 290-300.

Griffin, L. L., Brooker, R., & Patton, K. (2005). Working towards legitimacy: two decades of Teaching Games for Understanding. *Physical Education and Sport Pedagogy, 10,* 213-223.

Griffin, L. L., Butler, J., Lombardo, B., & Nastasi, R. (2003). An introduction to teaching games for understanding. In J. Butler, L. Griffin, B. Lombardo & R. Nastasi (Eds.), *Teaching games for understanding in physical education and sport* (pp. 1-9). VA: NASPE Publications.

Griffin, L.L., Mitchell, S.A., & Oslin, J.L. (1997). *Teaching sports concepts and skills: A tactical games approach.* Champaign, IL: Human Kinetics.

Guerin, S., & Kunkle, D. (2004). Emergence of constraint in self-organized systems. *Nonlinear Dynamics, Psychology and Life Sciences, 8,* 131-146.

Haffenden, A.M., & Goodale, M.A. (1998). The effects of pictorial illusion on prehension and perception. *Journal of Cognitive Neuroscience, 10,* 122-136.

Haken, H. (1996). *Principles of brain functioning.* Berlin: Springer.

Haken, H., Kelso, J.A.S., & Bunz, H. (1985). A theoretical model of phase transitions in human hand movements. *Biological Cybernetics, 51,* 347-356.

Hamill, J., Haddad, J.M., Heiderscheit, B.C., van Emmerik, R.E.A., & Li, L. (2006). Clinical relevance of variability in coordination. In K. Davids, S. Bennett, & K. Newell (Eds.), *Movement system variability* (pp. 133-152). Champaign, IL: Human Kinetics.

Handford, C., Davids, K., Bennett, S., & Button, C. (1997). Skill acquisition in sport: Some applications of an evolving practice ecology. *Journal of Sport Sciences, 15*(6), 621-640.

Hanisch, C., Konczak, J., & Dohle, C. (2001). The effect of the Ebbinghaus illusion on grasping behaviour of children. *Experimental Brain Research, 137*(2), 237-245.

Harris, L.R., & Jenkin, M. (1998). *Vision and action.* Cambridge, UK: Cambridge University Press.

Hasan, Z., & Thomas, J.S. (1999). Kinematic redundancy. In M.D. Binder (Ed.), *Peripheral and spinal mechanisms in the neural control of movement (Progress in brain research), Vol. 123* (pp. 379-388). Amsterdam: Elsevier.

Haywood, K.M. & Getchell, N. (2001). *Life span motor development* (3rd ed.). Champaign, IL: Human Kinetics.

Haywood, K.M., & Getchell, N. (2005). *Life span motor development* (4th ed.). Champaign, IL: Human Kinetics.

Hedges, L.V., & Olkin, I. (1985). *Statistical methods for meta-analysis.* Orlando, FL: Academic Press.

Heiderscheit, B.C., Hamill, J., & van Emmerik, R.E.A. (1998). Q-angle influences on the variability of lower extremity coordination during running. *Medicine and Science in Sports and Exercise, 31*(9), 1313-1319.

Hellison, D.R., & Templin, T.J. (1991). *A reflective approach to teaching physical education.* Champaign, IL: Human Kinetics.

Henderson, S.E. (1992). Clumsiness or developmental co-ordination disorder: A neglected handicap. *Current Paediatrics, 2,* 158-162.

Henderson, S.E., Sugden, D., & Barnette, A.L. (1992). *Movement assessment battery for children.* London: Psychological Corporation.

Henry, F.M., & Rogers, D.E. (1960). Increased response latency for complicated movements and a "memory drum" theory of neuromotor reaction. *Research Quarterly, 31,* 448-458.

Herbert, E.P., & Landin, D. (1994). The effects of learning model and augmented feedback on tennis skill acquisition. *Research Quarterly for Exercise and Sport, 65,* 250-257.

Herkowitz, J. (1984). Developmentally engineered equipment and playgrounds. In J.R. Thomas (Ed.), *Motor development during childhood and adolescence* (pp. 139-173). Minneapolis: Burgess.

Hodges, N.J., & Franks, I.M. (2001). Learning a coordination skill: Interactive effects of instruction and feedback. *Research Quarterly for Exercise and Sport, 72*(2), 132-142.

Hodges, N.J., & Franks, I.M. (2002). Modelling coaching practice: the role of instruction and demonstration. *Journal of Sports Sciences, 20,* 793-811.

Hoenkamp, E. (1978). Perceptual cues that determine the labeling of human gait. *Journal of Human Movement Studies, 4,* 59-69.

Holder, T. (1998). *Sources of information in the acquisition and organisation of interceptive actions.* Unpublished doctoral dissertation, University of Southampton, Southampton, UK.

Hopper, T. (2002). Teaching games for understanding: The importance of student emphasis over content emphasis. *Journal of Physical Education, Recreation and Dance, 73,* 44-48.

Horn, R., & Williams, A.M. (2004). Observational learning: Is it time we took another look? In A.M. Williams & N. Hodges (Eds.), *Skill acquisition in sport: Research, theory and practice* (pp. 175-206). Abingdon, UK: Routledge.

Horn, R., Williams, A.M., & Scott, M.A. (2002). Visual search strategy, movement kinematics and observational learning. *Journal of Sports Sciences, 20,* 253-269.

Horn, R., Williams, A.M., Scott, M.A., & Hodges, N. (2005). Visual search and coordination changes in response to video and point-light demonstrations without KR. *Journal of Motor Behavior, 37*(4), 265-274.

Immink, M.A., & Wright, D.L. (2001). Motor programming during practice conditions high and low in contextual interference. *Journal of Experimental Psychology: Human Perception and Performance, 27,* 423-437.

Iwatsubo, T., Kawamura, S., Miyamoto, K., & Yamaguchi, T. (2000). Numerical analysis of golf club head and ball at various impact points. *Sports Engineering, 3,* 195-204.

Jacobs, D.M., & Michaels, C.F. (2002). On the apparent paradox of learning and realism. *Ecological Psychology, 14,* 127-139.

James, W. (1890). *Principles of psychology* (Vols. 1 and 2). New York: Holt.

Janelle, C.M., Barba, D.A., Frehlich, S.G., Tennant, L.K., & Cauraugh, J.H. (1997). Maximizing feedback effectiveness through videotape replay and a self-controlled learning environment. *Research Quarterly for Exercise and Sport, 68,* 269-279.

Janelle, C.M., Champenoy, J.D., Coombes, S.A., & Mousseau, M.B. (2003). Mechanics of attentional cueing during observational learning to facilitate motor skill acquisition. *Journal of Sports Sciences, 21,* 825-838.

Jarvis, P., Holford, J. & Griffin, C. (2003). *The theory and practice of learning* (2nd ed.). London: Routledge, Taylor & Francis Ltd.

Jeannerod, M. (1981). Intersegmental co-ordination during reaching at natural visual objects. In J. Long & A. Baddeley (Eds.), *Attention and performance* (Vol. IX) (pp. 153-172). Hillsdale, NJ: Erlbaum.

Jeng, S.F., Holt, K.G., Fetters, L., & Certo, C. (1996). Self-optimization of walking in nondisabled children and children with spastic hemiplegic cerebral palsy. *Journal of Motor Behavior, 28*(1), 15-27.

Jette, A.M. (1994). Physical disablement concepts for physical therapy research and practice. *Physical Therapy, 74*(5), 380-386.

Johansson, G. (1973). Visual perception of biological motion and a model for its analysis. *Perception and Psychophysics, 14,* 201-211.

Johansson, G. (1975). Visual motion perception. *Scientific American, 232*(6), 76-88.

Johansson, G., von Hofsten, G., & Jannson, G. (1980). Event perception. *Annual Review of Psychology, 31,* 27-63.

Johnston, L.M., Burns, Y.R., Brauer, S.G., & Richardson, C.A. (2002). Differences in postural control and movement performance during goal directed reaching in children with developmental coordination disorder. *Human Movement Sciences, 21*(5-6), 583-601.

Johnston, T.D., & Edwards, L. (2002). Genes, interactions and the development of behaviour. *Psychological Review, 109,* 26-34.

Kærn, M., Elston, T.C., Blake, W.J., & Collins, J.J. (2005). Stochasticity in gene expression: From theories to phenotypes. *Nature Reviews Genetics, 6,* 451-464.

Kalkavan, A., & Fazey, J.A. (1995). An investigation of 'novice' and 'expert' catching performance with only auditory information sources. *Journal of Sports Sciences, 13* (61).

Kaplan, D., & Glass, L. (1995). *Understanding nonlinear dynamics.* New York: Springer Verlag.

Kauffman, S.A. (1993). *The origins of order: Self-organization and selection in evolution.* N.Y.: Oxford University Press.

Kauffman, S.A. (1995). *At home in the universe: The search for laws of complexity.* London: Viking.

Kawato, M. (1999). Internal models for motor control and trajectory planning. *Current Opinion in Neurobiology, 9*(6), 718-727.

Keele, S.W. (1968). Movement control in skilled motor performance. *Psychological Bulletin, 70,* 387-403.

Keele, S.W., & Posner, M.I. (1968). Processing of feedback in rapid movements. *Journal of Experimental Psychology, 77,* 353-363.

Keele, S.W., & Summers, J.J. (1976). The structure of motor programs. In G.E. Stelmach (Ed.), *Motor control: Issues and trends* (pp. 109-142). New York: Grune and Stratton.

Kelso, J.A.S. (1981). Contrasting perspectives on order and regulation in movement. In J. Long & A. Baddeley (Eds.), *Attention and performance IX* (pp. 437-458). Hillsdale, NJ: LEA.

Kelso, J.A.S. (1984). Phase transitions and critical behavior in human bimanual coordination. *American Journal of Physiology: Regulatory, Integrative and Comparative Physiology, 15,* R1000-R1004.

Kelso, J.A.S. (1992). Theoretical concepts and strategies for understanding perceptual-motor skill: From informational capacity in closed systems to self-organization in open, nonequilibrium systems. *Journal of Experimental Psychology: General, 121,* 260-261.

Kelso, J.A.S. (1995). *Dynamic patterns: The self-organisation of brain and behaviour.* Cambridge, MA: MIT Press.

Kelso, J.A.S. & Engström, D.A. (2006). *The complementary nature.* Cambridge, MA: Bradford Books.

Kelso, J.A., & Zanone, P.G. (2002). Coordination dynamics of learning and transfer across different effector systems. *Journal of Experimental Psychology: Human Perception and Performance, 28*(4), 776-797.

Kirk, D., & MacPhail, A. (2002). Teaching games for understanding and situated learning: Rethinking the Bunker-Thorpe model. *Journal of Teaching in Physical Education, 21,* 177-192.

Klapp, S.T. (1977). Reaction time analysis of programmed control. *Exercise and Sport Sciences Reviews, 5,* 231-253.

Konczak, J. (1990). Toward an ecological theory of motor development: The relevance of the Gibsonian Approach to vision for motor development research. In J. Clark & J. Humphrey (Eds.), *Advances in motor development research 3* (pp. 201-224). New York: AMS Press.

Konczak, J., Meeuwsen, H., & Cress, M. (1992). Changing affordances in stair climbing: The perception of maximum climbability in young and older adults. *Journal of Experimental Psychology: Human Perception and Performance, 18*(3), 691-697.

Kugler, P.N. (1986). A morphological perspective on the origin and evolution of movement patterns. In W. Wade & H.T.A. Whiting (Eds.), *Motor development in children: Aspects of coordination and control* (pp. 459-525). Dordrecht, Netherlands: Martinus Nijhoff.

Kugler, P.N., Kelso, J.A.S., & Turvey, M.T. (1982). On the control and coordination of naturally developing systems. In J.A.S. Kelso & J.E. Clark (Eds.), *The development of movement coordination and control* (pp. 5-78). New York: Wiley.

Kugler, P.N., Shaw, R.E., Vincente, K.J., & Kinsella-Shaw, J. (1990). Inquiry into intentional systems: I. Issues in ecological physics. *Psychological Research, 52*(2-3), 98-121.

Kugler, P.N., & Turvey, M.T. (1987). *Information, natural law, and the self-assembly of rhythmic movement.* Hillsdale, NJ: Erlbaum.

Lashley, K.S. (1917). The accuracy of movement in the absence of excitation from the moving organ. *American Journal of Physiology, 43,* 169-194.

Latash, M.L. (1996). The Bernstein problem: How does the central nervous system make its choices? In M.L. Latash & M.T. Turvey (Eds.), *Dexterity and its development* (pp. 277-304). Mahwah, NJ: LEA.

Latash, M.L. (2000). There is no motor redundancy in human movements. There is motor abundance. *Motor Control, 4,* 259-261.

Laurent, M., Montagne, G., & Durey, A. (1996). Binocular invariants in interceptive tasks: A directed perception approach. *Perception, 25,* 1437-1450.

Lebed, F. (2007). System approach to games and competitive playing. *European Journal of Sport Science, 6,* 33-42.

Lee, D.N. (1976). A theory of visual control of braking based on information about time-to-collision. *Perception, 5,* 437-459.

Lee, D.N. (1990). Getting around with light or sound. In R. Warrent & A.H. Wertheim (Eds.), *Perception and control of self-motion* (pp. 487-505). Hillsdale, NJ: Erlbaum.

Lee, D.N., & Lishman, R. (1975). Visual proprioceptive control of stance. *Journal of Human Movement Studies, 1,* 87-95.

Lee, T.D., Blandin, Y., & Proteau, L. (1996). Effects of task instructions and oscillation frequency on bimanual coordination. *Psychology Research, 59,* 100-106.

Lee, T.D., Chamberlin, C.J., & Hodges, N.J. (2001). Practice. In B. Singer, H. Hausenblas, & C. Jannelle (Eds.), *Handbook of sport psychology* (2nd ed., pp. 115-143). New York: Wiley.

Lee, T.D., & Magill, R.A. (1985). Can forgetting facilitate skill acquisition? In D. Goodman, R.B. Wilberg, & I.M. Franks (Eds.), *Differing perspectives in motor learning, memory and control* (pp. 3-22). Amsterdam: North-Holland.

Lewontin, R. (2000). *It ain't necessarily so: The dream of the human genome and other illusions.* London: Granta Books.

Liao, C., & Masters, R.S.W. (2001). Analogy learning: A means to implicit motor learning. *Journal of Sports Sciences, 19,* 307-319.

Liu, Y.-T., Mayer-Kress, G., & Newell, K.M. (2006). Qualitative and quantitative change in the dynamics of motor learning. *Journal of Experimental Psychology: Human Perception and Performance, 32,* 380-393.

Lyle, J. (2002). *Sports coaching concepts: A framework for coaches' behaviour.* Abingdon, UK: Routledge.

Magill, R.A. (2006). *Motor learning: Concepts and applications* (8th ed.). New York: McGraw-Hill.

Magill, R.A., & Schoenfelder-Zohdi, B.G. (1996). A visual model and knowledge of performance as sources of information for learning a rhythmic gymnastics skill. *International Journal of Sport Psychology, 27,* 7-22.

Maraj, B.K.V. (2003). Perceptual judgments for stair climbing as a function of pitch angle. *Research Quarterly for Exercise and Sport, 74*(3), 248-256.

Marisi, D.Q. (1977). Genetic and extragenetic variance in motor performance. *Acta Genetica Medica, 26,* 3-4.

Masters, R.S.W. (1992). Knowledge, knerves and know-how: The role of explicit versus implicit knowledge in the breakdown of a complex motor skill under pressure. *British Journal of Psychology, 83,* 343-358.

Masters, R., Law, J., & Maxwell, J. (2002). Implicit and explicit learning in interceptive actions. In K. Davids, G. Savelsbergh, S.J. Bennett, & J. van der Kamp (Eds.), *Interceptive actions in sport: Information and movement* (pp. 126-143). London: Routledge.

Matarić, M. (1998). Behavior-based robotics as a tool for synthesis of artificial behavior and analysis of natural behavior. *Trends in Cognitive Sciences, 2,* 82-87.

Maxwell, J. P., Masters, R. S. W., Kerr, E., & Weedon, E. (2001). The implicit benefit of learning without errors. *Quarterly Journal of Experimental Psychology, 54A,* 1049-1068.

McCullagh, P., & Weiss, M. R. (2001). Modeling: Considerations for motor skill performance and psychological responses. In R.N. Singer, H.A. Hasenblas, & C.M. Janelle (Eds.), *Handbook of sport psychology* (2nd ed., pp. 205-238). New York: Wiley.

McDonald, P.V., Oliver, S.K., & Newell, K.M. (1995). Perceptual-motor exploration as a function of biomechanical and task constraints. *Acta Psychologica, 88,* 127-166.

McGarry, T., Anderson, D.I., Wallace, S.A., Hughes, M.D., & Franks, I.M. (2002). Sport competition as a dynamical self-organizing system. *Journal of Sports Sciences, 20*(10), 771-781.

McGraw, M.B. (1943). *The neuromuscular maturation of the human infant.* New York: Columbia University Press (Reprinted by Hafner, 1963).

McMorris, T. (1998). Teaching Games for Understanding: Its contribution to the knowledge of skill acquisition from a motor learning perspective. *European Journal of Physical Education, 3,* 65-74.

Mechsner, F., Kerzel, D., Knoblich, G., & Prinz, W. (2001). Perceptual basis of bimanual coordination. *Nature, 414,* 69-73.

Michaels, C.F. (1998). The ecological/dynamical approach, manifest destiny and a single movement science. In A.A. Post, J.R. Pijpers, P. Bosch, & M.S.J. Boschker (Eds.), *Models in human movement sciences* (pp. 65-68). Amsterdam: Institute for Fundamental and Clinical Human Movement Sciences.

Michaels, C.F., & Beek, P. (1995). The state of ecological psychology. *Ecological Psychology, 7,* 259-278.

Michaels, C.F., & Carello, C. (1981). *Direct perception.* Englewood Cliffs, NJ: Prentice Hall.

Michels, L., Lappe, M., Vaina, L.M., Pelphrey, K.A., Mitchell, T.V., McKeown, M.J., et al. (2005). Visual areas involved in the perception of human movement from dynamic form analysis. *Neuroreport, 16*(10), 1037-1041.

Milner, A.D., & Goodale, M.A. (1995). *The visual brain in action.* Oxford: Oxford University Press.

Milner, A.D., Perrett, D.I., Johnston, R.S., Benson, P.J., Jordan, T.R., Heeley, D.W., et al. (1991). Perception and action in 'visual form agnosia'. *Brain, 114,* 39-49.

Missitzi, J., Geladas, N., & Klissouras, V. (2004). Heritability in neuromuscular coordination: Implications for motor control strategies. *Medicine and Science in Sports and Exercise, 36,* 233-240.

Mitra, S., Amazeen, P.G., & Turvey, M.T. (1998). Intermediate motor learning as decreasing active (dynamical) degrees of freedom. *Human Movement Science, 17*(1), 17-65.

Mononen, K., Vitasalo, J.T., Kontinnen, N., & Era, P. (2003). The effects of augmented kinematic feedback on motor skill learning in rifle shooting. *Journal of Sports Sciences, 21*(10), 867-876.

Montagne, G., Fraisse, F., Ripoll, H., & Laurent, M. (2000). Perception–movement coupling in an interceptive task: First-order time-to-contact as an input variable. *Human Movement Science, 19*, 59-72.

Montagne, G., Laurent, M., Durey, A., & Bootsma, R.J. (1999). Movement reversals in ball catching. *Experimental Brain Research, 129*, 87-92.

Montgomery, H.E., Clarkson, P., Barnard, M., Bell, J.D., Brynes, A.E., Dollery, C.M., et al. (1999). Angiotensin-converting enzyme gene insertion/deletion polymorphism and response to physical training. *Lancet, 353*, 541-545.

Montgomery, H.E., Marshall, R., Hemingway, H., Myerson, S., Clarkson, P., Dollery, C.M., et al. (1998). Human gene for physical performance. *Nature, 393*, 221-222.

Mon-Williams, M., Tresilian, J.R., & Wann, J.P. (1999). Perceiving limb position in normal and abnormal control: An equilibrium point perspective. *Human Movement Science, 18*, 397-419.

Muchisky, M., Gershkoff-Cole, L., Cole, E., & Thelen, E. (1996). The epigenetic landscape revisited: A dynamical interpretation. In C. Rovee-Collier & L.P. Lipsitt (Eds.), *Advances in infancy research* (pp. 121-160). Norwood, NJ: Ablex.

Muellbacher, W., Ziemann, U., Wissel, J., Dang, N., Kofler, M., Facchini, S., et al. (2002). Early consolidation in human motor cortex. *Nature, 415*, 640-643.

Müller, H., & Sternad, D. (2004). Decomposition of variability in the execution of goal-oriented tasks: Three components of skill improvements. *Journal of Experimental Psychology: Human Perception and Performance, 30*(1), 213-233.

Mullineaux, D.R., Bartlett, R.M., & Bennett, S. (2001). Research design and statistics in biomechancis and motor control. *Journal of Sports Sciences, 19*, 739-760.

Myerson, S., Hemingway, H., Budget, R., Martin, J., Humphries, S.E., & Montgomery, H.E. (1999). Human angiotensin I-converting enzyme gene and endurance performance. *Journal of Applied Physiology, 87*, 1313-1316.

Naylor, J., & Briggs, G. (1978). Effects of task complexity and task organization on the relative efficiency of part and whole training methods. *Journal of Experimental Psychology: Human Perception and Performance, 65*, 217-244.

Nazarov, I.B., Woods, D.R., Montgomery, H.E., Shneider, O.V., Kazakov, V.I., Tomilin, N.V., et al. (2001). The angiotensin converting enzyme I/D polymorphism in Russian athletes. *European Journal of Human Genetics, 9*, 797-801.

Netelenbos, J.B., & Savelsbergh, G.J. (2003). Children's search for targets located within and beyond the field of view: Effects of deafness and age. *Perception, 32*(4), 485-497.

Newell, A., & Rosenbloom, P.S. (1981). Mechanisms of skill acquisition and the law of practice. In J.R. Anderson (Ed.), *Cognitive skills and their acquisition* (pp. 1-55). Hillsdale, NJ: Erlbaum.

Newell, K.M. (1985). Coordination, control and skill. In D. Goodman, R.B. Wilberg, & I.M. Franks (Eds.), *Differing perspectives in motor learning, memory, and control* (pp. 295-317). Amsterdam: Elsevier Science.

Newell, K.M. (1986). Constraints on the development of coordination. In M.G. Wade & H.T.A. Whiting (Eds.), *Motor development in children: Aspects of coordination and control* (pp. 341-360). Dordrecht, Netherlands: Martinus Nijhoff.

Newell, K.M. (1989). On task and theory specificity. *Journal of Motor Behavior, 21*, 92-96.

Newell, K.M. (1991). Motor skill acquisition. *Annual Review of Psychology, 42*, 213-237.

Newell, K.M. (1996). Change in movement and skill: Learning, retention and transfer. In M.L. Latash & M.T. Turvey (Eds.), *Dexterity and its development* (pp. 393-430). Mahwah, NJ: Erlbaum.

Newell, K.M. (2003). Schema theory: Retrospectives and prospectives. *Research Quarterly for Exercise and Sport, 74,* 383-388.

Newell, K.M., Broderick, M.P., Deutsch, K.M., & Slifkin, A.B. (2003). Task goals and change in dynamical degrees of freedom with motor learning. *Journal of Experimental Psychology: Human Perception and Performance, 29*(2), 379-387.

Newell, K.M., & Corcos, D.M. (1993). Issues in variability and motor control. In K.M. Newell & D.M. Corcos (Eds.), *Variability and motor control* (pp. 1-12). Champaign, IL: Human Kinetics.

Newell, K.M., Deutsch, K.M., & Morrison, S. (2000). On learning to move randomly. *Journal of Motor Behavior, 32*(3), 314-320.

Newell, K.M., Deutsch, K.M., Sosnoff, J.J., & Mayer-Kress, G. (2006). Variability in motor output as noise: A default and erroneous proposition. In K. Davids, S. Bennett, & K.M. Newell (Eds.), *Movement system variability* (pp. 3-24). Champaign, IL: Human Kinetics.

Newell, K.M., Kugler, P.N., Emmerik, R.E.A.v., & McDonald, P.V. (1989). Search strategies and the acquisition of coordination. In S.A. Wallace (Ed.), *Perspectives on the coordination of movement* (pp. 85-122). Amsterdam: Elsevier Science.

Newell, K.M., Liu, Y.-T., & Mayer-Kress, G. (2001). Time scales in motor learning and development. *Psychological Review, 108*(1), 57-82.

Newell, K.M., Liu,Y.-T., & Mayer-Kress, G. (2005). Learning in the brain-computer interface: Insights about degrees of freedom and degeneracy from a landscape model of motor learning. *International Quarterly of Cognitive Science, 6,* 37-47.

Newell, K.M., & McDonald, P.V. (1991). Practice: A search for task solutions. In R. Christina & H.M. Eckert (Eds.), *American Academy of Physical Education Papers: Enhancing human performance in sport: New concepts and developments* (pp. 51-60). Champaign, IL: Human Kinetics.

Newell, K.M., Morris, L.R., & Scully, D.M. (1985). Augmented information and the acquisition of skill in physical activity. In R. Terjung (Ed.), *Exercise and sport science reviews* (Vol. 13, pp. 235-261). New York: Macmillan.

Newell, K.M. & Rovegno, I. (1990). Commentary-Motor learning: theory and practice. *Quest, 42,* 184-192.

Newell, K.M., & Slifkin, A.B. (1998). The nature of movement variability. In J.P. Piek (Ed.), *Motor behavior and human skill: A multidisciplinary perspective* (pp. 143-160). Champaign, IL: Human Kinetics.

Newell, K.M., & Vaillancourt, D. (2001). Dimensional change in motor learning. *Human Movement Science, 20,* 695-715.

New Zealand Government. (2003). Healthy Eating-Healthy Action (Oranga Kai- Oranga Pumau): A Strategic Framework. Ministry of Health, NZ: Wellington.

Niemeijer, A.S., Smits-Engelsman, B.C.M., Reynders, K., & Schoemaker, M.M. (2003). Verbal actions of physiotherapists to enhance motor learning in children with DCD. *Human Movement Science, 22*(4), 567-581.

Nouritt, D., Délignières, D., Caillou, N., Deschamps, T., & Lauriot, B. (2003). On discontinuities in motor learning: a longitudinal study of complex skill acquisition on a ski-simulator. *Journal of Motor Behavior, 35,* 151-170.

Ollis, S., Button, C., & Fairweather, M. (2005). The influence of professional expertise and task complexity upon the potency of the CI effect. *Acta Psychologica, 118,* 229-244.

Paine, R.W. & Tani, J. (2005). How hierarchical control self-organizes in artificial adaptive systems. *Adaptive Behavior, 13,* 211-225.

Pangrazi, R.P., & Dauber, V.P. (1989). *Dynamic physical education for elementary school children.* New York: Macmillan.

Pavani, F., Boscagli, I., Benvenuti, F., Rabuffetti, M., & Farnè, A. (1999). Are perception and action affected differently by the Titchener circles illusion? *Experimental Brain Research, 127*, 95-101.

Pelphrey, K.A., Mitchell, T.V., McKeown, M.J., Goldstein, J., Allison, T., & McCarthy, G. (2003). Brain activity evoked by the perception of human walking: Controlling for meaningful coherent motion. *Journal of Neuroscience, 23*(17), 6819-6825.

Peper, C.E., Bootsma, R.J., Mestre, D.R., & Bakker, F.C. (1994). Catching balls: How to get the hand to the right place at the right time. *Journal of Experimental Psychology: Human Perception and Performance, 20*(3), 591-612.

Pettifor, B. (1999). *Physical education methods for classroom teachers.* Champaign, IL: Human Kinetics.

Post, A.A., Pijpers, J.R., Bosch, P., & Boschker, M.S.J. (1998). Models in human movement sciences: Proceedings of the second international symposium of the institute for fundamental and clinical human movement science. Enschede: PrintPartners Ipskamp.

Potrac, P., Brewer, C., Jones, R.S., Armour, K., & Hoff, J. (2000). Toward an holistic understanding of the coaching process. *Quest, 52*, 186-199.

Prigogine, I., & Stengers, I. (1984). *Order out of chaos.* New York: Bantam Books.

Rankinen, T., Perusse, L., Gagnon, J., Chagnon, Y. C., Leon, A.S., Skinner, J.S., et al. (2000). Angiotensin-converting enzyme ID polymorphism and fitness phenotype in the HERITAGE Family Study. *Journal of Applied Physiology, 88,* 1029-1035.

Reed, E.S. (1988). Applying the theory of action systems to the study of motor skills. In O.G. Meijer & K. Roth (Eds.), *Complex movement behaviour: 'The' motor-action controversy* (pp. 45-86). Amsterdam: North Holland.

Regimbal, C., Deller, J., & Plimpton, C. (1992). Basketball size as related to children's preference, rated skill and scoring. *Perceptual and Motor Skills, 75,* 867-872.

Renshaw, I., & Davids, K. (2004). Nested task constraints shape continuous perception-action coupling control during human locomotor pointing. *Neuroscience Letters, 369*(2), 93-98.

Renshaw, I. & Davids, K. (2006). A comparison of locomotor pointing strategies in cricket bowling and long jumping. *International Journal of Sport Psychology, 37,* 38-57.

Ridley, M. (2004). *Nature via nurture: Genes, experience and what makes us human.* New York: Harper Collins.

Riley, M.A., & Turvey, M. (2002). Variability and determinism in motor behavior. *Journal of Motor Behavior, 34,* 99-125.

Rink, J.E. (2001). *Teaching physical education for learning* (4th ed.). Boston: WCB McGraw-Hill.

Rose, D., & Christina, R. (2005). *A multilevel approach to the study of motor control and learning* (2nd ed.). San Francisco: Benjamin Cummings.

Rosenblum, L.D., Carello, C., & Pastore, R.E. (1987). Relative effectiveness of three stimulus variables for locating a moving sound source. *Perception, 16,* 175-186.

Rosengren, K.S., Savelsbergh, G.J.P., & van der Kamp, J. (2003). Development and learning: A TASC-based perspective on the acquisition of perceptual motor behaviors. *Infant Behavior and Development, 26,* 473-494.

Runeson, S. (1977). On the possibility of "smart" perceptual mechanisms. *Scandinavian Journal of Psychology, 18,* 172-179.

Saltzman, E.L., & Kelso, J.A.S. (1987). Skilled actions: A task-dynamic approach. *Psychological Review, 94,* 84-106.

Sanders, R. (2000). Some ideas for coaches of pool, surf, and open water freestyle swimmers. Retrieved September 26, 2002, from www.coachesinfo.com.

Savelsbergh, G.J.P., & Bootsma, R.J. (1994). Perception–action coupling in hitting and catching. *International Journal of Sport Psychology, 25,* 331-343.

Savelsbergh, G.J.P., Netelenbos, J.B., & Whiting, H.T.A. (1991). Auditory perception and the control of spatially coordinated action in deaf and hearing children. *Journal of Child Psychology and Psychiatry, 32,* 489-500.

Savelsbergh, G.J.P., & van der Kamp, J.G. (2000). Information in learning to co-ordinate and control movements: Is there a need for specificity of practice? *International Journal of Sport Psychology, 31,* 467-484.

Savelsbergh, G.J.P., Whiting, H.T.A., & Bootsma, R.J. (1991). Grasping Tau. *Journal of Experimental Psychology: Human Perception and Performance, 17,* 315-322.

Scarantino, A. (2003). Affordances explained. *Philosophy of Science, 90,* 949-961.

Schaal, S. (1999). Is imitation learning the route to humanoid robots? *Trends in Cognitive Sciences, 3*(6), 233-242.

Schaal, S., Ijspeert, A., & Billard, A. (2003). Computational approaches to motor learning by imitation. *Philosophical Transactions: Biological Sciences, 358*(1431), 537-547.

Schiff, W., & Oldak, R. (1990). Accuracy of judging time to arrival: Effects of modality, trajectory, and gender. *Journal of Experimental Psychology: Human Perception and Performance, 16,* 303-316.

Schmidt, R.A. (1975). A schema theory of discrete motor skill learning. *Psychological Review, 82,* 225-260.

Schmidt, R.A. (1985). The search for invariance in skilled movement behavior. The 1984 C.H. McCloy Research Lecture. *Research Quarterly for Exercise and Sport, 56,* 188-200.

Schmidt, R.A. (1991). *Motor learning and performance: From principles to practice.* Champaign, IL: Human Kinetics.

Schmidt, R.A. (2003). Motor schema theory after 27 years: Reflections and implications for a new theory. *Research Quarterly for Exercise and Sport, 74*(4), 366-375.

Schmidt, R.C., Carello, C., & Turvey, M.T. (1990). Phase transitions and critical fluctuations in the visual coordination of rhythmic movements between people. *Journal of Experimental Psychology: Human Perception and Performance, 16,* 227-247.

Schmidt, R.C., & Fitzpatrick, P. (1996). Dynamical perspectives on motor learning. In H.N. Zelaznik (Ed.), *Advances in motor learning and control* (pp. 195-223). Champaign, IL: Human Kinetics.

Schmidt, R.A., & Lee, T. (2005). *Motor control and learning: A behavioral emphasis* (4th ed.). Champaign, IL: Human Kinetics.

Schmidt, R.A., & Wrisberg, C.A. (2004). *Motor learning and performance* (3rd ed.). Champaign, IL: Human Kinetics.

Schoenfelder-Zohdi, B.G. (1992). *Investigating the informational nature of a modeled visual demonstration.* Unpublished PhD dissertation, Louisiana State University, Louisana.

Schöllhorn, W.I., Beckmann, H., Michelbrink, M., Sechelmann, M., Trockel, M., & Davids, K. (2006). Does noise provide a basis for unification of motor learning theories? *International Journal of Sport Psychology, 37,* 186-206.

Schöllhorn, W.I., Nigg, B.M., Stefanyshyn, D.J., & Liu, W. (2002). Identification of individual walking patterns using time discrete and time continuous data sets. *Gait and Posture, 15,* 180-186.

Scholz, J.P., & Kelso, J.A.S. (1989). A quantitative approach to understanding the formation and change of coordinated movement patterns. *Journal of Motor Behavior, 21,* 122-144.

Scholz, J.P., Schoner, G., & Latash, M.L. (2000). Identifying the control structures of multijoint coordination during pistol shooting. *Experimental Brain Research, 135,* 382-404.

Schöner, G. (1994). Dynamic theory of action–perception patterns: The time-before-contact paradigm. *Human Movement Science, 13,* 415-440.

Schöner, G., Haken, H., & Kelso, J.A. (1987). A stochastic theory of phase transitions in human hand movement. *Biological Cybernetics, 53*(4), 247-257.

Scott, M.A. (2002). Visual regulation of the long jump approach phase. In K. Davids, G.J.P. Savelsbergh, S.J. Bennett, & J. van der Kamp (Eds.), *Interceptive actions in sport: Information and movement* (pp. 326-334). London: Routledge.

Scully, D.M. (1986). Visual perception of technical execution and aesthetic quality in biological motion. *Human Movement Science, 5,* 185-206.

Scully, D.M. (1987). *Visual perception of biological motion.* Unpublished PhD, University of IL at Urbana-Champaign, IL.

Scully, D.M. (1988). Visual perception of human movement: The use of demonstrations in teaching motor skills. *British Journal of Physical Education Research Supplement, 4,* 12-14.

Scully, D.M., & Newell, K.M. (1985). Observational learning and the acquisition of motor skills: Towards a visual perception perspective. *Journal of Human Movement Studies, 11,* 169-186.

Sharp, R.H. (1992). *Acquiring skill in sport.* London: Sports Dynamics.

Shaw, B.K., McGowan, R.S., & Turvey, M.T. (1991). An acoustic variable specifying time-to-contact. *Ecological Psychology, 3,* 253-261.

Shea, C.H., & Wulf, G. (1999). Enhancing motor learning through external-focus instruction and feedback. *Human Movement Science, 18,* 553-571.

Shea, C.H., & Wulf, G. (2005). Schema theory: A critical appraisal and reevaluation. *Journal of Motor Behavior, 37*(2), 85-101.

Shea, C.H., Wulf, G., Whitacre, C.A., & Park, J.H. (2001). Surfing the implicit wave. *Quarterly Journal of Experimental Psychology (A), 54*(3), 841-862.

Shea, J.B., & Morgan, R.L. (1979). Contextual interference effects on the acquisition, retention, and transfer of a motor skill. *Journal of Experimental Psychology: Human Learning and Memory, 5*(2), 179-187.

Sherrington, C.S. (1906). *The integrative action of the nervous system.* New Haven: Yale University Press (reprinted 1947).

Sidaway, B., & Hand, M.J. (1993). Frequency of modeling effects on the acquisition and retention of a motor skill. *Research Quarterly for Exercise and Sport, 64,* 122-126.

Siedentop, D., Herkowitz, J., & Pink, J. (1984). *Elementary physical education methods.* Englewood Cliffs, NJ: Prentice-Hall.

Sigmundsson, H., Hansen, P.C., & Talcott, J.B. (2003). Do 'clumsy' children have visual deficits? *Behavioral Brain Research, 139,* 123-129.

Singer, R.N. (1985). *Motor learning and human performance* (2nd ed.). New York: Macmillan.

Singer, R.N. (1988). Strategies and metastrategies in learning and performing self-paced athletic skills. *Sport Psychologist, 2,* 49-68.

Skinner, B.F. (1938). *The behavior of organisms.* New York: Appleton-Century.

Snoddy, G.S. (1926). Learning and stability: A psychophysical analysis of a case of motor learning with clinical applications. *Journal of Applied Psychology, 10,* 1-36.

Solomon, H.Y., & Turvey, M.T. (1988). Haptically perceiving the distances reachable with hand-held objects. *Journal of Experimental Psychology: Human Perception and Performance, 14,* 404-427.

Sonna, L.A., Sharp, M.A., Knapik, J.J., Cullivan, M., Angel, K.C., Patton, J.F., et al. (2001). Angiotensin-converting enzyme genotype and physical performance during US Army basic training. *Journal of Applied Physiology, 91,* 1355-1363.

Southard, D., & Higgins, T. (1987). Changing movement patterns: Effects of demonstration and practice. *Research Quarterly for Exercise and Sport, 58*(1), 77-80.

Sparrow, W.A. (2000). *Energetics of human activity.* Champaign, IL: Human Kinetics.

Starkes, J. (2000). The road to expertise: Is practice the only determinant? *International Journal of Sport Psychology, 31,* 431-451.

Strean, W.B., & Bengoechea, E.G. (2003). Beyond technical vs tactical: Extending the games-teaching debate. In J. Butler, L. Griffin, B. Lombardo, & R. Nastasi (Eds.), *Teaching Games for Understanding in physical education and sport* (pp. 181-188). VA: NASPE Publications.

Summers, J.J. (1998). Has ecological psychology delivered what it has promised? In J. Piek (Ed.), *Motor behavioral and human skill: A multidisciplinary approach* (pp. 385-402). Champaign, IL: Human Kinetics.

Summers, J.J. (2004). A historical perspective on skill acquisition. In A.M. Williams & N.J. Hodges (Eds.), *Skill acquisition in sport: Research, theory and practice* (pp. 1-26). Abingdon, UK: Routledge.

Taylor, R.R., Mamotte, C.D.S., Fallon, K., & van Bockxmeer, F.M. (1999). Elite athletes and the gene for angiotensin-converting enzyme. *Journal of Applied Physiology, 87,* 1035-1037.

Temprado, J.J. (2001). Co-ordination in the volleyball serve: Expert–novice differences. In K. Davids, G. Savelsbergh, S.J. Bennett & J. van der Kamp (Eds.), *Interceptive actions in sport: Information and movement* (pp. 259-272). London: Routledge.

Thelen, E. (1995). Motor development: A new synthesis. *American Psychologist, 50*(2), 79-95.

Thelen, E., Ridley-Johnson, R., & Fisher, D. (1983). Shifting patterns of bilateral coordination and lateral dominance in the leg movements of young infants. *Developmental Psychobiology, 16,* 29-46.

Thelen, E., & Smith, L.B. (1994). *A dynamic systems approach to the development of cognition and action.* Cambridge, MA: MIT Press.

Thorndike, E.L. (1927). The law of effect. *American Journal of Psychology, 39,* 212-222.

Thorpe, R. (1990). New directions in games teaching. In N. Armstrong (Ed.), *New directions in physical education: Vol. 1* (pp. 79-100). Champaign, IL: Human Kinetics.

Thorpe, R. (2001). Rod Thorpe on teaching games for understanding. In L. Kidman (Ed.), *Developing decision makers. An empowerment approach to coaching* (pp. 22-36). New Zealand: Innovative Print Communication Ltd.

Todorov, E., & Jordan, M.I. (2002). Optimal feedback control as a theory of motor coordination. *Nature Neuroscience, 5*(11), 1226-1235.

Tresilian, J.R. (1995). Perceptual and cognitive processes in time-to-contact estimation: analysis of prediction-motion and relative judgement tasks. *Perception and Psychophysics, 57*(2), 231-245.

Tresilian, J.R. (1999). Visually timed action: Time-out for 'tau'? *Trends in Cognitive Sciences, 3,* 301-310.

Turner, A.P., & Martinek, T.J. (1999). An investigation into Teaching Games for Understanding effects on skill, knowledge, and game play. *Research Quarterly for Exercise and Sport, 70*(3), 266-296.

Turvey, M.T. (1990). Coordination. *American Psychologist, 45,* 938-953.

Turvey, M.T. (1992). Ecological foundations of cognition: Invariants of perception and action. In H.L. Pick, P.v.d. Broek, & D.C. Knill (Eds.), *Cognition: Conceptual and methodological issues* (pp. 85-129). Washington, DC: American Psychological Association.

Turvey, M.T. (1996). Dynamic touch. *American Psychologist, 51,* 1134-1152.

Turvey, M.T., Burton, G., Amazeen, E.L., Butwill, M., & Carello, C. (1998). Perceiving the width and height of a hand-held object by dynamic touch. *Journal of Experimental Psychology: Human Perception and Performance, 24,* 35-48.

Turvey, M.T., Fitch, H., & Tuller, B. (1982). The Bernstein perspective: I. The problem of degrees of freedom and context-conditioned variability. In J.A.S. Kelso (Ed.), *Human motor behavior: An introduction* (pp. 239-252). Hillsdale, NJ: LEA.

Tyldesley, D., & Whiting, H.T.A. (1975). Operational timing. *Journal of Human Movement Studies, 1,* 172-177.

Ulrich, B.D., Thelen, E., & Niles, D. (1990). Perceptual determinants of action: Stair-climbing choices of infants and toddlers. In J.E. Clark & J.H. Humphrey (Eds.), *Advances in motor development research, 3* (pp. 1-15). New York: AMS Press.

Ulrich, B.D., Ulrich, D.A., Angulo-Kinzler, R., & Chapman, D.D. (1997). Sensitivity of infants with and without Down syndrome to intrinsic dynamics. *Research Quarterly for Exercise and Sport, 68*(1), 10-19.

Ulrich, D.A., & Sanford, C.B. (2000). *Test of Gross Motor Development: Examiner's manual.* Austin, TX: Pro-Ed.

van der Kamp, J. (1999). *The information-based regulation of interceptive timing.* PhD thesis. Amsterdam, Netherlands: Digital Printing Partners.

van der Kamp, J., Savelsbergh, G., & Davis, W. (1998). Body-scaled ratio as a control parameter for prehension in 5- to 9-year old children. *Developmental Psychobiology, 33*(4), 351-361.

van Emmerik, R.E.A., & van Wegen, E.E.H. (2000). On variability and stability in human movement. *Journal of Applied Biomechanics, 16,* 394-406.

van Gelder, T., & Port, R.F. (1995). It's about time: An overview of the dynamical approach to cognition. In R.F. Port & T.V. Gelder (Eds.), *Mind as motion: Explorations in the dynamics of cognition* (pp. 1-43). Cambridge, MA: MIT Press.

van Lieshout, C.F.M., & Heymans, P.G. (Eds.). (2000). *Developing talent across the life span.* Hove, UK: Psychology Press.

van Orden, G.C., Holden, J.G., & Turvey, M.T. (2003). Self-organization of cognitive performance. *Journal of Experimental Psychology: General, 132,* 331-351.

van Rossum, J.H.A. (1990). Schmidt's schema theory: The empirical base of the variability of practice hypothesis. A critical analysis. *Human Movement Science, 9,* 387-435.

Vereijken, B., van Emmerik, R.E.A., Whiting, H.T.A., & Newell, K.M. (1992). Free(z)ing degrees of freedom in skill acquisition. *Journal of Motor Behavior, 24,* 133-142.

Vereijken, B., & Whiting, H.T.A. (1990). In defence of discovery learning. *Canadian Journal of Sport Science, 15*(2), 99-106.

Vickers, J.N., Livingston, L.F., Umeris-Bohnert, S., & Holden, D. (1999). Decision training: The effects of complex instruction variable practice and reduced delayed feedback on the acquisition and transfer of a motor skill. *Journal of Sports Sciences, 17,* 357-367.

Waldrop, M.M. (1992). *Complexity.* London: Viking

Wallen, M., & Walker, R. (1995). Occupational therapy practice with children with perceptual motor dysfunction: Findings of a literature review and survey. *Australian Occupational Therapy Journal, 42,* 15-25.

Walter, C. (1998). An alternative view of dynamical systems concepts in motor control and learning. *Research Quarterly for Exercise Sciences, 69*(4), 326-333.

Ward, P., Williams, A.M., & Bennett, S. (2002). Visual search and biological motion perception in tennis. *Research Quarterly for Exercise and Sport, 73*(1), 107-112.

Warren, W. (1984). Perceiving affordances: Visual guidance of stair climbing. *Journal of Experimental Psychology: Human Perception and Performance, 10,* 683-703.

Warren, W.H. (1988). Action modes and laws of control for visual guidance. In O. G. Meijer & K. Roth (Eds.), *Complex Movement Behaviour: 'The' Motor-Action Controversy* (pp. 339-379). Amsterdam: North Holland.

Warren, W.H. (1990). The Perception-Action Coupling. In H. Bloch & B. I. Bertenthal (Eds.), *Sensory-Motor Organizations and Development in Infancy and Early Childhood* (pp. 23-37). Dordecht: Kluwer Academic Publishers.

Warren, W.H., Kim, E.E., & Husney, R. (1987). The way the ball bounces: Visual and auditory perception of elasticity and control of the bounce pass. *Perception and Psychophysics, 16,* 309-336.

Weinberg, R.S., & Hunt, V. (1976). The interrelationships between anxiety, motor performance, and electromyography. *Journal of Motor Behavior, 8,* 219-224.

Wenderoth, N., & Bock, O. (2001). Learning of a new bimanual coordination pattern is governed by three distinct processes. *Motor Control, 1,* 23-35.

Werner, P., Thorpe, R., & Bunker, D. (1996). Teaching games for understanding: Evolution of a model. *Journal of Physical Education, Recreation and Dance, 67,* 28-33.

West, B.J. (2006). Where medicine went wrong: Rediscovering the path to complexity. Studies in nonlinear phenomena (vol. 11). N.J., USA: World Scientific Publishing Co.

Whiting, H.T.A., Bijlard, M.J., & den Brinker, B.P.L.M. (1987). The effect of the availability of a dynamic model on the acquisition of a complex cyclic action. *Quarterly Journal of Experimental Psychology, 39A,* 43-59.

Wickens, C.D. (1997). *Engineering psychology and human performance* (3rd ed.). New York: HarperCollins.

Wickens, J., Hyland, B., & Anson, G. (1994). Cortical cell assemblies: A possible mechanism for motor programs. *Journal of Motor Behavior, 26*(2), 66-82.

Wightman, D.C., & Lintern, G. (1985). Part-task training for tracking and manual control. *Human Factors, 27,* 267-283.

Williams, A.M., Alty, P., & Lees, A. (2000). Effects of practice and knowledge of performance on the kinematics of ball kicking. In W. Spinks & T. Reilly (Eds.), *Science and Football IV* (pp. 320-328). London: E. & F.N. Spon.

Williams, A.M., Davids, K., & Williams, J.G. (1999). *Visual perception and action in sport.* London: Routledge, Taylor & Francis.

Willingham, D.B. (1998). A neuropsychological theory of motor skill learning. *Psychological Review, 105,* 558-584.

Wolpert, D.M., Ghahramani, Z., & Flanagan, J.R. (2001). Perspectives and problems in motor learning. *Trends in Cognitive Sciences, 5*(11), 487-494.

Woods, D.R., Hickman, M., Jamshidi, Y., Brull, D., Vassiliou, V., Jones, A., et al. (2001). Elite swimmers and the D allele of the ACE I/D polymorphism. *Human Genetics, 108,* 230-232.

Woods, D.R., Humphries, S.E., & Montgomery, H.E. (2000). The ACE I/D polymorphism and human physical performance. *Trends in Endocrinology and Metabolism, 11,* 416-420.

Woods, D.R., World, M., Rayson, M.P., Williams, A.G., Jubb, M., Jamshidi, Y., et al. (2002). Endurance enhancement related to the human angiotensin I-converting enzyme I-D polymorphism is not due to differences in the cardiorespiratory response to training. *European Journal of Applied Physiology, 86,* 240-244.

Woodworth, R.S. (1899). The accuracy of voluntary movement. *Psychological Review Monographs, 3* (Whole No. 13).

World Health Organization. (2002). *The World Health Report: Reducing risks, promoting healthy life.* Geneva: World Health Organization.

Wright, E.J. (1967). Effects of light and heavy equipment on acquisition of sports-type skills by young children. *Research Quarterly for Exercise and Sport, 38,* 705-714.

Wulf, G., Hoess, M., & Prinz, W. (1998). Instructions for motor learning: Differential effects of internal versus external focus of attention. *Journal of Motor Behavior, 30,* 169-179.

Wulf, G., Lauterbach, B., & Toole, T. (1999). The learning advantages of an external focus of attention in golf. *Research Quarterly for Exercise and Sport, 70*(2), 120-126.

Wulf, G., McConnel, N., Gartner, M., & Schwarz, A. (2002). Enhancing the learning of sport skills through external-focus feedback. *Journal of Motor Behavior, 34*(2), 171-182.

Wulf, G., McNevin, N.H., Fuchs, T., Ritter, F., & Toole, T. (2000). Attentional focus in complex skill learning. *Research Quarterly for Exercise and Sport, 71*(3), 229-239.

Wulf, G., McNevin, N., & Shea, C.H. (2001). The automaticity of complex motor skill learning as a function of attentional focus. *Quarterly Journal of Experimental Psychology, 54*(4), 1143-1154.

Wulf, G., & Shea, C.H. (2002). Principles derived from the study of simple skills do not generalize to complex skill learning. *Psychonomic Bulletin & Review, 9*(2), 185-211.

Yamanashi, T., Kawato, M., & Suzuki, R. (1980). Two coupled oscillators as a model for the coordinated finger tapping by both hands. *Biological Cybernetics, 37,* 219-225.

Yanovsky, M.J., & Kay, S.A. (2002). Molecular basis of seasonal time measurement in Arabidopsis. *Nature, 419,* 308-312.

Yates, F.E. (1979). Physical biology: A basis for modeling living systems. *Journal of Cybernetics and Information Science, 2,* 57-70.

Zaal, F.T., Bingham, G.P., & Schmidt, R.C. (2000). Visual perception of mean relative phase and phase variability. *Journal of Experimental Psychology: Human Perception and Performance, 26*(3), 1209-1220.

Zachry, T., Wulf, G., Mercer, J., & Bezodis, N. (2005). Increased movement accuracy and reduced EMG activity as the result of adopting an external focus of attention. *Brain Research Bulletin, 67*(4), 304-309.

Zanone, P.G., & Kelso, J.A.S. (1992). Evolution of behavioral attractors with learning: nonequilibrium phase transitions. *Journal of Experimental Psychology: Human Perception and Performance, 18,* 403-421.

Zanone, P.G., & Kelso, J.A.S. (1994). The coordination dynamics of learning: Theoretical structure and experimental agenda. In S. Swinnen, H. Heuer, J. Massion, & P. Casaer (Eds.), *Interlimb coordination-neural, dynamical and cognitive constraints* (pp. 461-491). New York: Academic Press.

Zanone, P.G., & Kelso, J.A.S. (1997). Coordination dynamics of learning and transfer: Collective and component levels. *Journal of Experimental Psychology: Human Perception and Performance, 23*(5), 1454-1480.

INDEX

Note: The italicized *f* and *t* following page numbers refer to figures and tables, respectively.

ABOUT THE AUTHORS

Keith Davids, PhD, is a professor of motor control and head of the School of Human Movement Studies at Queensland University of Technology in Brisbane, Australia. Over the past 25 years, Davids has focused his research and teaching in the area of motor learning and control. He has published five books and numerous book chapters and journal articles, and he has held teaching positions in Europe, New Zealand, and Australia.

He received his PhD in motor control in 1986 from Leeds University (UK) and has supervised the research of doctoral students from Australia, Germany, New Zealand, Portugal, Saudi Arabia, Singapore, and UK.

In his spare time Davids enjoys cooking, walking, and playing and coaching masters-level soccer in New Zealand and Australia. He and his wife, Anna, live in Queensland and have four children: Michael, Jacob, Charlie, and India.

Chris Button, PhD, is a senior lecturer and director of the Human Performance Centre, University of Otago, in Dunedin, New Zealand. He received his PhD in sport and exercise science in 2000 from Manchester Metropolitan University, UK. His doctoral research focused on coordination and interception skills applying ecological concepts to the study of interceptive actions.

Button is a biomechanist accredited by Sport and Exercise Science New Zealand. He is also a member of Royal Society of New Zealand. Button works with the coaches and athletes of the New Zealand Academy of Sport and provides sport science support to elite athletes and coaches in netball, football (soccer), swimming, and motor sports.

Button publishes his research in a variety of journals on sport science, psychology, and international movement science. He has received invitations to coordinate theoretical and practical seminars to the pre-Commonwealth Games Conference and the World Scientific Congresses of Science & Football/Golf.

Button lives with his wife, Angela, in Dunedin. He enjoys traveling, outdoor pursuits, and sports, especially football, skiing, and squash.

Simon Bennett, PhD, is a reader in behavioral neuroscience at the Research Institute for Sport and Exercise Sciences at Liverpool John Moores University (UK), where he researches and lectures on topics pertaining to visuomotor coordination and control.

Bennett received his PhD in 1996 from Manchester Metropolitan University (UK). Both his PhD research and postdoctoral work have focused on the control and acquisition of interceptive skills. Bennett has coauthored more than 60 papers published in sport science, sensorimotor neuroscience, and movement science journals; he has also coedited 3 books and several book chapters.

In his leisure time, Bennett enjoys spending time outdoors, cycling, skiing, and traveling. He lives in Alsager, Stoke-on-Trent, UK.